EADI Global Development Series

The **EADI Global Development book series** seeks to broaden our understanding of the processes that advance or impede human development, whether from a political, economic, sociological or anthropological perspective. Development Studies is a multi- and inter-disciplinary field of study. The European Association of Development Research and Training Institutes (EADI) reaches with over 120 development research institutes and regular conferences the most important institutes and researchers in this field.

The book series aims to better understand the interplay between social, economic, political, technological, ecological, cultural and gendered (inter-sectional) aspects of societal change at the local, national, regional and global levels. It focusses on the link between theory, policy and practice. New formats include: **"From past to present - and vice versa"** (development processes are not ahistorical); **"From theory to practice - and vice versa"** (dialogues between academics, policymakers and practitioners); and **"Development roundtable"** (a forum where major contributors engage in a debate about a specific topic. Original and thought-provoking perspectives based on evidence are encouraged).

The series editors invite proposals for manuscripts across all disciplines at bookproposals@eadi.org.

Ward Vloeberghs · Sylvia I. Bergh
Editors

Social Accountability Initiatives in Morocco, Tunisia, and Lebanon

Civic Innovation in the Arab World After 2011

palgrave
macmillan

Editors
Ward Vloeberghs
Erasmus University College
Erasmus University Rotterdam
Rotterdam, The Netherlands

Sylvia I. Bergh
International Institute of Social Studies
Erasmus University Rotterdam
Rotterdam, The Netherlands

Research Group Multilevel Regulation
Centre of Expertise Global and Inclusive Learning
The Hague University of Applied Sciences
The Hague, The Netherlands

ISSN 2947-8529 ISSN 2947-8537 (electronic)
EADI Global Development Series
ISBN 978-3-031-51321-3 ISBN 978-3-031-51322-0 (eBook)
https://doi.org/10.1007/978-3-031-51322-0

This Palgrave Macmillan imprint is published by the registered company Springer Nature Switzerland AG
The registered company address is: Gewerbestrasse 11, 6330 Cham, Switzerland

Paper in this product is recyclable.

Acknowledgements

We would like to thank the International Institute of Social Studies (ISS) at Erasmus University Rotterdam for the Research Innovation Facility grant that made this book possible. In particular, we are grateful to our colleague Kees Biekart and other members of the Civic Innovation Research Group for their continuous support and feedback on our approach and findings. Similarly, we thank The Hague University of Applied Sciences (and the now sadly defunct Centre of Expertise on Global Governance) for helping us organise a well-attended hybrid seminar in February 2022 (in collaboration with ISS and Erasmus University College). We also received very useful feedback at the hybrid session we held at the Knowledge Platform Security and Rule of Law's Annual Conference in October 2022. In addition, two persons in particular deserve to be mentioned: Elodie Hermsen provided able research assistance which helped us to submit a successful book proposal; and our copy-editor Marieke Krijnen took care of every detail to enable us to submit a polished manuscript. The original inspiration for this book project grew out of Panel P4922, 'Local governance and social accountability reforms in the wake of the Arab Spring', which was held at the Middle East Studies Association (MESA) Annual Meeting in Washington DC on 20 November 2017. The panel was organised by Sylvia I. Bergh, chaired by Dawn Chatty, and included Mariz Tadros as an excellent discussant. Mariz Tadros also gave very valuable inputs to help us refine our research questions. And of course, we are forever indebted to

Francesco Colin, Hicham Jadaoun, Intissar Kherigi, and Tasnim Chirchi for their insightful chapters and their patience with us while we deliberated on how to best proceed with this project during the Covid-19 pandemic, and in what form to publish the findings. We are very pleased that we found Palgrave Macmillan ready to publish them in this book, and are grateful to the editors of the EADI Global Development book series for their willingness to include the book in their series. Special thanks are due to our editors at Palgrave Macmillan, Alina Yurova, Lucy Everitt and Shreenidhi Natarajan for their expert assistance and patience throughout the process. Finally, we thank the colleagues in charge of Open Access funding at Erasmus University Rotterdam for making this book available to everyone.

Contents

Notes on Contributors

Dr. Sylvia I. Bergh is Associate Professor in Development Management and Governance at the International Institute of Social Studies (ISS), Erasmus University Rotterdam (EUR), and Senior Researcher at the Research Group Multilevel Regulation and the Centre of Expertise on Global and Inclusive Learning at The Hague University of Applied Sciences. She has published widely on state-society relations in the MENA region.

Dr. Tasnim Chirchi is a lecturer in Sociology at Ibn Haldun University in Turkey, specialising in political sociology. She holds a Ph.D. in Sociology from the Université du Québec in Montreal. She previously taught sociology and anthropology in Canada and Tunisia and served as Director of the Jasmine Foundation, a non-governmental organization that works on promoting accountable governance in the context of Tunisia's democratic transition as well as on strengthening the participation of women and youth in public decision-making processes.

Francesco Colin is a Ph.D. researcher at the International Institute of Social Studies (ISS-EUR) and a senior fellow at the Moroccan Institute for Policy Analysis in Rabat. His doctoral research focuses on civic engagement and active citizenship through local petitions in Morocco. He also contributes to different research projects on political participation, social accountability, decentralisation, and the impact of technology on local governance.

Hicham Jadaoun is a trainer, facilitator, researcher and evaluation specialist with extended professional experience. He is an accredited trainer in mental toughness, social and behavioural change and design thinking. He holds a master's degree in public health from the American University of Beirut and has worked with governments, NGOs and the International Committee of the Red Cross across sectors including leadership, education, gender, economic recovery, social cohesion, governance and social accountability. Hicham has a strong record in mixed-methods and participatory research and led projects in Lebanon, Jordan, Iraq, Syria, Turkey, Tunisia, Libya, Mauritania, Niger, United Arab Emirates, Kingdom of Saudi Arabia, Democratic Republic of the Congo, Uganda and Zimbabwe.

Dr. Intissar Kherigi is an associate researcher at Sciences Po Paris and lecturer at the Southern Mediterranean University in Tunisia. She holds a Ph.D. in political science from Sciences Po University in Paris, with a focus on decentralisation reforms and policy-making in Tunisia. She holds a master's in human rights from the London School of Economics and Political Science, and a bachelor's in law from Cambridge University. She has conducted several research projects in Tunisia over the last 10 years on various themes, including local governance, decentralization, public participation and youth participation.

Dr. Ward Vloeberghs is Senior Lecturer in Political Science at Erasmus University College Rotterdam, The Netherlands where he serves as Head of the Social and Behavioural Sciences Department. He taught at universities in Belgium, Lebanon and Morocco. His research explores symbolic and material articulations of power among (Arab) political elites.

Abbreviations

A4EA	Action for Empowerment and Accountability
ANSA	Arab Network for Social Accountability
ATCP	Association Tunisienne des Contrôleurs Publics
ATIDE	Association Tunisienne pour l'Intégrité et la Démocratie des Élections
ATMDAS	Association Troisième Millénaire pour le Développement de l'Action associative au Sud-Est
CARE	Cooperative for Assistance and Relief Everywhere
CBO	Community-Based Organisation
CDAI	Commission du Droit d'Access à l'Information
CSO	Civil Society Organisation
FGD	Focus Group Discussion
GDP	Gross Domestic Product
GIZ	German Development Cooperation
GPSA	Global Partnership for Social Accountability
IFEDA	Centre d'Information, de Formation d'Études et de Documentation sur les Associations
IMPACT	Inter-Ministerial and Municipal Platform for Assessment, Coordination and Tracking
INAI	Instance d'Accès à l'Information
INGO	International Non-Governmental Organisation
INLUCC	Instance nationale de lutte contre la corruption
INPPLC	Instance Nationale de la Probité, de la Prevention et Lutte contre la Corruption
LADE	Lebanese Association for Democratic Elections
LCPS	Lebanese Center for Policy Studies

LTA	Lebanese Transparency Association
MENA	Middle East and North Africa
MEPI	Middle East Partnership Initiative
MoSA	Ministry of Social Affairs
MSS	Mechanism of Social Stability
NGO	Non-Governmental Organisation
OCHA	United Nations Office for the Coordination of Humanitarian Affairs
OECD	Organisation for Economic Co-operation and Development
OGP	Open Government Partnership
OMSAR	Office of the Minister of State for Administrative Reform
OPEMH	Observatoire pour la protection de l'environnement et les monuments historiques
PAI	Participatory investment programme
PARE	Programme d'Appui à la Relance Economique
PHC	Primary Health Care
PJD	Parti de la Justice et du Développement (Justice and Development Party)
PM	Prime Minister
SA	Social Accountability
SAI	Social Accountability Initiative
SDG	Sustainable Development Goal
SOLIDE	Support of Lebanese in Detention and Exile
UGTT	Union Générale Tunisienne du Travail
UN	United Nations
UNDP	United Nations Development Programme
UNHCR	United Nations High Commissioner for Refugees
UNICEF	United Nations Children's Fund
UPR	Universal Periodic Review

List of Tables

CHAPTER 1

Introduction: Social Accountability and Civic Innovation in the Arab World

Ward Vloeberghs and Sylvia I. Bergh

Abstract The Middle East and North Africa region has been absent form stocktaking exercises on social accountability initiatives (SAI), an umbrella term to designate citizen-led tools aimed at socio-political change. We argue that this sidelining is unwarranted, given the proliferation of participatory governance initiatives, civic associations and popular mobilisation in Arab societies after 2011. Whereas the struggle for improved

W. Vloeberghs (✉)
Erasmus University College, Erasmus University Rotterdam, Rotterdam, The Netherlands
e-mail: vloeberghs@euc.eur.nl

S. I. Bergh
International Institute of Social Studies, Erasmus University Rotterdam, Rotterdam, The Netherlands

Research Group Multilevel Regulation, Centre of Expertise Global and Inclusive Learning, The Hague University of Applied Sciences, The Hague, The Netherlands

S. I. Bergh
e-mail: bergh@iss.nl

W. Vloeberghs and S. I. Bergh (eds.), *Social Accountability Initiatives in Morocco, Tunisia, and Lebanon*, EADI Global Development Series,
https://doi.org/10.1007/978-3-031-51322-0_1

accountability in the Arab world remains under-researched, analysis of authoritarian regime tactics has proliferated. The fact is, however, that many Arab societies have experimented with mechanisms to apply political pressure on corrupt elites while international donors have launched diverse SAIs, including community score cards and participatory and gender-responsive budgeting initiatives. In this chapter, we first identify this double gap: not only has the literature on SAIs overlooked the MENA region but scholarship on the Middle East has largely failed to recognise initiatives launched across the region over the past decade as SAIs. Then, we aim to address the blind spot of Arab SAI's as pathways towards improved governance. Finally, we present an overview of extant literature and introduce a set of four research questions to better understand what social accountability means for people on the ground. These questions focus on the various meanings of social accountability (*musā'ala* vs *muhāsaba*), its modes of mobilisation, the responses from authorities to such initiatives and their overall outcomes.

Keywords Public service delivery · Social accountability · Democratisation · Civic innovation · Middle East North Africa region · Arab world

1.1 Background

On 25 April 2022, Walid Fayyad, Lebanon's Energy Minister, had just finished dinner when he was physically assaulted outside a Beirut restaurant by a well-known activist ('Lebanon Energy Minister shoved', 2022). Although other activists were quick to condemn this aggression, by early 2023, headlines of desperate citizens confronting politicians or violently reclaiming their bank deposits had become scaringly mainstream in Lebanon. Such incidents of 'direct accountability' show what can happen when livelihoods collapse. Fortunately, misgovernance does not only inspire harm or destruction; it can also spark unprecedented unity and cooperation.[1] This is as true in Lebanon as in other (Arab) countries, sometimes in settings where it is least expected (Findell-Aghnatios & Majzoub, 2022; 'Vive la résistance', 2023).

Over the past decade, ordinary citizens across the Arab world have increasingly taken matters of public service delivery into their own hands amidst what they perceive as betrayal by corrupt officials, impunity of elites incapable of good governance and lawmakers unwilling of democratic reform. This book focuses on the wide variety of international donor programmes, community-level participatory governance mechanisms, civil society activism, grassroots mobilisation and social movements aimed at forcing public actors to explain or justify their conduct. Below, we discuss such efforts from a cumulative perspective under the umbrella term of social accountability (SA) and analyse them as tools of civic innovation contributing to socio-political change.

To clarify the concept of SA, we can say that accountability is about doing what you say and saying what you do. A more scholarly definition views accountability as 'a relationship between an actor and a forum, in which the actor has an obligation to explain and justify his or her conduct, the forum can pose questions and pass judgment, and the actor may face consequences' (Bovens, 2007, p. 450). Given the historic transformation of political authority in Western Europe from personal to institutional rule, the principle of accountability was usually closely associated with formal mechanisms fixing taxation and representation: to determine the level of taxation, the monarch needed a count of his or her citizens' possessions. Later, as the balance of power shifted from king or queen to parliament, the legislative came to hold the executive to account.

Adding the adjective 'social' to accountability further emphasises the relational nature of the concept by drawing attention to the possibility of involving ordinary citizens in this process. Citizens are often organised at the level of a (local) community or in common interest associations at the level of the neighbourhood that hold authorities, such as municipalities or ministries, to account. Furthermore, SA implicitly refers to two additional dimensions often found in the scholarly literature: answerability and enforceability (Kuppens, 2016). Answerability is an *ex ante* dimension of accountability, since it refers to the obligation of officials to inform citizens about policy measures and justify why they are needed. By contrast, enforceability is an *ex post* dimension of accountability since it refers to the sanctions (formal or informal) that can be imposed on power holders who transgress their mandate.

However, these two dimensions are not always present in equal measure across social accountability initiatives (SAIs), and scholars continue to disagree about which of these (the practice of explaining or the ability to punish) is the most crucial condition for accountability to exist. Moreover, SAIs can vary significantly in ambit and format, ranging from participatory budgeting—where citizens have the power to co-decide on government budget allocation (Wampler et al., 2021)—to grievance-redress or transparency mechanisms, where citizens target specific power holders or institutions to exact more information or redress (Vian, 2020), to contentious action as part of social movements, which targets a wider class of elites (Almén & Burell, 2018; Volpi & Clark, 2019).

Given the diverse operationalisations of SA and because of its broad use across actors, sectors and regions, one key question we address below and in the rest of this book is: what does SA look like for people on the ground in the Arab world?

1.2 A 'Double Gap' in the Scholarly Literature

To a Tunisian street vendor named Mohamed Bouazizi, accountability seemed so unattainable that he set himself on fire in protest at the harassment and humiliation local authorities subjected him to, including the confiscation of his wares. His tragic act of desperation—staged in a modest Tunisian town in December 2010—proved the catalyst for Tunisia's so-called Jasmine Revolution and triggered subsequent uprisings across the Middle East that became known as the Arab Spring (Bayat, 2017; Lynch et al., 2022).

The decade since the Arab Spring protests of 2011 has often been analysed, especially by Western scholars, as a popular call for democratisation (Ahmed & Capoccia, 2014; Howard & Hussain, 2013; Huber & Pisciotta, 2022). It is said that Arab regimes responded to this rallying cry for democracy with a counter-revolution consisting of repression or state violence (Allinson, 2022; Al-Rasheed, 2011; Heydemann & Leenders, 2013; Hinnebusch, 2018; Stacher, 2020).

However, to define the Arab uprisings as a wave of democratisation is a mischaracterisation of developments (Abushouk, 2016; Allam et al., 2022; Maboudi, 2022). Democracy was never an explicit demand of the regional protests. Rather, demonstrators asked for dignity, freedom, social justice and an end to corruption. The deficit of a democratisation prism of analysis has been further underlined by Tunisia's backsliding under President Kais Saied, even though the country had been hailed as the only one that successfully transitioned from autocracy to democracy (Bou Nassif, 2022; Ridge, 2022).

In this book, we argue that rather than a wave of democratisation, the uprisings in Arab societies highlight a remarkable drive of citizens and local communities to challenge the social status quo by seizing the opportunity to launch local campaigns grounded in concrete actions—ranging from leaderless protests to new formats of mediating state power. The willingness and capacity of citizens to organise themselves *despite* authoritarian rule or dysfunctional public governance structures have been remarkable over the past 15 years or so. Across the Arab Middle East and North Africa (MENA), citizens have launched campaigns to directly improve public service delivery or hold public officeholders to account. In this book, we study these dynamics and those initiatives by ordinary citizens and small associations, as they are the prime agents of what we label 'social accountability initiatives'.

We maintain that the scholarly literature suffers from a double gap: not only has the literature on SAIs neglected the MENA region, but there has also been a blind spot when it comes to SAIs. Below, we argue that the limited attention to SA in Arab countries is unwarranted, given the proliferation of participatory governance initiatives, civic associations and popular mobilisation in the decade after 2011.

One common thread running through this wave of revolts was a surge in calls to challenge existing ruling regimes, often by targeting political elites or state institutions. These various forms of collective action were underpinned and propelled by wide discontent with the uneven distribution of civic, political and social citizenship rights between different groups and societal classes. Citizens united to claim a greater level of justice and freedom as well as accountable governance.

While there is now a substantial body of literature on the underlying causes of these uprisings, and valuable studies are emerging on the main actors and their practices, the struggle for improved accountability has remained under-researched. To some extent, the lack of scholarly interest can be explained by key Arab regimes' counter-revolutionary tactics to suppress demands for social change (Bulliet, 2015; Hinnebusch, 2018; Josua & Edel, 2021). The fact is, however, that even in such authoritarian states, citizens have experimented with mechanisms to apply political pressure on incumbents and with attempts to foster public scrutiny, notwithstanding the threat of violent repression.

Thus, over the past decade, many societies across the MENA region have witnessed the creation of new 'participatory' institutions (e.g. participatory urban planning systems, municipal service centres and consultative committees for gender equity and equal opportunities in Morocco and Tunisia), increased decentralisation to the municipal level and the establishment or strengthening of economic and social councils or ombudsman offices. Similarly, international donors have scaled up their work on SAIs, including community score cards in the education (Egypt and Morocco), health (Egypt) and water fields (Yemen). Elsewhere, participatory and gender-responsive budgeting initiatives have been launched.

In short, even though SAIs have 'conquered' the region—albeit often at limited scales—scholars have largely focused on (authoritarian) regime resilience and thereby ignored innovative tools in citizen-led transformations of the status quo. This neglect is all the more striking given the agreement among analysts that many of the root causes of the 2011 uprisings have not disappeared (Cavatorta & Clark, 2022; Dunne, 2020). On the contrary, some of the collisions that erupted in 2011 have resurfaced or given rise to renewed forms of popular protest in 2019 and beyond, from Sudan to Algeria. Hereafter, we review the existing literature on SA in more detail to highlight the gap this book intends to fill.

Geographically speaking, stocktaking exercises on SA have documented an impressive corpus of initiatives across many regions of the world, including Africa (Claasen & Alpín-Lardiés, 2010; Dewachter et al., 2018; Kanyane et al., 2022; McNeil & Mumvuma, 2006), Asia (Ankamah, 2016; Cammett et al., 2022; Dhungana, 2020; Peisakhin & Pinto, 2010; Sirker & Cosic, 2007), Europe (Kurze & Vukusic, 2013; Loia & Maione, 2022; Novikova, 2007) and Latin America (Gonçalves, 2014; Mainwaring & Welna, 2003; Peruzzotti & Smulovitz, 2006; Puschel et al., 2020). However, the MENA region has been conspicuously absent from these efforts.

Thematically speaking, the 'state of the art' covers many policy sectors—from education (Boelen, 2018; Hansen et al., 2019; Pandey et al., 2009; Reinikka & Svensson, 2011) to food security (Mutersbaugh, 2005; Pande & Houtzager, 2016; Razzaque et al., 2023) and public health (Björkman Nyqvist et al., 2016; Jacobs et al., 2020; Lodenstein et al., 2017; Mahmud, 2007) to natural resources (Isham & Kahkonen, 2002; Mejía Acosta, 2013; Moldalieva & Heathershaw, 2020; Ribot & Larson, 2005) or finance (El-Halaby & Hussainey, 2015; Neu et al., 2019). Yet, here too, very little attention has been paid to initiatives conducted in the MENA, which were initially concentrated in education, health or water management and municipal governance (Bousquet et al., 2012).

This is not to say that no attempts were made to explore SA strategies in the MENA region. Fully in line with other parts of the world, international donors and practitioners preceded scholars in promoting and analysing SA in the MENA (Atammeh et al., 2013; Beddies et al., 2011; Bousquet et al., 2012; Meknassi, 2014; United Nations Development Programme [UNDP], 2004). The World Bank in particular has sponsored the establishment of an Arab regional network to complement its Affiliated Networks for Social Accountability (ANSA) initiated in 2006. This materialised, spurred on by unfolding developments, in November 2012.

Although the 2011 uprisings brought momentum to the politics of accountability in the region, the post-Arab Spring literature was mostly channelled into topics linked to democratic transitions and (post-) authoritarianism. This has come to include a wide array of issues, such as authoritarian upgrading, regime survival, counter-revolution, sectarianism, migration (Abdel-Samad & Flanigan, 2019) and Western (EU, US) policy towards the MENA (e.g. Bouris et al., 2022; Dalacoura, 2012; Freyburg, 2011; Freyburg & Richter, 2015; Hashemi & Postel, 2017; Hassan, 2015; Heydemann & Leenders, 2013; Roccu & Voltolini, 2019; Teti et al., 2018; Volpi, 2013).

At first, less attention was paid to the internal dynamics of social change, partly because of the ongoing reconfiguration of social forces. However, this has now begun to change. When domestic developments became the object of focus, interest tended to cluster around themes such as citizenship (Alessandri et al., 2016; Butenschøn & Meijer, 2018; Challand, 2013; Meijer & Zwaini, 2015), social movements (Beinin & Vairel, 2013; Geha, 2019; Rougier & Lacroix, 2015), Islamist parties (Cavatorta & Merone, 2013; Lynch & Schwedler, 2020; Vannetzel, 2017), spatial politics (Al Sayyad & Guvenc, 2015; Bogaert, 2018; Rabbat, 2012; Schwedler, 2013; Singerman, 2011), women (Allam, 2018; el-Husseini, 2016; Joseph & Zaatari, 2022) and youth (Herrera, 2014; Korany et al., 2016; Sika, 2017). Hence, even though scholars have started to explore how citizens across the MENA rethink institutional governance (Ahmed & Capoccia, 2014) and improve socio-economic well-being through pressure from below (Harders, 2013; Volpi & Jasper, 2017), one decade after the Arab uprisings, to our knowledge, no systematic effort has zoomed in exclusively on SAIs.

A second reason this book squarely emphasises SA initiatives in the MENA is that we have witnessed a multitude of such initiatives across the region over the past decade. Yet, only a few of these actions have been identified as SAIs. In the wake of the Arab uprisings, substantial consideration has been given to social movements and social media activism as well as practices of civil resistance or citizen protest. While all these phenomena may have been involved in facilitating SA, few of these activities have been labelled or recognised as SAIs. This may be due, at least partially, to an obsession with (waves of) democratisation and authoritarian rule. A shift in attention is needed to move beyond authoritarianism. There are good reasons to believe that micro-level politics plays a major role in producing state-level outcomes—thus, 'informal networks are an important variable for political change' (Medani, 2013, p. 223).

Several scholars have studied either state-led (Bellin, 2012; Kamrava, 2014; Stacher, 2015; Thyen, 2018) or citizen-led responses to the 2011 uprisings (Achcar, 2013; Cambanis & Mokh, 2020; Cavatorta & Clark, 2022; Gerges, 2016; Tripp, 2013). Consequently, we have seen a proliferation of studies on the strategies of governments (the counter-revolution paradigm, the deep-state syndrome, regime remaking tactics) on the one hand and on grassroots actors (youth, Islamists, women, civil society organisations [CSOs]) on the other. Most of these efforts echo how scholars have traditionally kept track of social change and democratic governance progress in the MENA: either by investigating pressures from below (Bayat, 2010; Ben Néfissa et al., 2005; Brynen et al., 1998; Cronin, 2008; Halpern, 1963; Hudson, 1977; Khadduri, 1970; Sharabi, 1988) or by adopting the view from above (Binder, 1964; Dekmejian, 1975; Issawi, 1956; Maboudi, 2022; Perthes, 2004; Salamé, 1994; Valbjørn & Bank, 2012; Zartman et al., 1982).

However, very few studies published after the 2011 watershed have offered a more comprehensive picture of social change by combining perspectives and integrating both top-down and bottom-up dynamics (Mako & Moghadam, 2021). It is evident, nevertheless, that grassroots activism does not exist in a void and cannot therefore be separated from policy-making at the higher level. We believe that SA mechanisms are particularly relevant to documenting and understanding power shifts in state–citizen relations (Bergh, 2019; Heydemann, 2020; Loewe et al., 2021). Successful SAIs clearly illustrate how such challenges to the status quo are never the result of only one set of actors getting actively engaged; rather, as suggested by Grandvoinnet et al. (2015), such shifts in state–society relations are always the outcome of interactions between civic mobilisation and state action.

In order to fill this gap in our knowledge, the book proposes a systematic analysis of SA in three key countries by contextualising the contrasting understandings of SA in Arab societies. To do so, we explore what SA means in political as well as practical terms for people on the ground.

Some might argue that the three cases highlighted in this book are similar, since they share relatively open and pluralistic institutions, thus opening up questions on how SAIs have played out in authoritarian countries. We counter this by pointing out that Morocco and increasingly Tunisia are hardly liberal democracies and have their own authoritarian features. We do not intend to minimise the contributions of authoritarianism studies, but we wish to ensure that social dynamics and informal renegotiations of the social contract are not neglected. We did not include clear-cut authoritarian polities in the volume (such as Egypt and Syria), which have been studied elsewhere (Khodary, 2022a, 2022b; Sika, 2023). These studies have shown that even non-pluralistic regimes must contend with bottom-up demands to a certain degree.

Although we do address the often sobering net result (Chalcraft, 2021) of these manifestations of civic innovation, popular resistance or collaborative governance campaigns, we are most interested in the description and comparison of dynamics in which citizens take part to improve public service delivery, and their modes of action. In doing so, we question the common impression that accountability does not matter in Arab societies.

1.3 Research Questions and Structure of the Volume

This volume engages several disciplinary fields, including public policy, Middle East Studies and development studies, to create a nuanced and effective framework underpinning the three case studies. Throughout the book and across the case studies, we document what SA means for stakeholders and practitioners, both conceptually and practically, by engaging four main subquestions linked to the multiple meanings of SA, mobilisation methods, responses by authorities and the outcomes of these civic innovation tools, respectively.

First, we set out to map the multiple meanings of the SA concept with the objective of gaining a grip on the terminology. Our working definition of SA is 'any citizen-led action beyond elections that aims to enhance the accountability of state actors' (Vloeberghs & Bergh, 2021, p. 8). With regard to the countries under review here, this often boils down to six mechanisms: transparency, access to information, participation, answerability, rule of law and performance monitoring.

At this point, we must acknowledge the various terms which currently circulate to define accountability. The debate on how best to translate accountability into Arabic matters for our research because the two main corresponding words—*musāʾala* and *muḥāsaba*—each carry specific connotations. *Musāʾala* implicitly assumes questioning (*sāʾala*) and also hints at responsibility (*masʾūliya*), as the responsible is literally the one being asked (*al-masʾūl*). *Muḥāsaba*, on the contrary, has a connotation of reckoning and accountancy, as it relates more to settling a bill (*al-ḥisāb*). To cut a long discussion short, we note that SA is mostly translated as *musāʾala ijtimāʿiyya*. This term has been popularised in recent years, thanks also to the institutional backing of actors like the World Bank and UNDP. As such, the chapters of this book document what people on the ground understand under this specific term.

A second subquestion relates to the mobilisation methods of SAIs. We noted how after 2010, ordinary citizens started to ask public officeholders questions, not only about corrupt or clientelist practices but also about waste management, unemployment, social injustice and human right abuses. Many of these initiatives, in our eyes, fit the definition of SAIs. We wanted to verify our intuition and document such initiatives to better understand and compare the driving forces behind these campaigns. As indicated, to us, the democratisation paradigm and corresponding answers from an authoritarianism perspective dominated by strategies of repression seemed inaccurate, or at least incomplete. It appeared oblivious to the possibility that—regardless of their actual success in bringing about social change—civic innovation efforts were a new phenomenon in the region. Thus, we became curious not only about the means of mobilisation but also about the authorities' reactions to it.

This is why the third subquestion focuses on responses by authorities: how did activists get officials to commit to providing better information or services? What kinds of responses did campaigns elicit from officials, and were these mostly cooperative or confrontational? And when there was collaboration of some kind, was this genuine or tokenism? This is where a discussion of co-optation and sabotage mechanisms becomes relevant.

The fourth and final subquestion of each chapter addresses the outcomes of the various mobilisation formats. As a logical extension of the third subquestion (official responses), the actual result of such initiatives is discussed. Which measures work on the ground? Under what conditions do SAIs manage to improve public services for the local community? Do such (new) tools offer any (new) hope of achieving political change in contexts marked by corrupt elites or undemocratic decision-making?

We asked each chapter author(s) to systematically address these questions for their country context, i.e. in Morocco (Chapter 3), Tunisia (Chapter 4) and Lebanon (Chapter 5), using qualitative research methodologies (for details, please see the individual chapters). The next chapter (Chapter 2) briefly charts the surge of SA as a concept and then presents the theoretical framework used in the country case study chapters. Following the three case study chapters, we offer a conclusion (Chapter 6) in which we synthesise the differences and similarities among SAIs in the three countries and indicate what these insights tell us about SA in the wider region. We also engage in a comparative effort to assess the outcomes produced by SAI in the three countries by pointing to the issue of 'lack of teeth' and the difficulty of scaling up SAIs across local contexts. Here, we also highlight institutional obstacles to SA at the level of national authorities (some of which may be intentional) and the (mostly unintended) limitations caused by international donors' funding and implementation modalities. Finally, this volume ends with some suggestions for (international, regional and national) policy-makers, donors, local stakeholders and practitioners to make SAIs more effective.

Note

1. For example, the advocacy organisation Kulluna Irada (we are all will[ingness]) is an initiative promoting political reform rooted in 'transparency, accountability and citizen participation as major constituents of good governance' (Kulluna Irada, n.d.).

References

Abdel-Samad, M., & Flanigan, S. T. (2019). Social accountability in diaspora organizations aiding Syrian migrants. *International Migration, 57*(4), 329–344. https://doi.org/10.1111/imig.12494

Abushouk, A. I. (2016). The Arab Spring: A fourth wave of democratization? *Digest of Middle East Studies, 25*(1), 52–69. https://doi.org/10.1111/dome.12080
Achcar, G. (2013). *The people want: A radical exploration of the Arab uprising*. University of California Press.
Ahmed, A., & Capoccia, G. (2014). The study of democratization and the Arab Spring. *Middle East Law and Governance, 6*(1), 1–31. https://doi.org/10.1163/18763375-00601002
Alessandri, E., Balfour, R., Bouchet, N., & Youngs, R. (2016). *New forms of democratic citizenship in the Middle East and North Africa: An alternative approach for the EU and United States* (EU Spring Working Paper No. 3). http://aei.pitt.edu/84226/1/new_forms_of_democratic_on_euspring_template.pdf
Allam, N. (2018). *Women and the Egyptian revolution: Engagement and activism during the 2011 Arab uprisings*. Cambridge University Press.
Allam, N., Berman, C., Clarke, K., & Schwedler, J. (2022). Between two uprisings: The study of protest in the Middle East, 2010–2020. In M. Lynch, J. Schwedler, & S. Yom (Eds.), *The political science of the Middle East: Theory and research since the Arab uprisings* (pp. 62–85). Oxford University Press.
Allinson, J. (2022). *The age of counter-revolution: States and revolutions in the Middle East*. Cambridge University Press.
Almén, O., & Burell, M. (2018). Social accountability as social movement outcome: Protests in a Chinese city. *Social Movement Studies, 17*(6), 716–735. https://doi.org/10.1080/14742837.2018.1521716
Al-Rasheed, M. (2011). Sectarianism as counter-revolution: Saudi responses to the Arab Spring. *Studies in Ethnicity and Nationalism, 11*(3), 513–526. https://doi.org/10.1111/j.1754-9469.2011.01129.x
Al Sayyad, N., & Guvenc, M. (2015). Virtual uprisings: On the interaction of new social media, traditional media coverage and urban space during the 'Arab Spring.' *Urban Studies, 52*(11), 2018–2034. https://doi.org/10.1177/0042098013505881
Ankamah, S. S. (2016). Toward a framework of improving horizontal and social accountability mechanisms: Case studies in Asia. *Asian Education and Development Studies, 5*(3), 288–304. https://doi.org/10.1108/AEDS-09-2015-0043
Atammeh, J., Elwan, S., Hamouti, N., Hammam, G., Al Husseini, J., Ives, K., al-Khatib, A., Mitri, D., & Zedan, S. (2013). *Baseline assessment of social accountability in the Arab world*. Final report for the Affiliated Network of Social Accountability in the Arab World (ANSA-AW) and CARE Egypt. INTEGRITY Research & Consultancy. https://www.aman-palestine.org/cached_uploads/download/migrated-files/itemfiles/f4792496d188a649cc1a68bbf9750495.pdf

Bayat, A. (2010). *Life as politics. How ordinary people change the Middle East*. Amsterdam University Press. https://doi.org/10.5117/9789053569115

Bayat, A. (2017). *Revolutions without revolutionaries*. Stanford University Press.

Beddies, S., Felicio, M., Dedu, G., Fall, F., & Vagneron, C. (2011). *Middle East and North Africa local service delivery initiative: Promoting social accountability and demand for good governance* (Arab World Brief No. 9454). World Bank. http://mars.gmu.edu/bitstream/handle/1920/12776/622270BRI0Midd0Box0361475B00PUBLIC0%5b1%5d.pdf?sequence=1&isAllowed=y

Beinin, J., & Vairel, F. (Eds.). (2013). *Social movements, mobilization, and contestation in the Middle East and North Africa*. Stanford University Press.

Bellin, E. (2012). Reconsidering the robustness of authoritarianism in the Middle East: Lessons from the Arab Spring. *Comparative Politics, 44*(2), 127–149. https://doi.org/10.5129/001041512798838021

Ben Néfissa, S. B., Abd Al-Fattah, N., Hanafi, S., & Milani, C. (Eds.). (2005). *NGOs and governance in the Arab world*. American University in Cairo Press.

Bergh, S. I. (2019). Social accountability, citizenship, and social protection in the MENA region: Exploring the linkages. In R. Jawad, N. Jones, & M. Messkoub (Eds.), *Social policy in the Middle East and North Africa: From social assistance to universal social protection* (pp. 220–242). Edward Elgar. https://doi.org/10.4337/9781786431998.00016

Binder, L. (1964). *The ideological revolution in the Middle East*. Wiley.

Björkman Nyqvist, M., Guariso, A., Svensson, J., & Yanagizawa-Drott, D. (2016). *Effect of a micro entrepreneur-based community health delivery program on under-five mortality in Uganda: A cluster-randomized controlled trial* (CEPR Discussion Paper No. DP11515). https://ssrn.com/abstract=2843534

Boelen, C. (2018). Coordinating medical education and health care systems: The power of the social accountability approach. *Medical Education, 52*(1), 96–102. https://doi.org/10.1111/medu.13394

Bogaert, K. (2018). *Globalized authoritarianism: Megaprojects, slums, and class relations in urban Morocco*. University of Minnesota Press.

Bou Nassif, H. (2022). Why the military abandoned democracy. *Journal of Democracy, 33*(1), 27–39. https://doi.org/10.1353/jod.2022.0002

Bouris, D., Huber, D., & Pace, M. (Eds.). (2022). *Routledge handbook of EU-Middle East relations*. Routledge.

Bousquet, F., Thindwa, J., Felicio, M., & Grandvoinnet, H. (2012). *Supporting social accountability in the Middle East and North Africa: Lessons from transitions* (MENA Knowledge and Learning Quick Notes Series No. 53). World Bank. https://documents1.worldbank.org/curated/en/678031468275940310/pdf/677290BRI00PUB0ocial0Accountability.pdf

Bovens, M. (2007). Analyzing and assessing accountability: A conceptual framework. *European Law Journal, 13*(4), 447–468. https://doi.org/10.1111/j.1468-0386.2007.00378.x

Brynen, R., Korany, B., & Noble, P. (Eds.). (1998). *Political liberalization and democratization in the Arab world* (Vol. 2: Comparative experiences). Lynne Rienner.

Bulliet, R. W. (2015). Monarchs and mamluks, or how do you say 'thank you' for $20 billion. *Middle East Law and Governance, 7*(1), 16–24. https://doi.org/10.1163/18763375-00701004

Butenschøn, N. A., & Meijer, R. (Eds.). (2018). *The Middle East in transition: The centrality of citizenship*. Edward Elgar.

Cambanis, T., & Mokh, S. (2020). Redefining citizenship, security and stability. *Journal of International Affairs, 73*(2), 43–60.

Cammett, M., Chakrabarti, P., & Romney, D. (2022). *Social accountability and public goods provision: Testing informal mechanisms to improve community welfare in the slums of Delhi*. https://papers.ssrn.com/sol3/papers.cfm?abstract_id=4130343

Cavatorta, F., & Clark, J. A. (2022). Political and social mobilization in the Middle East and North Africa after the 2011 uprisings. *Globalizations*. Advance online publication. https://doi.org/10.1080/14747731.2021.2012910

Cavatorta, F., & Merone, F. (2013). Moderation through exclusion? The journey of the Tunisian Ennahda from fundamentalist to conservative party. *Democratization, 20*(5), 857–875. https://doi.org/10.1080/13510347.2013.801255

Chalcraft, J. (2021). Revolutionary weakness in Gramscian perspective: The Arab Middle East and North Africa since 2011. *Middle East Critique, 30*(1), 87–104. https://doi.org/10.1080/19436149.2021.1872858

Challand, B. (2013). Citizenship against the grain: Locating the spirit of the Arab uprisings in times of counterrevolution. *Constellations, 20*(2), 169–187. https://doi.org/10.1111/cons.12032

Claasen, M., & Alpín-Lardiés, C. (Eds.). (2010). *Social accountability in Africa: Practitioners' experiences and lessons*. African Books Collective.

Cronin, S. (Ed.). (2008). *Subalterns and social protest: History from below in the Middle East and North Africa*. Routledge.

Dalacoura, K. (2012). The 2011 uprisings in the Arab Middle East: Political change and geopolitical implications. *International Affairs, 88*(1), 63–79. https://doi.org/10.1111/j.1468-2346.2012.01057.x

Dekmejian, R. H. (1975). *Patterns of political leadership: Egypt, Israel, Lebanon*. SUNY Press.

Dewachter, S., Holvoet, N., Kuppens, M., & Molenaers, N. (2018). Beyond the short versus long accountability route dichotomy: Using multi-track accountability pathways to study performance of rural water services in Uganda. *World Development, 102*, 158–169. https://doi.org/10.1016/j.worlddev.2017.09.018

Dhungana, N. (2020). Doing civil society-driven social accountability in a disaster context: Evidence from post-earthquake Nepal. *Politics and Governance, 8*(4), 395–406. https://doi.org/10.17645/pag.v8i4.3154

Dunne, M. (2020). Fear and learning in the Arab uprisings. *Journal of Democracy, 31*(1), 182–192. https://doi.org/10.1353/jod.2020.0015

El-Halaby, S., & Hussainey, K. (2015). The determinants of social accountability disclosure: Evidence from Islamic banks around the world. *International Journal of Business, 20*(3), 202–223.

El-Husseini, R. (2016). Is gender the barrier to democracy? Women, Islamism, and the 'Arab Spring.' *Contemporary Islam, 10*(1), 53–66. https://doi.org/10.1007/s11562-015-0324-4

Findell-Aghnatios, A., & Majzoub, T. (2022). *From inside and outside: Palestinian youth reshaping old electoral systems*. Arab Reform Initiative. https://www.arab-reform.net/publication/from-inside-and-outside-palestinian-youth-reshaping-old-electoral-systems/

Freyburg, T. (2011). Transgovernmental networks as catalysts for democratic change? EU functional cooperation with Arab authoritarian regimes and socialization of involved state officials into democratic governance. *Democratization, 18*(4), 1001–1025. https://doi.org/10.1080/13510347.2011.584737

Freyburg, T., & Richter, S. (2015). Local actors in the driver's seat: Transatlantic democracy promotion under regime competition in the Arab world. *Democratization, 22*(3), 496–518. https://doi.org/10.1080/13510347.2014.1000875

Geha, C. (2019). Politics of a garbage crisis: Social networks, narratives, and frames of Lebanon's 2015 protests and their aftermath. *Social Movement Studies, 18*(1), 78–92. https://doi.org/10.1080/14742837.2018.1539665

Gerges, F. A. (Ed.). (2016). *Contentious politics in the Middle East: Popular resistance and marginalized activism beyond the Arab uprisings*. Springer.

Gonçalves, S. (2014). The effects of participatory budgeting on municipal expenditures and infant mortality in Brazil. *World Development, 53*, 94–110. https://doi.org/10.1016/j.worlddev.2013.01.009

Grandvoinnet, H., Aslam, G., & Raha, S. (Eds.). (2015). *Opening the black box: The contextual drivers of social accountability* (New Frontiers of Social Policy series). World Bank. https://doi.org/10.1596/978-1-4648-0481-6

Halpern, M. (2015) *Politics of social change in the Middle East and North Africa*. Princeton University Press. (Original work published 1963).

Hansen, H. F., Geschwind, L., Kivistö, J., Pekkola, E., Pinheiro, R., & Pulkkinen, K. (2019). Balancing accountability and trust: University reforms in the Nordic countries. *Higher Education, 78*, 557–573. https://doi.org/10.1007/s10734-019-0358-2

Harders, C. (2013). Bringing the local back in: Local politics between informalization and mobilization in an age of transformation in Egypt. In M. Bouziane, C. Harders, & A. Hoffmann (Eds.), *Local politics and contemporary transformations in the Arab world* (pp. 113–136). Palgrave Macmillan. https://doi.org/10.1057/9781137338693.0013

Hashemi, N., & Postel, D. (Eds.). (2017). *Sectarianization: Mapping the new politics of the Middle East*. Hurst.

Hassan, O. (2015). Undermining the transatlantic democracy agenda? The Arab Spring and Saudi Arabia's counteracting democracy strategy. *Democratization, 22*(3), 479–495. https://doi.org/10.1080/13510347.2014.981161

Herrera, L. (Ed.). (2014). *Wired citizenship: Youth learning and activism in the Middle East*. Routledge. https://doi.org/10.4324/9780203747575

Heydemann, S. (2020). Rethinking social contracts in the MENA region: Economic governance, contingent citizenship, and state-society relations after the Arab uprisings. *World Development, 135*, 105019. https://doi.org/10.1016/j.worlddev.2020.105019

Heydemann, S., & Leenders, R. (Eds.). (2013). *Middle East authoritarianisms: Governance, contestation, and regime resilience in Syria and Iran*. Stanford University Press.

Hinnebusch, R. (Ed.). (2018). *After the Arab uprisings: Between democratization, counter-revolution and state failure*. Routledge.

Howard, P. N., & Hussain, M. M. (2013). *Democracy's fourth wave? Digital media and the Arab Spring*. Oxford University Press.

Huber, D., & Pisciotta, B. (2022). From democracy to hybrid regime. Democratic backsliding and populism in Hungary and Tunisia. *Contemporary Politics*. Advance online publication. https://doi.org/10.1080/13569775.2022.2162210

Hudson, M. C. (1977). *Arab politics: The search for legitimacy*. Yale University Press.

Isham, J., & Kahkonen, S. (2002). Institutional determinants of the impact of community-based water services: Evidence from Sri Lanka and India. *Economic Development and Cultural Change, 50*(3), 667–691. https://doi.org/10.1086/342357

Issawi, C. (1956). Economic and social foundations of democracy in the Middle East. *International Affairs, 32*(1), 27–42. https://doi.org/10.2307/2607810

Jacobs, B., Sam Oeun, S., Ir, P., Rifkin, S., & Van Damme, W. (2020). Can social accountability improve access to free public health care for the poor? Analysis of three Health Equity Fund configurations in Cambodia, 2015–17.

Health Policy and Planning, 35(6), 635–645. https://doi.org/10.1093/heapol/czaa019

Joseph, S., & Zaatari, Z. (Eds.). (2022). *Routledge handbook on women in the Middle East*. Taylor & Francis.

Josua, M., & Edel, M. (2021). The Arab uprisings and the return of repression. *Mediterranean Politics, 26*(5), 586–611. https://doi.org/10.1080/13629395.2021.1889298

Kamrava, M. (Ed.). (2014). *Beyond the Arab Spring: The evolving ruling bargain in the Middle East*. Hurst.

Kanyane, M., Mutema, E. P., & Zikhali, T. (2022). Social accountability in local government: Lessons from Vuwani (South Africa) and Gweru (Zimbabwe). *Journal of Public Affairs, 22*(3), e2581. https://doi.org/10.1002/pa.2581

Khadduri, M. (1970). *Political trends in the Arab world: The role of ideas and ideals in politics*. Johns Hopkins University Press.

Khodary, Y. (2022a). Social accountability in challenging environments: Case studies from Egypt. *Middle East Law and Governance, 15*(2), 129–152.

Khodary, Y. (2022b). Social accountability initiatives in Egypt: Unlocking the 'black box' of contextual factors. In S. I. Bergh, S. Pellissery, & C. Sathyamala (Eds.), *The state of accountability in the Global South: Challenges and responses* (pp. 40–58). Edward Elgar.

Korany, B., El-Sayyad, M., & Serag, B. (2016). *A ticking bomb: Egypt's youth unemployment* (SAHWA Policy Paper, 06, 2016). AUC Forum, The American University in Cairo. https://doi.org/10.24241/swpp.2016.4.1

Kulluna Irada. (n.d.). *Mission and blueprint*. Retrieved 21 March 2023 from https://kulluna-irada.org/mission-and-blueprint

Kuppens, M. (2016). *Exploring the social accountability concept: A literature review* (IOB Working Paper 2016.06). Institute of Development Policy and Management, University of Antwerp. https://medialibrary.uantwerpen.be/oldcontent/container2673/files/Publications/WP/2016/06-Kuppens.pdf

Kurze, A., & Vukusic, I. (2013). Afraid to cry wolf: Human rights activists' struggle of transnational accountability efforts in the Balkans. In O. Simić & Z. Volčič (Eds.), *Transitional justice and civil society in the Balkans* (Springer Series in Transitional Justice). Springer.

Lebanon Energy Minister Walid Fayyad 'shoved' as blackouts blight the country. (2022). The New Arab. https://english.alaraby.co.uk/news/lebanon-energy-minister-walid-fayyad-shoved-beirut

Lodenstein, E., Dieleman, M., Gerretsen, B., & Broerse, J. E. (2017). Health provider responsiveness to social accountability initiatives in low- and middle-income countries: A realist review. *Health Policy and Planning, 32*(1), 125–140. https://doi.org/10.1093/heapol/czw089

Loewe, M., Zintl, T., & Houdret, A. (2021). The social contract as a tool of analysis: Introduction to the special issue on 'Framing the evolution of new social contracts in Middle Eastern and North African countries.' *World Development, 145*, 104982. https://doi.org/10.1016/j.worlddev.2020.104982

Loia, F., & Maione, G. (2022). Social accountability of local governments in smart cities: A multiple case study. In A. Visvizi & O. Troisi (Eds.), *Managing smart cities: Sustainability and resilience through effective management* (pp. 181–197). Springer.

Lynch, M., & Schwedler, J. (2020). Introduction to the special issue on 'Islamist politics after the Arab uprisings.' *Middle East Law and Governance, 12*(1), 3–13. https://doi.org/10.1163/18763375-01201008

Lynch, M., Schwedler, J., & Yom, S. (Eds.). (2022). *The political science of the Middle East: Theory and research since the Arab uprisings*. Oxford University Press.

Maboudi, T. (2022). *The 'fall' of the Arab Spring: Democracy's challenges and efforts to reconstitute the Middle East*. Cambridge University Press.

Mahmud, S. (2007). Spaces for participation in health systems in rural Bangladesh: The experience of stakeholder community groups. In A. Cornwall & V. S. P. Coelho (Eds.), *Rights, resources and the politics of accountability*. Zed Books.

Mainwaring, S., & Welna, C. (Eds.). (2003). *Democratic accountability in Latin America*. Oxford University Press.

Mako, S., & Moghadam, V. M. (2021). *After the Arab uprisings: Progress and stagnation in the Middle East and North Africa*. Cambridge University Press.

McNeil, M., & Mumvuma, T. (2006). *Demanding good governance: A stocktaking of social accountability initiatives by civil society in Anglophone Africa*. World Bank. https://documents1.worldbank.org/curated/en/164301468007541296/pdf/389190Demanding1Good1Governance01PUBLIC1.pdf

Medani, K. (2013). Teaching the 'new Middle East': Beyond authoritarianism. *PS, Political Science & Politics, 46*(2), 222–224. https://doi.org/10.1017/S1049096513000176

Meijer, R., & Zwaini, L. (2015). *Citizenship rights and the Arab uprisings: Towards a new political order*. Report for the Dutch Ministry of Foreign Affairs. https://english.iob-evaluatie.nl/binaries/iob-evaluatie-eng/documents/publications/2015/09/01/400---substudy-citizenship-rights-and-the-arab-uprising/citizenship-rights-and-the-arab-uprisings-%E2%80%93-towards-a-new-political-order.pdf

Mejía Acosta, A. (2013). The impact and effectiveness of accountability and transparency initiatives: The governance of natural resources. *Development Policy Review, 31*, s89–s105. https://doi.org/10.1111/dpr.12021

Meknassi, S. F. (2014). *Acceder à l'information c'est notre droit. Guide pratique pour promouvoir l'accès à l'information publique au Maroc*. UNESCO. https://unesdoc.unesco.org/ark:/48223/pf0000227162

Moldalieva, J., & Heathershaw, J. (2020). Playing the 'game' of transparency and accountability: Non-elite politics in Kyrgyzstan's natural resource governance. *Post-Soviet Affairs, 36*(2), 171–187. https://doi.org/10.1080/1060586X.2020.1721213

Mutersbaugh, T. (2005). Fighting standards with standards: Harmonization, rents, and social accountability in certified agrofood networks. *Environment & Planning A, 37*(11), 2033–2051. https://doi.org/10.1068/a37369

Neu, D., Saxton, G., Rahaman, A., & Everett, J. (2019). Twitter and social accountability: Reactions to the Panama Papers. *Critical Perspectives on Accounting, 61*, 38–53. https://doi.org/10.1016/j.cpa.2019.04.003

Novikova, I. (2007). *Stocktaking of social accountability initiatives in Europe and Central Asia, ECSSD/WBI/SDV*. World Bank.

Pande, S., & Houtzager, P. P. (2016). *Civil society innovation and resilience in the struggle for the right to food in India* (IDS Working Paper 475). Institute of Development Studies. https://opendocs.ids.ac.uk/opendocs/bitstream/handle/20.500.12413/12141/Wp475.pdf?sequence=1&isAllowed=y

Pandey, P., Goyal, S., & Sundararaman, V. (2009). Community participation in public schools: Impact of information campaigns in three Indian states. *Education Economics, 17*(3), 355–375. https://doi.org/10.1080/09645290903157484

Peisakhin, L., & Pinto, P. (2010). Is transparency an effective anti-corruption strategy? Evidence from a field experiment in India. *Regulation & Governance, 4*(3), 261–280. https://doi.org/10.1111/j.1748-5991.2010.01081.x

Perthes, V. (Ed.). (2004). *Arab elites: Negotiating the politics of change*. Lynne Rienner.

Peruzzotti, E., & Smulovitz, C. (Eds.). (2006). *Enforcing the rule of law: Social accountability in the new Latin American democracies*. University of Pittsburgh Press.

Puschel, K., Riquelme, A., Sapag, J., Moore, P., Díaz, L. A., Fuentes-López, E., Burdick, W., Norcini, J., Jiménez de la Jara, J., Campos, H., Valdez, J. E., Llosa, M. P., Lamus-Lemus, F., Yulitta, H., & Grez, M. (2020). Academic excellence in Latin America: Social accountability of medical schools. *Medical Teacher, 42*(8), 929–936. https://doi.org/10.1080/0142159X.2020.1770712

Rabbat, N. (2012). The Arab Revolution takes back the public space. *Critical Inquiry, 39*(1), 198–208. https://doi.org/10.1086/668055

Razzaque, F., Sarker, A. E., & Hossain, F. (2023). Conceptualizing the role of social accountability in public service delivery: A comparative study of Bangladesh, India, and Pakistan. In M. S. Haque, W. Wong, & K. Ko (Eds.), *Handbook on Asian public administration* (pp. 253–269). Edward Elgar.

Reinikka, R., & Svensson, J. (2011). The power of information in public services: Evidence from education in Uganda. *Journal of Public Economics, 95*(7–8), 956–966. https://doi.org/10.1016/j.jpubeco.2011.02.006

Ribot, J., & Larson, A. (Eds.). (2005). *Democratic decentralisation through a natural resource lens: Cases from Africa*. Routledge.

Ridge, H. M. (2022). Dismantling new democracies: The case of Tunisia. *Democratization, 29*(8), 1539–1556. https://doi.org/10.1080/13510347.2022.2093346

Roccu, R., & Voltolini, B. (Eds.). (2019). *The EU in the Mediterranean after the Arab uprisings: Frames, selective engagement and the security-stability nexus*. Routledge.

Rougier, B., & Lacroix, S. (Eds.). (2015). *Egypt's revolutions. Politics, religion, and social movements*. Palgrave Macmillan.

Salamé, G. (1994). Small is pluralistic: Democracy as an instrument for civil peace. In G. Salamé (Ed.), *Democracy without democrats? The renewal of politics in the Muslim world* (pp. 84–111). I.B. Tauris.

Schwedler, J. (2013). Spatial dynamics of the Arab uprisings. *PS, Political Science & Politics, 46*(2), 230–234. https://doi.org/10.1017/S104909651300019X

Sharabi, H. (1988). *Neopatriarchy: A theory of distorted change in Arab society*. Oxford University Press.

Sika, N. (2017). *Youth activism and contentious politics in Egypt: Dynamics of continuity and change*. Cambridge University Press.

Sika, N. (2023). Mobilization, repression and policy concessions in authoritarian regimes: The cases of Egypt and Jordan. *Political Studies*. Advance online publication. https://doi.org/10.1177/00323217221141426

Singerman, D. (Ed.). (2011). *Cairo contested: Governance, urban space, and global modernity*. The American University in Cairo Press.

Sirker, K., & Cosic, S. (2007). *Empowering the marginalized: Case studies of social accountability initiatives in Asia* (WBI working paper 42994). World Bank. https://documents1.worldbank.org/curated/en/922061468206055176/pdf/429940WBWP0Mar10Box327342B01PUBLIC1.pdf

Stacher, J. (2015). Fragmenting states, new regimes: Militarized state violence and transition in the Middle East. *Democratization, 22*(2), 259–275. https://doi.org/10.1080/13510347.2015.1010810

Stacher, J. (2020). *Watermelon democracy: Egypt's turbulent transition*. Syracuse University Press.

Teti, A., Abbott, P., & Cavatorta, F. (2018). Understanding the context: Hopes and challenges in 2011. In A. Teti, P. Abbott, & F. Cavatorta, *The Arab Uprisings in Egypt, Jordan and Tunisia* (pp. 27–54). Palgrave Macmillan.

Thyen, K. (2018). Managing contention: Divergent government responses to youth protests in the Arab world. *Middle East Law and Governance, 10*(1), 91–116. https://doi.org/10.1163/18763375-01001003

Tripp, C. (2013). *The power and the people: Paths of resistance in the Middle East*. Cambridge University Press.

United Nations Development Programme. (2004). *Public sector transparency and accountability in selected Arab countries: Policies and practices* (ST/ESA/PAD/SER.E/71). https://publicadministration.un.org/publications/content/PDFs/E-Library%20Archives/2005%20Public%20Sector%20Transp%20and%20Accountability%20in%20SelArab%20Countries.pdf

Valbjørn, M., & Bank, A. (2012). The new Arab cold war: Rediscovering the Arab dimension of Middle East. *Review of International Studies, 38*, 3–24. https://doi.org/10.1017/S0260210511000283

Vannetzel, M. (2017). The Muslim Brotherhood's 'virtuous society' and state developmentalism in Egypt: The politics of 'goodness.' *International Development Policy Journal, 8*, 220–245. https://doi.org/10.4000/poldev.2327

Vian, T. (2020). Anti-corruption, transparency and accountability in health: Concepts, frameworks, and approaches. *Global Health Action, 13*(supl), 1694744.

Vive la résistance. How young Sudanese are still fighting for democracy. (2023). *The Economist*. https://www.economist.com/middle-east-and-africa/2023/01/19/how-young-sudanese-are-still-fighting-for-democracy

Vloeberghs, W., & Bergh, S. I. (2021, March 10). *Weapons of discontent? Sketching a research agenda on social accountability in the Arab Middle East and North Africa* (ISS Working Paper No. 671). https://repub.eur.nl/pub/135292

Volpi, F. (2013). Explaining (and re-explaining) political change in the Middle East during the Arab Spring: Trajectories of democratization and of authoritarianism in the Maghreb. *Democratization, 20*(6), 969–990. https://doi.org/10.1080/13510347.2012.668438

Volpi, F., & Clark, J. A. (2019). Activism in the Middle East and North Africa in times of upheaval: Social networks' actions and interactions. *Social Movement Studies, 18*(1), 1–16. https://doi.org/10.1080/14742837.2018.1538876

Volpi, F., & Jasper, J. M. (2017). *Microfoundations of the Arab uprisings: Mapping interactions between regimes and protesters*. Amsterdam University Press.

Wampler, B., McNulty, S., & Touchton, M. (2021). *Participatory budgeting in global perspective*. Oxford University Press.

Zartman, I. W., Tessler, M., Entelis, J. P., Stone, R. A., Hinnebusch, R., & Akhavi, S. (Eds.). (1982). *Political elites in Arab North Africa: Morocco, Algeria, Tunisia, Libya, and Egypt*. Longman.

CHAPTER 2

Social Accountability in Review: From Conceptual Models to Grounded Practices of Civic Innovation

Ward Vloeberghs and Sylvia I. Bergh

Abstract This chapter offers a working definition of social accountability as any citizen-led action beyond elections that aims to enhance the accountability of state actors. We view social accountability as a broad array of predominantly bottom-up initiatives, aimed at improving the

W. Vloeberghs (✉)
Erasmus University College, Erasmus University Rotterdam, Rotterdam, The Netherlands
e-mail: vloeberghs@euc.eur.nl

S. I. Bergh
International Institute of Social Studies, Erasmus University Rotterdam, Rotterdam, The Netherlands

Research Group Multilevel Regulation, Centre of Expertise Global and Inclusive Learning, The Hague University of Applied Sciences, The Hague, The Netherlands

S. I. Bergh
e-mail: bergh@iss.nl

W. Vloeberghs and S. I. Bergh (eds.), *Social Accountability Initiatives in Morocco, Tunisia, and Lebanon*, EADI Global Development Series,
https://doi.org/10.1007/978-3-031-51322-0_2

quality of governance (especially oversight and responsiveness) through active citizen participation. We also trace the evolution of SA as a concept in the literature over the past decades and, then, discuss some influential theoretic approaches to SAIs, pointing out strengths and weaknesses of each model. Finally, we suggest organising Arab SAIs into one of three categories: (1) transparency; (2) advocacy; or (3) participatory governance and we review each of these existing action formats by discussing their main strengths and flaws.

Keywords Social accountability · Civic innovation · Widgets vs watchdogs · Contextual drivers · Social contract theory · Empowerment

2.1 Social Accountability Initiatives as Democratic Renewal

Academics have traditionally explored avenues for political change from two angles. The first looks for ways to involve citizens more directly in decision-making to fix loopholes of representative democracy. This has typically taken shape in multiple modes of deliberative democracy (Fishkin, 2018) or by reaching back to ancient democratic principles to design new mechanisms of collective governance (Landemore, 2020; Springborg, 2019). A second recipe for democratic renewal has been to redesign citizen participation by focusing on transparency and oversight. Such ideas emphasise the need to involve citizens as well as other stakeholders in the decision-making process. This perspective highlights the need for institutions to achieve a certain quality standard in their delivery of public services. Institutions are thus evaluated as good or bad by 'the extent to which they realise four explicitly democratic goods, namely *inclusiveness*, *popular control*, *considered judgement* and *transparency*' (Smith, 2009, p. 12, emphasis in original). Both approaches to democratic renewal share a bottom-up perspective on political change by acknowledging the need to involve citizens in novel ways.

Scholars of civic innovation

> are interested in how innovative practices of community and solidarity economies, sometimes in alliances with transformative empowerment strategies … are allowing new imaginaries of well-being and possibility to

> flourish. These alternative discourses ... try hard and sometimes selectively succeed to create inroads into the mainstream development discourse. Most importantly, they contain the potential for social change that needs to be understood and acted upon. (Biekart et al., 2016, p. 4)

In this volume, we argue that civic innovation in the Arab world remains poorly studied, although everyday practices in the decade following the Arab uprisings illustrate an abundance of strategies aimed at not only coping with but also altering the social status quo. Examples from the region abound: the 'You Stink' protests in Lebanon, the al-Bawsala platform in Tunisia or the Transparency Maroc campaigns. To narrow down civic innovation, we focus on one specific form of civic innovation here: social accountability initiatives (SAIs).

A consensual scholarly definition of SAIs is lacking. We understand them as 'any citizen-led action beyond elections that aims to enhance the accountability of state actors' (Vloeberghs & Bergh, 2021, p. 8). Thereby, we intentionally adopt a scope that is broader than that of some authors, as we believe casting the net wide benefits our effort to map the politics of accountability in the Arab world during the period 2011–2021.[1]

Tellingly, while the *Oxford handbook of public accountability*, published in 2014, consists of 43 chapters, none of these chapters explore social accountability (SA). The book dedicates exactly one short paragraph and a handful of index entries to the term. By contrast, the *Oxford handbook of the quality of government* (Bågenholm et al., 2021) not only features a dedicated chapter on SA but also includes no fewer than 17 entries pertaining to SA in its index. This is revealing, first, because it shows that the term has gained tremendously in prominence and importance over the past decade. The passage from that handbook is also telling because it suggests a narrow understanding of the concept and future research agenda. It argues that SA has mainly been used 'to examine administrative processes in developing countries' and that the main research priority 'is whether similar routines of civic engagement can open up new accountability dimensions in civil services in developed countries' (Damgaard & Lewis, 2014, p. 238).

In the research project on which this book is based, we identified a different research priority mainly because we observed a general trend in the literature: SA was being studied in many regions (especially Asia, Latin America and Africa) but not in the Middle East and North Africa (MENA). For some reason, scholarship on SA seemed to avoid the Arab world (see Chapter 1 for a detailed review of the literature and this gap). We found this odd, especially after the spectacular series of Arab uprisings in 2011 (Ottaway & Ottaway, 2019). Many protests resurfaced in 2019, and several of these grievances are ongoing today, despite meagre coverage in the mainstream media.

To fill this gap in our knowledge, this book proposes a systematic analysis of SA in three key countries by contextualising the contrasting understandings of SA in Arab societies. To do so, we explore what SA means in political as well as practical terms for people on the ground (see Chapter 1 for the detailed research questions). Before we turn to the three case study chapters, this chapter briefly charts the surge of SA as a concept and then presents the theoretical framework of SA used in the subsequent chapters. The final section discusses SAIs, arguing that they fall into one of three broad categories—(1) transparency; (2) advocacy; or (3) participatory governance—and discussing their possible outcomes.

2.2 From Accountability to Social Accountability

The most recent mutation of accountability into social accountability as a governance concept has been driven by the recognition that institutional protocols can fail to provide responsible governance on countrywide scales. Institutional arrangements—such as oversight of the legislative and/or judicial branch over the executive branch—are themselves the outcomes of centuries of citizens' attempts to hold rulers accountable for their decisions by prioritising the rule of law above the 'rule of men'.

Traditionally, political scientists have approached the study of accountability as the analysis of citizens holding governments responsible during elections. Citizens are theorised to express a retrospective judgement via the ballot box by either punishing or rewarding executive representatives for their performance (Maravall, 2007). This delegated chain of authority so typical of representative democracies—from voting citizens via chosen politicians to executive policy-makers managing service delivery—has been labelled the 'long route of accountability' (World Bank, 2003).[2]

The ensuing shift in the study of accountability came early in the new millennium, at the impetus of experts who hailed the concept of the 'short route of accountability' as a way to combat corruption, clientelism and state capture (Ackerman, 2005). Strengthening the direct links between citizens and service providers was thought to empower the former while fostering transparency and participation. Thus, the notion of democratic oversight came to include the idea that citizens can act as principal agents of improved governance—especially if local participatory mechanisms can be devised to increase the dissemination of information that enables them to demand the realisation of their entitlements.

Yet, neither the ability of short routes to supplement longer routes of accountability nor the existence of horizontal accountability (in which branches or agencies of the state keep each other in check), nor the availability of vertical accountability mechanisms (institutionalised occasions on which citizens provide feedback to representatives, e.g. elections or referenda) have, by themselves, led to improved democratic governance. In any polity, the size or complexity of the bureaucracy can present overwhelming obstacles to (congressional) oversight attempting to guarantee conscientious behaviour by executive officeholders. Moreover, for direct accountability to function, other factors—such as principled public servants, politically engaged citizens and dense civil society networks—need to prevail (Bauhr & Grimes, 2014). By contrast, where corruption is rife, self-interested individuals may derail even well-conceived oversight procedures.

It is no coincidence, then, that the notion of accountability is a central concept for democratisation theorists, who have defined its scope as being much broader than procedural elections. Schedler (1999), for one, suggests that accountability has three main features: information, justification and punishment or compensation. From this perspective, it should not be a surprise that, in her exploration of authoritarianism as democracy's polar opposite, Glasius (2018, p. 525) defines authoritarianism as those practices that sabotage the very notion of accountability.

Because of the difficulty of establishing institutional oversight as a safeguard for accountable governance on a large scale, and given the global persistence of corruption and authoritarianism, SAIs have gained traction over the past few decades—especially in settings marked by weak or imperfect state capacity. Such civic-engagement initiatives intend to bolster citizens and local communities in acting as instigators of state responsiveness (Hydén & Samuel, 2011).

Today, even though scholars acknowledge that all circulating definitions of SA have conceptual flaws—which, moreover, complicate attempts to measure the impact of such initiatives—there is agreement that SA is an

> evolving umbrella category that includes a range of tools: citizen monitoring and oversight of public and/or private sector performance, user-centred public information access/dissemination systems, public complaint and grievance redress mechanisms, and citizen participation in actual resource allocation decision-making, such as participatory budgeting. (Fox, 2022, p. 55)

In short, SA encompasses any citizen-led action beyond elections that aims to enhance the accountability of state actors. However, the sheer diversity of these action formats explains why conceptualising SA has proven such an arduous task.

2.3 Social Accountability: A Theoretical Synopsis

The surge of SA in reaction to the deficit of traditional public services and goods delivery has been so spectacular that scholars have struggled to keep track of the phenomenon. As a result, SA is 'a broad category, without clear boundaries' (Fox, 2022, p. 53). To complicate matters further, the heterogeneity of SA mechanisms has been matched by the diversity of its observers: not only have social scientists, lawyers and economists picked up SA, so too have education specialists and health professionals. In addition to scholars, policy-makers (politicians, experts, public managers and international donors as well as civil society organisations [CSOs]) have contributed to the debate.

SA, then, denotes programmes aimed at making 'government institutions actually listen and respond to citizen voice' through mechanisms of citizen participation (Fox, 2022, p. 54). The underlying assumptions are that practices of citizen oversight should be normalised, that campaigns widely differ in their capacity and autonomy to actually implement oversight, that initiatives are often uneven in addressing service delivery superficially or structurally and that well-intended initiatives can trigger unintended consequences, leaving the actors involved (be they citizens or authorities) more exposed or vulnerable than before their engagement.

One actor, the World Bank, has stood out in terms of knowledge production on SA, and extant scholarship widely credits the organisation with the global spread of the concept. Building on this lead, the United Nations provided a major boost by including the concept in its Sustainable Development Goals in 2015. Goal 16 calls for building 'effective, *accountable* and inclusive institutions', thus increasing funds earmarked for SAIs (United Nations, 2023, emphasis added). Nowadays, the World Bank continues to provide scholars and practitioners with leading expertise in the field and hosts the Global Partnership for Social Accountability (GPSA)[3]—even though some scholars have adopted a critical stance towards the international promotion of a reform agenda advocating SA as a governance tool (Gaventa & McGee, 2013; Joshi & McCluskey, 2018; Rodan & Hughes, 2012). We will turn to some of this criticism below.

A useful way to start thinking about SA in conceptual terms is by distinguishing between upward and downward accountability (Hickey & King, 2016). The former corresponds to bottom-up initiatives by non-state actors (i.e. citizens, local communities or CSOs) whereas the latter denotes top-down mechanisms (e.g. anti-corruption bureaus, open budgeting, legislative oversight, capacity-building, grievance-redress mechanisms and legal or fiscal public-sector reform). Development economists sometimes speak of the demand side and supply side of accountable governance to indicate this same division. However, such reliance on market metaphors also suggests an 'invisible hand' that will, somehow, regulate demand and supply in governance—and this has proven unrealistic (Fox, 2015). Instead, the most effective SAIs are those that integrate elements of both the demand and supply sides in their project design (Hickey & King, 2016, p. 1226).

The distinction introduced by Hickey and King not only highlights a difference in SA interventions depending on the kind of actors involved but also helps set apart initiatives that are arguably predominantly technical in nature from others that are more eminently political. On the one hand, there are SA interventions driven by external actors (CSOs, international donors) who 'projectise' communities' involvement in monitoring activities, such as public expenditure tracking surveys or citizen report cards. These are what Joshi and Houtzager (2012) have labelled 'widgets'. This type of SA is often marked by a top-down logic. The authors believe that this first category is too technical and depoliticised, and they contrast it with SAIs labelled 'watchdogs', which focus on active political engagement by local social forces rooted in a specific context. In this configuration, social actors confront the state as part of a long-term pattern shaped by past exchanges and current imperatives. Joshi and Houtzager (2012) maintain that widgets create conceptual as well as empirical problems in terms of impact evaluation. They advocate for a more dynamic view by examining 'social accountability actions as one part of a broader and longer process of engagement between collective actors and the state' (Joshi & Houtzager, 2012, p. 155) because they believe '[it] is those very political processes that lie at the heart of successful accountability actions from below' (p. 152). In SA theory and practice, there has been a clear trend 'away from a narrow technical blueprint approach towards a more context-sensitive, politically "savvy" approach but it is unclear whether this "watchdog approach" has already trickled down to the reality on the ground' (Kuppens, 2016, p. 23).

In practice, most 'approaches cut across these [conceptual] boundaries' (Grandvoinnet et al., 2015 p. 27). Grandvoinnet et al. (2015, p. 118) emphasise that SA trajectories are unique because they are 'typically circular and iterative: each incremental change reconfigures the contextual conditions for the next [SA trajectory]'. However, they managed to isolate a set of recurrent factors. When clustered, these characteristics amount to five so-called contextual drivers that are constitutive elements present in nearly all SA arrangements. These five drivers are: citizen action, state action, state–citizen interface, civic mobilisation and information (see Fig. 2.1).

Three principles animate the permanent reconfiguration of these five core elements. First, SA is a result of the interplay between state action and citizen action. Second, information, the state–citizen interface and civic mobilisation act as levers on state action and citizen action. Third, there is a fundamental imbalance of power among the actors involved, with the state coming out on top. This being said,

> links between these constitutive elements are not straightforward, and there is no generic sequence among them. For example, SA may be spurred by citizens but also by the state, and both state and citizens may initiate any of the three 'levers': information may be made available by state action or through civic mobilization, and it may be generated or exposed by citizen action; mobilization may be spurred by information or precede it. Creation of the interface may be the starting point or the ending point of an SA approach. (Grandvoinnet et al., 2015, p. 37)

The beauty of this model is that it captures the complexity of SA mechanisms while at the same time pinpointing some of its striking features in one single image. One such strength is the visualisation of information as a crucial variable of SA.

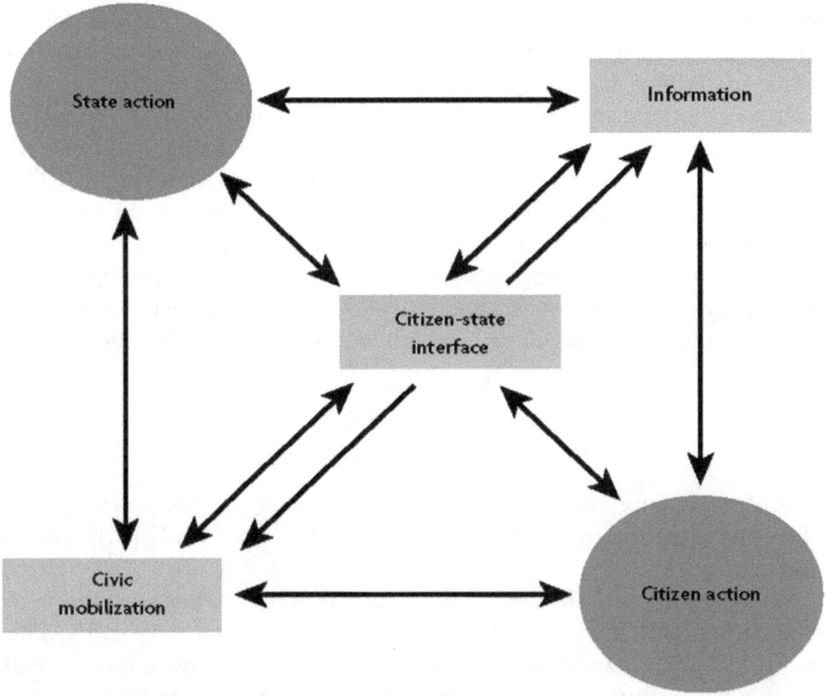

Fig. 2.1 Social accountability as the interplay of five elements (*Source* Grandvoinnet et al. [2015])

In an accountable and responsive state that engages citizens in decision making, information flows are needed from citizens to the state, from the state to citizens, between the various parts of civil society, and within the state apparatus. A wide range of information is needed to ensure accountability, and it is often highly technical in nature (for example, laws, policies, standards, targets, performance, assets, budgets, revenues, and expenditures). In many cases, the information needed for social accountability may not even exist. ... Ensuring that citizens and civil society have access to information, understand it, and make good use of it takes considerable efforts and skills. For these reasons, intermediaries – whether a person, an organization, or the media – are almost always needed to improve access to information, simplify it, clarify it, and point out its implications. (Grandvoinnet et al., 2015, p. 38)

Social scientists like David Apter (1968) have long hinted at the delicate balance between information and coercion in altering levels of accountability in society and bringing about political change. Adding to this, Grandvoinnet and colleagues highlight the crucial role of intermediaries (like brokers, women, challengers and so on) in bringing about SA, especially in settings where state capacity is uneven (Gaventa et al., 2023).

Unavoidably, however, schematised models are nothing but simplified renderings of complex social realities. They thus need to be refined and adapted to represent concrete SA mechanisms in a specific setting, i.e. the MENA region in our case. In the following section, we therefore propose a more refined typology of SAIs which we found on the ground.

2.4 Social Accountability Typology and Outcomes

Roughly speaking, SAIs in the MENA region fall into one of the following categories: (1) transparency; (2) advocacy; or (3) participatory governance.

Transparency initiatives range from formal oversight bodies or right-to-information legislation to ombuds(wo)men and citizen report cards. They aim to increase citizens' access to information as a way to reduce corruption and other abuses of power. For example, the Moroccan Open Budget Index aims to measure the availability of national budget information to citizens and the degree to which citizens are included in its development and implementation (see Chapter 3). Lately, however, scholars have started to question the conviction that transparency automatically induces good governance. Empirical testing of this supposedly causal relationship by Bauhr and Grimes (2014, 2017) suggests that public exposure of endemic corruption may in fact erode institutional confidence and demobilise the demos rather than enhancing pressures for accountability. Although there are reasons to assume that transparency can breed indignation and willingness to act

> among citizens already highly interested and involved in political matters …, our analysis suggests that this effect is not universal. Especially in settings in which corruption is the modus operandi, transparency may instead give rise to resignation and a withdrawal from political life. (Bauhr & Grimes, 2014, p. 309)

This insight undermines the assumption that citizens will act as principal agents of public indignation or that they will press for reform when provided with access to potentially explosive information. Instead, it suggests that information alone is not enough; for SAIs and transparency reforms to be effective, they need to be accompanied by other institutional arrangements that encourage fellow citizens to hold officeholders accountable.

Advocacy initiatives focus on informal pressures used by citizens to claim public goods and services. They usually adopt a more confrontational approach as they tend to address contentious actions by public bodies or state employees. Such initiatives range from popular protests and demonstrations to civil disobedience or public-interest litigation. An example from Tunisia is the Manich Msemeh public campaign. Launched in 2017, it was a protest against an amnesty law which would absolve public officials and businesspeople from corruption charges committed under the previous regime (see Chapter 3). The success of these tools often depends on context-based factors, such as the capacity and commitment of CSOs to engage with both civil and political society, the interests of power holders involved, the levels of inequality between citizens and the character of state–citizen relations (Hickey & King, 2016, pp. 1227–1228). In assessing these contextual factors, Hickey and King (2016) suggest the existence of two different types of context. One is favourable to the effective implementation of SA, i.e. a situation in which civil society has capacity and the government is willing to engage. A contrasting type of context is characterised by a much weaker government willingness and the absence of a legal framework and/or political system facilitating access to information, making it a much less favourable setting for successful experiments with SA.

This finding shows that the attitude of incumbent officeholders and the institutional structure are crucial: whereas denunciation and advocacy can be powerful tools, without the availability of credible enforcement mechanisms, calls for SA can be ignored, defused or diverted. Without sufficient 'bite', SAIs can be captured by established elites.

Finally, participatory governance mechanisms provide groups of (under-represented) citizens with opportunities to engage directly in the policy process. Moreover, participatory institutions are said to improve the poor's well-being (Touchton & Wampler, 2014). Such tools include participatory budgeting or community co-management of education, water or health facilities, thus emphasising the collective dimension of SA.

Whereas examples exist in which such mechanisms have led to tangible development impacts, empirical evidence on participatory governance outcomes is mixed (Fox, 2015). In particular, the assumptions 'community participation is democratic' and 'decentralisation brings government closer to the people' turn out to be weak. This does not mean that SA tools systematically fail to trigger virtuous circles of mutual empowerment, but for that to happen some conditions should be met.

Fox (2015) advocates for a 'sandwich strategy' that consists of both *voice* (citizen capacity for collective action in support of accountability) and *teeth* (defined as the institutional capacity to respond to citizen voice) in these words:

> The sandwich strategy's point of departure is that anti-accountability forces, deeply embedded in both state and society, are often stronger than pro-accountability forces. To break these 'low-accountability traps', resistance is likely and therefore conflict would be both expected and necessary. While initial opportunities for change are necessarily context-driven and can be opened either from society or from the state, the main determinant of a subsequent pro-accountability power shift is whether or not pro-change actors in one domain can empower the others .... In this scenario of mutual empowerment reformists within the state need to have actual capacity to deliver to their societal counterparts, by providing tangible support and the political space necessary to provide some degree of protection from the likely reprisals from vested interests. (Fox, 2015, p. 356)

The strength of Fox's model lies in his recognition that incumbent power holders and anti-accountability forces are deeply embedded in both state and society. However, the question is whether his model goes beyond a revamping of prevailing perspectives on SA as widgets. Even though Fox acknowledges that 'many accountability campaigns are led primarily by pressure from below', his strategy emphasises a state-first, top-down reasoning.

In many societies (including those in the MENA region), the main question is not how openings from above can meet mobilisation from below. Rather, it is the other way round: how to ensure that when pressure builds from below, there will be receptive openings at the top? In the words of Bauhr and Grimes (2014), how to channel indignation into socio-political transformation by avoiding resignation?

Indeed, the question of which SA strategies yield the best results lingers on as a leading theme throughout the literature (Khodary, 2022; Smith & Benavot, 2019; Yang & Pandey, 2011). Not all scholars agree that increased emphasis on context and dynamics from below are salutary. In fact, there is emerging consensus that initiatives which combine bottom-up forms of accountability with reforms that strengthen the responsiveness of public-sector officials tend to work best. In this vein, Fox has pleaded for a shift away from tactical towards strategic SA approaches. This is more than a semantic shift. Tactical approaches are bounded interventions, focusing mostly on local arenas on the assumption that access to information alone will drive collective action to trigger improved public-sector performance. By contrast, strategic approaches deploy multiple tactics, encourage environments that enable accountability and coordinate citizen voice initiatives with governmental reforms, bolstering pro-accountability coalitions that bridge the state–society divide through iterative, often contested processes (Fox, 2015, p. 352).

Trajectories of social change like these are the desired outcome of most SAIs. Such improved levels of governance and development amount to what some have called 'new social contracts'. These authors emphasise that

> social accountability is more likely to emerge when the political settlement ... becomes more inclusive of broader social groups. At this stage, it becomes possible to discuss state–society relations in terms of a 'social contract' which refers both to the legitimacy of political rule, including the capacity of citizens to hold rulers to account, and to the pursuit of social justice as a fundamental principle of government. (Hickey & King, 2016, p. 1233)

Indeed, it seems 'likely that citizen-led forms of accountability will emerge as citizens come to see the goods that are distributed to them through various social protection instruments as entitlements rather than as a form of patronage' (Hickey & King, 2016, p. 1236). More recent work suggests that while citizens expect authorities to deliver the three P's (provision, protection, participation), when urged to rank priorities they tend to value the first P (provision of socio-economic services) more than the other two P's (protection and participation) (Loewe & Albrecht, 2022).

It is important to acknowledge the extent to which Hickey and King (2016) incorporate insights from authors discussed above. Like Fox (2015), they recognise that successful SAIs 'are as likely to require demand- as well as supply-led sources of power' (Hickey & King, 2016, p. 1235). Yet, at the same time, like Joshi and Houtzager (2012), they point out that few SA studies have 'paid any in-depth attention to the role of context and politics in shaping their success' (Hickey & King, 2016: p. 1237). Successful SAIs clearly illustrate how, as suggested by Grandvoinnet et al. (2015), challenges to the status quo are never the result of only one set of actors becoming actively engaged. Rather, shifts in state–society relations are always the outcome of interactions between civic mobilisation and state action.

Inspired by recent research projects that take a grounded and relational approach to studying SA, such as the five-year Action for Empowerment and Accountability (A4EA) research programme (see Anderson, 2023), we aim to address the role of context and politics, as well as the nature of these interactions, in this volume.

Notes

1. Among others, Boräng and Grimes (2021) offer a narrower definition by excluding campaigns waged at a (trans)national level as well as efforts initiated by non-state actors. While we are aware that the latter are usually analysed as contentious politics (see Allam et al., 2022), we maintain that such campaigns are intimately connected to calls by communities or citizens for better delivery of public services and stronger accountability by decision-makers—at least in the countries under analysis here. In this sense, we align with the view of Jonathan Fox on what accountability is and what it is not: 'social accountability refers to both formal and informal channels through which citizen voice is expressed directly to power-holders, often in the context of public service provision' (Fox, 2022, p. 30).
2. See also Bergh et al. (2022) for a more detailed discussion of various types of and approaches to the study of (social) accountability.
3. This initiative was launched in 2012 to foster 'constructive engagement between governments and civil society in order to create an enabling environment in which citizen feedback is used to solve fundamental problems in service delivery and to strengthen the

performance of public institutions'. The GPSA makes funding available to CSOs only in countries where governments have consented to 'opt in'. As of March 2023, this covered 55 countries across all continents, including five countries that are part of the MENA (Jordan, Mauritania, Morocco, Tunisia and Yemen). The GPSA is supporting over 50 projects in 34 countries (including one on education in Morocco and two on health and education in Tunisia). See https://www.thegpsa.org.

References

Ackerman, J. M. (2005). *Social accountability in the public sector: A conceptual discussion and learning module* (World Bank Social Development Paper No. 82). World Bank. https://www.worldbank.org/content/dam/Worldbank/Event/MNA/yemen_cso/english/Yemen_CSO_Conf_Social-Accountability-in-the-Public-Sector_ENG.pdf

Allam, N., Berman, C., Clarke, K., & Schwedler, J. (2022). Between two uprisings: The study of protest in the Middle East, 2010–2020. In M. Lynch, J. Schwedler, & S. Yom (Eds.), *The political science of the Middle East: Theory and research since the Arab uprisings* (pp. 62–85). Oxford University Press.

Anderson, C. (2023). Understanding accountability in practice: Obligations, scrutiny, and consequences'. *Development Policy Review, 41*(S1), 1–17. https://doi.org/10.1111/dpr.12687

Apter, D. (1968). Why political systems change. *Government and Opposition, 3*(4), 411–427. https://doi.org/10.1111/j.1477-7053.1968.tb01340.x

Bågenholm, A., Bauhr, M., Grimes, M., & Rothstein, B. (Eds.). (2021). *The Oxford handbook of the quality of government*. Oxford University Press.

Bauhr, M., & Grimes, M. (2014). Indignation or resignation: The implications of transparency for societal accountability. *Governance, 27*(2), 291–320. https://doi.org/10.1111/gove.12033

Bauhr, M., & Grimes, M. (2017). Transparency to curb corruption? Concepts, measures and empirical merit. *Crime, Law and Social Change, 68*(4), 431–458. https://doi.org/10.1007/s10611-017-9695-1

Bergh, S. I., Hout, W., Pellissery, S., & Sathyamala, C. (2022). Introduction—Public accountability in the Global South: Approaches and practices. In S. I. Bergh, S. Pellissery, & C. Sathyamala (Eds.), *The state of accountability in the Global South: Challenges and responses* (pp. 1–21). Edward Elgar. https://www.elgaronline.com/display/book/9781789907513/book-part-9781789907513-9.xml

Biekart, K., Harcourt, W., & Knorringa, P. (Eds.). (2016). *Exploring civic innovation for social and economic transformation*. Routledge.

Boräng, F., & Grimes, M. (2021). Social accountability and quality of government. In A. Bågenholm, M. Bauhr, M. Grimes, & B. Rothstein (Eds.), *The Oxford handbook of the quality of government* (pp. 268–289). Oxford University Press.

Damgaard, B., & Lewis, J. (2014). Citizen participation in public accountability. In M. Bovens, R. Goodin, & T. Schillemans (Eds.), *Oxford handbook of public accountability* (pp. 258–272). Oxford University Press.

Fishkin, J. S. (2018). *Democracy when the people are thinking: Revitalizing our politics through public deliberation*. Oxford University Press.

Fox, J. A. (2015). Social accountability: What does the evidence really say? *World Development, 72*, 346–361.

Fox, J. A. (2022). *Accountability keywords* (Accountability Research Center Working Paper 11). https://accountabilityresearch.org/wp-content/uploads/2022/01/Working-Paper-11_Keywords_May-24.pdf

Gaventa, J., Joshi, A., & Anderson, C. (2023). Citizen action for accountability in challenging contexts: What have we learned? *Development Policy Review, 41*, e12697. https://doi.org/10.1111/dpr.12697

Gaventa, J., & McGee, R. (2013). The impact of transparency and accountability initiatives. *Development Policy Review, 31*(S1), s3–s28. https://doi.org/10.1111/dpr.12017

Glasius, M. (2018). What authoritarianism is… and is not: A practice perspective. *International Affairs, 94*(3), 515–533. https://doi.org/10.1093/ia/iiy060

Grandvoinnet, H., Aslam, G., & Raha, S. (Eds.). (2015). *Opening the black box: The contextual drivers of social accountability* (New Frontiers of Social Policy series). World Bank.

Hickey, S., & King, S. (2016). Understanding social accountability: Politics, power and building new social contracts. *The Journal of Development Studies, 52*(8), 1225–1240. https://doi.org/10.1080/00220388.2015.1134778

Hydén, G., & Samuel, J. (Eds.). (2011). *Making the state responsive: Experience with democratic governance assessments*. United Nations Development Programme.

Joshi, A., & Houtzager, P. (2012). Widgets or watchdogs? *Public Management Review, 14*(2), 145–162.

Joshi, A., & McCluskey, R. (2018). *The art of 'bureaucraft': Why and how bureaucrats respond to citizen voice* (Research Briefing). Institute of Development Studies (IDS). https://opendocs.ids.ac.uk/opendocs/handle/20.500.12413/13446

Khodary, Y. (2022). Social accountability in challenging environments: Case studies from Egypt. *Middle East Law and Governance, 15*(2), 129–152.

Kuppens, M. (2016). *Exploring the social accountability concept: A literature review* (IOB Working Paper 2016.06). Institute of Development Policy and Management, University of Antwerp. https://medialibrary.uantwerpen.be/oldcontent/container2673/files/Publications/WP/2016/06-Kuppens.pdf

Landemore, H. (2020). *Open democracy: Reinventing popular rule for the twenty-first century*. Princeton University Press.

Loewe, M., & Albrecht, H. (2022). The social contract in Egypt, Lebanon and Tunisia: What do the people want? *Journal of International Development, 35*(5), 838–855.

Maravall, J.-M. (2007). Accountability and the survival of governments. In C. Boix & S. C. Stokes (Eds.), *The Oxford handbook of comparative politics* (Vol. 4, pp. 910–939). Oxford University Press.

Ottaway, D., & Ottaway, M. (2019). *A tale of four worlds: The Arab region after the uprisings*. Oxford University Press.

Rodan, G., & Hughes, C. (2012). Ideological coalitions and the international promotion of social accountability: The Philippines and Cambodia compared. *International Studies Quarterly, 56*(2), 367–380.

Schedler, A. (1999). Conceptualizing accountability. In A. Schedler, L. Diamond, & M. F. Plattner (Eds.), *The self-restraining state: Power and accountability in new democracies* (pp. 13–28). Lynne Rienner.

Smith, G. (2009). *Democratic innovations: Designing institutions for citizen participation*. Cambridge University Press.

Smith, W. C., & Benavot, A. (2019). Improving accountability in education: The importance of structured democratic voice. *Asia Pacific Education Review, 20*(2), 193–205.

Springborg, P. (2019). Constitutionalism ancient and oriental. In D. Landau & H. Lerner (Eds.), *Comparative constitution making* (pp. 363–383). Edward Elgar.

Touchton, M., & Wampler, B. (2014). Improving social well-being through new democratic institutions. *Comparative Political Studies, 47*(10), 1442–1469.

United Nations. (2023, September 5). *Goal 16*. https://sdgs.un.org/goals/goal16

Vloeberghs, W., & Bergh, S. I. (2021, March 10). *Weapons of discontent? Sketching a research agenda on social accountability in the Arab Middle East and North Africa* (ISS Working Paper Series/General Series, 671). https://repub.eur.nl/pub/135292

World Bank. (2003). *World development report 2004: Making services work for poor people*. World Bank. https://documents1.worldbank.org/curated/en/832891468338681960/pdf/268950WDR00PUB0ces0work0poor0people.pdf

Yang, K., & Pandey, S. K. (2011). Further dissecting the black box of citizen participation: When does citizen involvement lead to good outcomes? *Public Administration Review, 71*(6), 880–892.

CHAPTER 3

Social Accountability in Morocco: Recurring Pressures and Sporadic Concessions

Francesco Colin

Abstract Amongst the institutional and societal changes that Morocco experienced in the last decades, accountability is becoming pivotal. The first article of the 2011 Constitution correlates responsibility with the rendering of accounts. However, important limitations to institutional accountability remain. This chapter aims to delve into local meanings and practices of social accountability, asking what accountability looks like for people in Morocco. After providing contextual information on Morocco's overall accountability environment, the chapter looks at four dimensions of citizen engagement with social accountability: the multiple meanings that citizens ascribe to this notion, how these translate into diverse mobilisation methods, how authorities respond to citizen engagement and the overall outcome of these processes. This research showed that while the limited efficacy of institutional protocols for accountability taints citizens' hopes for change, they still engage in a plethora of

F. Colin (✉)
International Institute of Social Studies (ISS), Erasmus University Rotterdam, The Hague, The Netherlands
e-mail: colin@iss.nl

W. Vloeberghs and S. I. Bergh (eds.), *Social Accountability Initiatives in Morocco, Tunisia, and Lebanon*, EADI Global Development Series,
https://doi.org/10.1007/978-3-031-51322-0_3

social accountability initiatives. Yet, such initiatives are far from systematically producing results. Local officials' complicated relationship with civil society and limited ad hoc concessions further nuance the assessment of bottom-up demands for accountability. Regardless, civil society actors remain resolute in their struggles for change.

Keywords Responsibility · Tokenism · Citizens' power · Civic action · Morocco · Social accountability

3.1 Introduction

This chapter focuses on the notion and practices of social accountability (SA) in Morocco. Within this research, SA refers to citizens holding state officials (elected or appointed) to account for service delivery outside of elections. After the uprisings of 2011, Morocco implemented a series of institutional changes that—amongst other objectives—aim at 'completing the process of establishment of the rule of law and of democratic institutions' (from the Royal Speech of 17 June 2011 announcing the constitutional reform; my translation). Accountability occupies a prime position, as the first article of the 2011 Constitution establishes the correlation between responsibility and the rendering of accounts. This has resulted in a series of reforms and institutional changes formally aimed at reinforcing both top-down and bottom-up accountability processes. Beyond this institutional recognition, international donors working in Morocco have paid substantial attention to accountability issues. Notably, donors working with citizens and civil society directly have invested substantially in the support of bottom-up actions and processes of accountability. At the same time, both institutional changes and donor action are taking place in a context of wide and enduring social mobilisation. Actions such as demonstrations for improved public service delivery or broader actions demanding that decision-makers uphold their responsibility have been common in Morocco since well before the 2011 Constitution. This context of diverse actions, in which different stakeholders collaborate and clash depending on their goals and strategies, provides a rich field of meanings and practices of accountability in Morocco.

Fundamentally, this research explores the different ways in which citizens and civil society actors talk about and engage in accountability initiatives, how authorities respond to them and whether these efforts manage to exact accountability. The research revolves around the following main research question: *What does accountability look like for the people on the ground?*

This key question has been further unpacked into four subquestions, namely:

1. Multiple meanings: what do local citizens understand by the word 'accountability'? How do citizens engaged in SA mechanisms refer to it and ascribe meaning to it?
2. Mobilisation methods: how did local activists get the attention of fellow citizens (mobilising them) and of the officials in power responsible for providing certain types of information or services?
3. Responses from authorities: how did local activists maintain momentum in terms of mobilisation and how did they get power holders and officials to commit to providing the information and services?
4. Outcomes: how did activists get power holders to deliver on their commitments? Did they succeed in exacting accountability at all, and if so, to what extent? And are there some signs of their commitments being institutionalised? What are the reasons for successes and/or failures?

This chapter is divided into five sections. This short introduction will be followed by a methodology section, in which the main research methods will be presented and positioned in the actual research process. Next, I present a non-exhaustive account of SA initiatives in Morocco with the goal of providing a broader picture of the experiences in the Moroccan context, followed by an empirical section in which I answer the research questions by presenting the data gathered during the fieldwork. Finally, a conclusion summarises the main findings while sketching out the lines of further research on this topic in Morocco.

3.2 Methodology

This section will outline the methodological approach of the research, presenting the methodological choices made, the methods employed for data collection, the limitations faced while conducting fieldwork and the ensuing adjustments made throughout the research. The goal of this section is to position the findings of the study within the wider context in which the research has been carried out.

Overall, this research is grounded in a strongly qualitative approach. It is based on fieldwork in Morocco conducted between August and November 2021 that explored the question and subquestions mentioned above. Given my focus on the multiple understandings and practices of SA in Morocco, I used qualitative research methods that enable research participants to provide dense descriptions of their interpretations of the notion of SA, of their actions and of the wider context these occur in. The strong qualitative focus aimed at 'getting closer' to the phenomenon at the centre of the research in order to improve its understanding (Aspers & Corte, 2019). This methodological choice was also translated into the development of this chapter, which relies heavily on direct quotes from research participants. Bringing to the fore the latter's voices represents a concrete engagement with the main goal of this research: finding out what accountability looks like for the people on the ground.

The data collection process started with desk research aimed at obtaining a wide picture of SA initiatives in Morocco, using general and academic search engines (Google, Scopus and Google Scholar) as well as the main social media in Morocco (Facebook and Twitter). In an attempt to be as inclusive as possible, these searches were conducted in English, French and Arabic. Table 3.1 summarises the search terms employed.

Following the desk research, 16 semi-structured interviews were conducted with key civil society actors, scholars, journalists and activists who have engaged with SA initiatives. A broad interview guide based on the four subquestions guided these interviews but was not followed strictly. Indeed, interviewees were given broad room to discuss and explore local meanings and practices of accountability. Two interviews were held with two participants at the same time, as both worked for the same organisation. Half of the interviews were conducted remotely (via telephone or online), since some interviewees preferred to minimise the risk of exposure to Covid-19 and others could not travel to meet in person (also due to Covid-19 restrictions). Ten interviewees gave permission to

Table 3.1 Search-term matrix for desk review

English	*French*	*Arabic*
Accountability Morocco	Redevabilité Maroc	*musāʾala al-Maghrib* *muḥāsaba al-Maghrib*
Accountability initiative Morocco	Initiative redevabilité Maroc	*mubādara musāʾala al-Maghrib* *mubādara muḥāsaba al-Maghrib*
Social accountability Morocco	Redevabilité sociale Maroc	*musāʾala al-ijtimāʿiyya al-Maghrib* *muḥāsaba al-ijtimāʿiyya al-Maghrib*

record the interview for transcription purposes, while six interviewees did not. In these cases, I took notes that were used in the analysis, but I could not quote them verbatim. I conducted interviews in both English and French, using specific Arabic words at times.

Following the interviews, I presented some preliminary findings in an online validation workshop with five interviewees, aimed at substantiating the preliminary interpretation of the data and collecting further inputs for the analysis. A presentation of preliminary research findings was followed by a discussion that covered both the specific research findings and the overall context for SA in Morocco.

In terms of limitations, the Covid-19 pandemic (and the related policy response) presented an obstacle to the fieldwork, as some interviewees preferred not to meet face-to-face and the policy response of the Moroccan government included limitations on intercity travel and a curfew that, at times, did not allow for in-person meetings. However, resorting to remote interviewing mostly mitigated this limitation. The local political context also influenced the fieldwork process. First, local and general elections held on 8 September 2021 monopolised the debate during most fieldwork activities. This made it harder to focus on accountability *beyond* the elections. Second, some interviewees believed that accountability was a sensitive topic and that debating it could result in retaliation from public authorities. A notable case is a participant who refused to do the interview since I did not possess an authorisation issued by a Moroccan administration. Even though I informed him that I had submitted an application for a research permit and that Moroccan authorities were aware of my research, this interviewee was advised by a police officer he knew not to do the interview if I lacked written authorisation.

3.3 Accountability in the Moroccan Context

This section briefly tackles the wider socio-political environment in Morocco and reviews some of the main contextual factors that influence the development and effectiveness of SA initiatives. Hickey and King (2016, p. 1277) review the variety of contextual elements that may have an impact on SAI, including

> the role of different kinds of political institutions, the type and capacity of civil society actors involved in promoting social accountability, and a wide range of different 'relational' factors, whether in the form of state–society relations or relations between groups and citizens.

Therefore, this section will start by reviewing the legal framework of accountability in Morocco, including public policies and the prerogatives of institutional bodies related to accountability mechanisms. Then it will delve into the 'relational factors' that influence SA dynamics, such as the political will to act, officials' support, political opposition and CSOs' capacities.

3.3.1 *The Reform of the Constitutional Framework: Plus ça Change…?*

As mentioned in the introduction, most interviewees underlined the central role of the 2011 Constitution in relation to accountability dynamics in Morocco. Even if the societal demands for increased accountability preceded the last constitutional reform (scholar, personal communication, 6 September 2021, in person), the fundamental law may be seen as a step towards Morocco's democratisation: it establishes the 'correlation between the responsibility for and the rendering of accounts' (article 1, paragraph 2, Moroccan Constitution 2011) as a founding principle of the state. Further, it makes provisions for a series of bodies and mechanisms with the mission of monitoring and evaluating the performance of public powers and allowing citizens to exercise their sovereignty and act as a counterpower. Indeed, a plethora of institutions are officially mandated to oversee the actions of public authorities (and, ideally, hold them to account), including the Court of Auditors (Cour des Comptes), the Competition Council (Conseil de la Concurrence) and the National Authority of Integrity, of Prevention and the Struggle against Corruption (Instance Nationale de la Probité, de la Prevention et Lutte contre la Corruption; INPPLC). In addition, the 2011 Constitution introduced new measures granting citizens and civil society organisations (CSOs) new roles and innovative tools to engage with the state. For instance, civil society is identified as a partner of the state in the development, monitoring and evaluation of public policies (article 12), while citizens are granted the right to participate by submitting petitions and legislative motions (articles 14 and 15, respectively). The right to access information is also established (article 27). Furthermore, the 2011 Constitution states that public services are subordinated to, amongst others, the principles of transparency, responsibility and rendering of accounts (article 154). The relevance of the 2011 shift is summarised well by this interviewee:

> I think we have to talk about a pre-2011 and a post-2011. We have always talked about accountability in the sense of incriminating corrupt officials. ... There always was this debate in Morocco about the possibility of seeing public officials, and especially to bring politicians (ministers, political leaders, etc.) before the courts and punish them in a criminal way. ... The context in which accountability was included in the 2011 Constitution, in the first article, in the second paragraph... it was very, very important to put it in that place. ... So, the context gave accountability more of a political meaning than a criminal one. ... it was another way of expressing the new step of democratisation of the Moroccan political system. That is to say, to link governance, to link power (in part) to the popular will and to the decision and intervention of the people. (Journalist, personal communication, 9 August 2021, in person)

The involvement of citizens and CSOs in the political system is determined by a framework of 'participatory democracy', which is both evoked as a founding principle of the state (article 1, paragraph 2, Moroccan Constitution 2011) and materialised in the laws and regulations that implement the rights mentioned above. Specifically, a series of organic laws define the right to present petitions and legislative motions and the right to access information and its scope.

Overall, the renewal of Morocco's constitutional framework greatly advanced the legal arsenal that citizens and civil society can use to become more engaged in its political system. However, the concrete realisation of these rights and the implementation of this ambitious framework were immediately recognised as being a challenge (Bendourou, 2012). Furthermore, the 2011 Constitution also crystallised a specific power balance, reaffirming the central role of the king in Morocco's political system (as, amongst others, the head of state, commander of the faithful and supreme arbiter between institutions; see articles 41 and 59 in the 2011 Constitution on the monarchy) while failing to provide any means to balance his power or even debate or question his decisions. In short, not only does the 2011 Constitution provide the monarch with decisional power in most strategic areas of the country's governance, but it also explicitly affirms that the king is inviolable—thereby curtailing any possibility to hold him to account, in spite of his far-reaching prerogatives. As another interviewee describes:

> The head of state has enormous powers on the judicial level, on the religious level, on the military level, etc. There is nothing in the Constitution that allows to question him, at least, to do a minimum of *musāʾala* … or of social accountability. (Scholar, personal communication, 6 September 2021, in person)

Hence, the intention of correlating responsibility and the rendering of accounts outlined in the first article of the Constitution are put into question by the consolidation of the monarch's position in Morocco's political system. The fact that the 2011 constitutional reform does not provide any mechanism to hold the monarch to account represents a first ceiling to accountability in the Moroccan context: both newly created and reinforced state institutions and citizens and civil society formally lack the prerogatives to exact accountability from the primary decision-maker in Morocco.

3.3.2 Institutions for Top-Down Accountability: Great Prerogatives, Meagre Results

Although they lack in providing counterbalance to the prerogatives of the monarchy, the innovations brought forward by the 2011 Constitution play a key role in defining the wider environment in which accountability dynamics interplay in Morocco. As introduced above, the main institutional bodies with prerogatives related to accountability dynamics are the Court of Auditors, the Competition Council and the INPPLC. While the constitutional reform renewed the mandates of these institutions and increased their prerogatives, research participants presented concrete examples of how and why all three ultimately fail to achieve their objectives. Such a limited performance record fundamentally questions their power and ability to exact accountability.

The example of gas prices at the Competition Council is a case in point. The Competition Council is an independent institution that aims at ensuring transparency and equity in economic relations through the analysis and regulation of competition in markets and the control of anticompetitive behaviour and operations related to monopolies. It was established as an advisory body in 2000 by Law no. 06-99 on the freedom of prices and competition. In 2014, a new law aimed to amplify its prerogatives, including the capacity to act on its own initiative and, crucially, the power to sanction enterprises found guilty of anticompetitive practices by imposing fines amounting to up to the 10 per cent of their revenues ("Le Conseil de la Concurrence", 2015). In 2015, a parliamentary inquiry investigated the increase in fuel prices after the liberalisation of the sector and concluded that the main providers had expanded their profit margin. This inquiry estimated that an excess profit of around 17 billion dirhams (MAD)—approximately 1.56 billion euros (EUR)—was made compared to the previous market situation (Berrada, 2018). After seizing this case, the Competition Council imposed a fine of 9 per cent of the turnover of these companies at the end of July 2020. However, in the following days some of its members stated that the president had not followed internal procedures. The king put the decision on hold, swiftly appointing an ad hoc commission to investigate the proceedings. This commission concluded that there had been various irregularities in the decision-making process. However, further details about these irregularities are not available, since the investigation was conducted behind closed doors and the report was submitted only to the king (El Hourri, 2021a). Ultimately, this process prompted a revision of the Council's internal regulations and of the legal framework regulating competition ("Conseil de la Concurrence", 2021).

One of the central elements that short-circuits the institutional protocol around accountability is the preference for extrajudicial dynamics over legal avenues. Instead of following the normal procedure (in this case an appeal to the administrative tribunal), the dispute was managed in a top-down fashion through a royally appointed commission. As two interviewees outlined:

> Miraculously, [the Competition Council] delivers a sanction. But they decided on the sanction on a Thursday in July, and the following Monday it was blocked. The behaviour of the president has been denounced and an ad hoc committee was appointed by the head of state and then the president was replaced. All this to tell you that the implementation of laws, even when they are very limited… the extra-institutional power has the capacity to make sure that the law is useless, through appointments, through commissions. (Scholar, personal communication, 6 September 2021, in person)

> You saw how [the former president of the Competition Council] was dismissed... In a way that has no basis: creating a commission composed by the president of the Parliament, the head of the government... to investigate and then to say 'ah, he didn't respect [the internal regulations] and now he is dismissed'. And now we don't have a Council. (Journalist, personal communication, 9 August 2021, in person)

Moreover, the review of the internal regulations of the Competition Council arguably decreased the transparency of its decision. Specifically, even though the Council is still legally bound to publish its decision, the proceedings of its deliberation are now excluded from publication and covered under professional secrecy (El Hourri, 2021b). Infringement of such secrecy may lead to fines between 1,200 and 20,000 dirhams for Council members, as stated by Law project no. 40–21. The situation is further complicated by an evident conflict of interest, since the current government is headed by the owner of one of the companies implicated in the affair and will have to oversee the revision of the competition law (Dalil, 2021). At the time of writing, even after the nomination of the new president of the Council in March 2021, no decision had been taken on the fine for the fuel companies involved in anticompetitive practices.

The case of the Competition Council highlights the limitations that these institutions face: extrajudicial practices, ad hoc decisions and an overall environment that is not favourable to exacting accountability. Specifically, the malfunction of institutional bodies to enforce accountability is seen as going beyond a flawed legal framework. Different interviewees identified a lack of political will to ensure accountability at the institutional level, which is evident both from the inaction of these bodies and from the barriers put up to further pieces of legislation that could ameliorate the situation. In the words of three different interviewees:

> We have some reports prepared by the Court of Auditors. The reports produced by this institution are very good, they're very legal, they're incredible. They tell you 'look what this company has done, [look what] this deputy has done, etc.' And all is very well written and they provide the accounts of the thefts that there have been, but in the end... these reports go directly to the archive. There are no actions. (Civil society actor 10, personal communication, 24 September 2021, in person)

> The great witness of this situation is the law that criminalises the illicit enrichment of officials. It was the obvious case where we felt that there was no longer this political will to exercise accountability over officials. It was a bill that was introduced in the last months of the first Benkirane government by the Minister of Justice and that remained frozen in Parliament. ... In spite of the significant modifications made to the text, which practically emptied it of its meaning and made it ineffective, it remains blocked. Overall, this reflects the absence, the loss of the political will to exercise this principle [of accountability]. (Journalist, personal communication, 9 August 2021, in person)

> There is a general situation of impunity and the problem is not just technical or with the laws. It's many things combined and, ultimately, it's the political system that does not tolerate accountability as it is. (Scholar, personal communication, 6 September 2021, in person)

In sum, institutional bodies aimed at exacting accountability suffer from a weak political will to engage with these mechanisms and a limited efficacy of the rule of law. Their increased prerogatives have yet to be matched by improved results: the fact that the political system is not open to a systematic exercise of accountability obstructs the action of these bodies.

3.3.3 Institutional Mechanisms for Bottom-Up Accountability: A Missed Opportunity

Besides increasing the prerogatives of the institutions in charge of top-down accountability, the 2011 Constitution also outlines several innovations that open bottom-up institutional avenues for accountability.

Citizens and CSOs can use these mechanisms to attempt achieving accountability. In particular, institutional petitions[1] can be used to make specific requests of national authorities (i.e. the Head of Government and the Presidents of the two chambers of the Parliament) or to propose the discussion of specific issues in the council of local governments. Citizens can also submit requests to obtain certain pieces of information to national and local authorities, as regulated by Organic Law no. 31-13.[2] Requests can be filed directly at the administration concerned, via email to the administration's contact point for access to information and via the dedicated online portal Chafafiya ('Transparency').

Citizens and CSOs have been using these mechanisms to demand accountability from decision-makers. However, as in the case of the institutions in the previous subsection, concrete experiences with these mechanisms call into question their promises. Both institutional petitions and requests to access information encounter key obstacles and generally do not lead to concrete results, casting doubt on the use of these tools as systematic mechanisms to achieve accountability.

The issues related to the right to information partly depend on its regulation (the features of Organic Law no. 31-13) and on how officials approach such requests. Organic Law no. 31-13 defines the procedures to access information held by national and local authorities as well as the limitations to this right in the form of a list of 'exceptions'. Critics have pointed out that such a list of exceptions is ambiguous and leaves substantial room for manoeuvre for authorities to decide which information gets published—and which does not ("Droit d'accès à l'information", 2019). However, the Access to Information Law's main issue is that it does not establish sanctions for officials that fail to provide information (Belghazi, 2014). In the words of an interviewee: 'If you look at the Access to Information Law alone: … it has been designed to reduce as much as possible its scope and the access to information' (scholar, personal communication, 6 September 2021, in person). Even the appeal process cannot compel officials to provide information. The administrative court can be used to enforce a legal decision to provide the information, but only once internal appeal processes have been exhausted and only if the citizen can bear the legal costs.

Simply put, officials in charge of providing information can decide whether to provide the information without the risk of incurring a sanction. In practice, citizens' ability to access information depends on the inclination of the information officer they reach. Indeed, research participants highlighted a general attitude that obstructs the right to access information. As summarised by this interviewee:

> The grounds rule are set, but things are different when it comes to practice. And it's not about the regulation, it's about the culture. Even in the Moroccan culture we got used not to share information. When you ask for something, especially when you ask for the budget etc., the answer is 'why you need it?' ... I am a Moroccan citizen, I have this constitutional right, but that's the response. (Civil society actor 5, personal communication, 3 September 2021, online)

The lack of a culture of transparency has already been identified (Shalaby & Bergh, 2020). Together with the issues in the legislative framework this creates a situation in which citizens have no guarantees that they will receive a response. Even the Commission for the Right to Access to Information (Commission du Droit d'Access à l'Information, CDAI)—which is supposed to monitor, ensure and improve the implementation of the right to access information—does not have the power to enforce decisions. The experience of two interviewees highlights these difficulties:

> We filed 80 requests through the portal. We got 17 responses and 63 non-responses. About those 17, either the response is negative or positive, but there is a response. It was an exercise for everyone, both the ministries and us, to see who responds to what. For those 63 that did not reply, we followed the appeal process: first we wrote to the head of the administration, then CDAI. After [asking the head of the administration], we got zero responses, then [after asking the CDAI] we also got zero responses. (Civil society actor 5, personal communication, 3 September 2021, online)

> The deadlines for receiving information are about 20 days, which can be extended by another 20. I can tell you that nothing is respected in this regard ... we have been asking for four months for the convention of delegation of the management [procurement contracts] of water, electricity and sanitation in Casablanca. We made a complaint to the National Commission for the Right to Access to Information [CDAI], which is the body that manages these cases, and it told us that it will follow up on the case, but we will certainly be called upon to go to court for this. (Civil society actor 7, personal communication, 16 September 2021, in person)

These accounts show that requests to access information do not generate a systematic response. This is partly due to shortcomings in the regulation of the right to access information but is ultimately an issue related to the lack of response of those responsible for providing information. In turn, this limits the potential of exercising the right to access information as a strategy for SA.

Similar considerations apply for institutional petitions to place an item on the agenda of local government councils. The regulation of this right provides a certain degree of insurance that claims filed through this mechanism will be taken into consideration by officials—provided that they comply with strict criteria. In other words, if citizens and CSOs comply with the formal conditions to present a petition, they should be guaranteed that authorities will take the topic of the petition into consideration. Indeed, institutional petitions have been used as a strategy to hold local governments to account for their actions (or lack thereof). For instance, an association in Sefrou presented a petition to demand the municipality's intervention in solving the issue of uncontrolled waste dumping; another association in Figuig presented a petition to the municipal council demanding better management of the water resources dedicated to local oases. Nonetheless, the regulatory limitations of this right and contextual constraints put into question the feasibility of institutional petitions as a systematic avenue for bottom-up accountability.

The regulation of the right to petition is fundamentally flawed in its lack of coercive force, but there are also challenges related to the implementation of citizens' initiatives. At the national level, citizens can present a petition that will have to be taken into consideration by the relevant authorities. Yet, there is no guarantee that they will come to a decision on the petition (Colin, 2023). Furthermore, since the promulgation of the organic laws necessary to implement the right to petition in 2016, out of 12 initiatives presented to authorities only three were accepted, and none has been implemented so far.[3] At the local level, where the conditions make it much easier to present a petition to the local council, the implementation of citizens' initiatives still faces considerable issues. Notably, the limited autonomy of local governments, especially in terms of budget capacity, represents a main obstacle. Most petitions that were accepted, particularly those related to infrastructure and service delivery, did not result in actual improvements on the ground. For example, the citizens of a rural municipality next to Larache submitted a petition for the sanitation of the groundwater tables, but over five years since its approval by the municipal council the issue still needs to be solved, due to the lack of funds. In the end, although institutional petitions can be a viable option to voice citizens' concerns to authorities, especially at the local level, actual results are rarely achieved.

The overall assessment of institutional mechanisms' potential to bring about SA is that the promises on paper largely fall behind the actual results of these mechanisms on the ground. Citizens and CSOs have seized these tools, which has sometimes led to increased accountability, but neither requests to access information nor institutional petitions currently represent an effective tool to obtain SA.

3.4 Reviewing Social Accountability Initiatives: What Does Accountability Look Like for the People in Morocco?

This section reviews some of the SA initiatives that have been developed in Morocco since the early 2000s and then proceeds to provide the main findings in response to the research questions. This review includes initiatives that explicitly define their actions as fostering SA as well as other grassroots dynamics that attempt to exact accountability from power holders at different levels. The goal of this review is to present a wide range of initiatives, not limited to 'classic' tools and actions. The inclusion of localised dynamics also aims at identifying how SA takes shape in Morocco. Indeed, in contexts where typical accountability initiatives may not thrive, particular attention should be paid to how citizens and CSOs develop alternative and spontaneous forms of political engagement (Gaventa & Oswald, 2019, p. 11).

The initiatives have been divided into three broad categories: transparency, advocacy and participatory governance initiatives (Vloeberghs & Bergh, 2021). The choice of inclusion in one category rather than another was guided by the main focus of the initiative, but there could be overlaps with other categories. Indeed, many initiatives were developed with a multidimensional approach (such as advocacy initiatives aimed at increased participation or transparency initiatives that enable participation in governance), reminding us that the borders between these categories are often blurred. Table 3.2 showcases the initiatives reviewed in the framework of this research.

Table 3.2 Review of social accountability initiatives in Morocco

Transparency initiatives—increasing access to information and oversight capacity

- Open Budget Index, developed by the International Budget Partnership (and implemented locally by Transparency Maroc) to measure the availability of information concerning the national budget as well as citizens' inclusion in its development and its overall implementation
- Legal aid centres for victims of corruption and for whistle-blowers (Centre d'Assistance Juridique et d'Action Citoyenne, CAJAC), developed by Transparency Maroc in Rabat and Nador since 2009, including an online desk to submit complaints
- Series of training sessions on public finances targeting professionals in the media sector, aimed at increasing the quality of their media coverage of questions related to public finance, organised by Transparency Maroc with the support of Oxfam Novib in 2016
- Publication of disaggregated electoral data to foster independent analysis of electoral outcomes by the think tank Tafra
- Nouabook.ma, an online platform developed by the association SimSim – Participation Citoyenne, that provides a space to pose questions to (and receive answers from) Moroccan MPs
- Article27.ma, an online platform developed by the association SimSim – Participation Citoyenne to follow up on the implementation of the right to access information and facilitate citizens' submission of requests to access information
- Project 'Mobilisation Citoyenne Pour La Redevabilité Des Finances Publiques' (2016–2018), carried out by the association Espace Associatif and the Association Troisième Millénaire pour le Développement de l'Action associative au Sud-Est (ATMDAS), aimed at reinforcing citizens' participation in public finance through different activities—including training in mechanisms to monitor budgets, a national meeting on civil society strategies to hold municipalities to account and regional advocacy campaigns—in the Souss-Massa region, the Beni Mellal-Khénifra region and the Rabat-Salé-Kénitra region, as well as different studies on local budgets
- Project 'Paroles de jeunes', carried out by Transparency Maroc in collaboration with the Heinrich Böll Foundation office in Rabat (2018–2021), aimed at reinforcing youth's awareness of issues related to the lack of SA as well as their capacity to act and demand accountability through artistic means
- Project aimed at reviewing and following up on the ecological commitments of political parties, carried out by the association Prometheus Institute for Democracy and Human Rights (2021–2022)

Advocacy initiatives—informal pressure for accountability

- Consumers' boycott of products of the main dairy producers and water and gas distributors in Morocco, which originated in a demonstration against the rising cost of living but became a wider demonstration against social injustice and unfulfilled promises of the county's elites (2018)
- Birthday parties to celebrate the anniversary of citizens' demands of local authorities to repair potholes, in Taddart Anza, Inezgane (Agadir) and Ouled Nemma (Fqih Bensalah province) (2019)
- A call on political parties to express their commitments to women's rights by feminist collective Masaktach (2021)
- 'Wanted' posters made by the ultras group Cap Soleil to denounce the malpractices of the football team Difaâ Hassani El Jadidi with pictures of its management team, reading 'resigning and taking accountability' (2021)
- Recent social media campaigns for accountability (2021): #Justiceforyoussef to demand accountability from police officers involved in the death of a young man; #MeTooUniv to support the voice of victims of harassment in Moroccan universities and hold perpetrators to account
- Project to be carried out by Transparency Maroc to develop civil society networks aimed at advocating for increased accountability of state institutions (2021–2023)

(continued)

Table 3.2 (continued)

Participatory governance initiatives—direct participation to improve governance systems

- Participatory budgeting: the well-known participatory experience born in Porto Alegre has been implemented in different Moroccan cities, starting in the city of Tiznit in 2003–2004 due to the autonomous initiative of the municipality (Moussalih, 2021). Next were Tétouan, Chefchaouen and Larache in the framework of a project by the Foundation An-Mar. Finally, it has been deployed in Tangiers after a petition of the Centre Ibn Batouta
- Implementation of SCORE Cards by CARE Maroc in Dar Bouazza (Casablanca) to empower citizens to hold local officials to account (2013–2014)
- LEAD Project, developed by CARE Maroc aimed at the development of an SA tool targeted at the improvement of primary education institutions in urban (Casablanca-Settat region) and rural (Marrakech-Safi region) areas (2015–2018)
- Accountability dashboard, an online platform developed by the association ICT4Dev to link citizens' and associations' avenues for local participation to the achievement of the Sustainable Development Goals; three sub-platforms have also been developed for the cities of Sefrou, Tangiers and Tan-tan to provide a space for citizens and associations to facilitate the direct presentation of institutional petitions to their respective municipalities
- Project 'Li Tgal Yddar' (meaning 'what is promised is due') carried out by the association Racines in collaboration with the Heinrich Böll Foundation office in Rabat (2015–2017), aimed at increasing citizens' capacity to demand and obtain accountability, especially in relation to the management of taxes and in the framework of the electoral cycle
- Project 'Les Jeunes et la redevabilité sociale, manière de renforcer la démocratie et la participation citoyenne' (2019–2020), aimed at training youth to use SA as a tool to strengthen local democracy, carried out by the Reseau Al Amal (Al Hoceima)
- Project 'Les leaders de changement' (2019–2020) carried out by the Centre Ibn Batouta (Tangiers) and aimed at reinforcing SA and local participation of youth through training
- Alloeco.org, an online platform developed by the Observatory for the Protection of the Environment and of Historical Monuments in Tangiers (Observatoire pour la protection de l'environnement et les monuments historiques, OPEMH) to allow citizens to submit complaints related to environmental protection (2019)
- Project 'Agendas Associatifs Locaux pour l'Égalité: pour un monitoring, plaidoyer, et partenariat efficaces et responsables autour du Plan Gouvernemental de l'Égalité' (2015–2018) by Espace Associatif and the ATMDAS, aimed at reinforcing the role of civil society actors in the monitoring and implementation at the local level of the Governmental Plan for Equality, including Social Accountability Training (2018)

The presentation of the main findings will follow the four research questions that guided the study. These questions are linked by the overarching research goal of exploring what accountability looks like for the people on the ground and will therefore be explored by putting the voice of the research participants at the centre.

3.4.1 Multiple Meanings

The first research question explored the multiple meanings that citizens ascribe to accountability as well as the diversity and nuances of the terminology used on the ground. 'Accountability' and accountability dynamics have different connotations for interviewees; moreover, different terms are used depending on the context and the language employed.

From a linguistic perspective, accountability is translated in French as *redevabilité*. SA follows the same reference and is translated as *redevabilité sociale*. This is also the term international donors mainly use. The Arabic translation of accountability falls between *musāʾala*, more related to the practice of questioning, and *muḥāsaba*, which mainly refers to the rendering of (financial) accounts. The different nuances of the terms and their implications for the meaning of accountability were highlighted by several interviewees:

> In Arabic, it is difficult to translate... we use *musāʾala ijtimāʿiyya*, which means 'social questioning' if you wish. But when you translate it as *musāʾala ijtimāʿiyya* you lose the question of rendering of accounts, of accountability ... For civil society that worked on social accountability, me included, the translation that is most used is *musāʾala ijtimāʿiyya*. (Scholar, personal communication, 6 September 2021, in person)

When asked whether accountability translates into Arabic as *muḥāsaba*, one interviewee said: 'That's how it's written in the constitution, ... that is, linking responsibility (*masʾūliyya*) with accountability (*muḥāsaba*). But accountability doesn't translate very well... *musāʾala* is closer to accountability. It is as if you're almost guilty already [laughs]' (journalist, personal communication, 9 August 2021, in person).

In spite of the different nuances, it seems that the meaning related to the rendering of accounts—and consequently of holding power holders to account—is the most common amongst interviewees. For instance: 'In my mind, accountability is holding people accountable to their promises' (civil society actor 2, personal communication, 11 August 2021, in person).

> For me social accountability is the rendering of accounts from the part of public authorities, trade unions, political parties, NGOs, on any programme that is implemented. There is a duty to be accountable for the objectives that have been assigned, for the whole cycle of these policies, of development projects, or of a societal project, as in the case of political parties. (Civil society actor 15, personal communication, 15 October 2021, online)

In parallel, some interviewees evoked SA in relation to the role of civil society in monitoring and evaluating public policies. In this sense, SA is seen rather as a technical tool to observe and evaluate public policies. In the words of one interviewee: 'We believe that [SA] is one of the most important pillars for civic democracy. It is meant to monitor and evaluate local policies and action plans, and to help citizens understand the extent of implementation of policies' (civil society actor 3, personal communication, 1 September 2021, online). Another respondent stated:

> Accountability goes beyond a sanction if you break the law. It is also about how much you are satisfied with the promises that have been made. And here, civil society is still building the tools to measure and learning to evaluate... because it is about the evaluation of the public policies. (Civil society actor 2, personal communication, 11 August 2021, in person)

At the same time, different interviewees recognised that these concepts are not really discussed in Moroccan society. Further, they acknowledged that they are mostly imported and used in the framework of international cooperation—and often 'laundered' by political elites to void their original meaning and impact (civil society actor 14, personal communication, 5 October 2021, online). Furthermore, while citizens recognise practices related to the lack of accountability (such as corruption, unfulfilled electoral promises or non-transparent practices), they are less aware that they can demand accountability from power holders (civil society actor 4, personal communication, 2 September 2021, online). This is partially attributed to a self-imposed lack of legitimacy to take action and partially to the feeling that even if they do demand accountability, nothing will change. As one interviewee states, in relation to the lack of accountability:

> If you see that the majority of Moroccans do not vote, if you see that even 50 per cent of those who are registered on the electoral lists do not vote, it is because of this: because they say why am I going to vote, if when they steal, nobody makes them responsible for their actions? (Civil society actor 10, personal communication, 24 September 2021, in person)

More generally, other interviewees clarified that SA is not recognised as an explicit societal demand in Morocco: 'Honestly we don't talk much about social accountability in Morocco' (civil society actor 14, personal communication, 5 October 2021, online). 'From the side of citizens too, very few people are really looking for this social rendering [of accounts], this social accountability' (scholar, personal communication, 6 September 2021, in person).

The supposed lack of a societal demand for accountability sheds light on another key interpretation of SA in Morocco: it is understood as a claim that needs to emerge from citizens and CSOs, as a 'counter[vailing]-power' (journalist, personal communication, 9 August 2021, in person) that can spur actions aimed at reinforcing the rule of law and moving towards a more solidary society (civil society actor 14, personal communication, 5 October 2021, online). In the words of one interviewee: 'Accountability is at the heart of participation and political action, but it needs to be a demand that is brought forward by citizens' (civil society actor 4, personal communication, 2 September 2021, online). Another respondent stated:

> We work on social accountability, but not explicitly in relation to the concept. Rather, we use [the notion of] citizen power and we think that informed citizens who know their rights well are the starting point to make many things evolve in our country. ... Social accountability is a bit the other side of the coin of citizen power. Because if there is one, there is the other. If there is citizen power, it will demand accountability. And if there is accountability, surely there is citizen power behind it. (Civil society actor 16, personal communication, 15 October 2021, online)

As hinted by the quote above, another key feature of SA initiatives in Morocco is that often, those who are engaged in them do not refer to them explicitly as SA. Amongst the variety of bottom-up initiatives aimed at holding officials to account, including those reviewed in the beginning of this section, SA is explicitly mentioned mostly when actions are carried out in the framework of a project with international donors. In spite of the overall lack of a societal demand for accountability highlighted by research participants, an increasing number of initiatives aim at identifying the responsibility of power holders in different instances—with the final goal of holding them to account for their decisions and actions.

Ultimately, the understanding that SA is a demand that needs to emerge from the citizenry binds together its multiple meanings related to measuring and evaluating public policies, the questioning of people in positions of responsibility and the process of holding them to account for their promises and actions. However, the emergence of such a demand is dependent on citizens self-identifying as rights bearers—which cannot always be taken for granted. Nonetheless, over the course of the fieldwork interviewees provided different examples of actions that they identified as SA initiatives, even if this term was not explicitly employed. In the following section, I review the different methods used by citizens and civil society actors to engage in SA initiatives.

3.4.2 Mobilisation Methods

The second research question aimed at reviewing the strategies that citizens and civil society actors employ to demand accountability and mobilise the population around common issues. Even if the rather limited capacity to mobilise has been identified as an issue for civil society in Morocco (civil society actor 1, personal communication, 11 August 2021, online; civil society actor 16, personal communication, 15 October 2021, online), this research found a wide set of mobilisation strategies showcasing different approaches, scopes and arenas of action. By reviewing the initiatives listed above I identified three broad mobilisation strategies: building tools and creating spaces, raising awareness and boosting pressure. Although I reviewed the mobilisation strategies separately, actors engaged in SA initiatives do not limit themselves to one strategy or another. Rather, citizens and CSOs combine multiple strategies, aiming at the best possible combination to achieve the desired result.

Building Tools and Creating Spaces for Social Accountability

One of the main strategies is to develop and apply specific SA tools. This has been more common for organisations that engaged explicitly in SA initiatives—especially in the case of donor-funded projects. For instance, CARE Maroc developed a project aimed at the integration of SA in primary education, which included the development of a tool to facilitate collaboration amongst stakeholders aimed at solving schools' issues in a participatory fashion. The tool was named Bayan Attaakoud Al Madrassi, which roughly translates as 'schools' contractual declaration'. By bringing together 'users' and administrators, this tool sought to build consensus on realistic objectives to improve the quality of education and the physical environment in the primary schools targeted by the project (CARE International Maroc, 2019, p. 26). The collaborative spirit upholding this tool is summed up by an interviewee who worked on the project:

> The goal was to develop a tool that can be used to create a dynamic between the stakeholders of the school, such as the pupils, the parents, the teachers, the administrators, the directors, etc.... to take charge of the problems in a contractual spirit. (Scholar, personal communication, 6 September 2021, in person)

This 'contractual spirit' represents a key feature of this tool. Specifically, it aims at going beyond promises and moving towards more binding forms of engagement between stakeholders. However, different research participants explained that securing the participation of public officials (in this case of the Ministry of Education) is challenging and cannot be taken for granted (see Sect. 4.3 for more on authorities' response to SA initiatives). Therefore, it is quite rare for this type of SA initiatives to reach the stage of signing a binding engagement between societal stakeholders (such as parents' associations or schools) and authorities.

Another prominent feature of mobilisation strategies closely linked to the development of tools for SA is to create a space that gathers citizens, civil society actors and (elected and appointed) decision-makers. These gatherings seek to reduce the gap between citizens and officials, increasing available information for citizens and creating a space to question the work of decision-makers. Civil society actors mediate the encounter between decision-makers and the citizenry, opening the possibility of a dialogue between the two. In the words of an interviewee: 'We are aiming to connect the elected officials, authorities and citizens in order to give the latter more access to information in relation to the Municipal Councils' (civil society actor 8, personal communication, 17 September 2021, in person). Another said:

> We had, for example, a space where representatives of the municipalities presented their action plan. There were questions on the follow-up and

> evaluation of the projects that are in the process of implementation, or the projects that are already implemented, as well as on the follow-up of the advisory opinions of the bodies directly linked to the municipalities. (Civil society actor 3, personal communication, 1 September 2021, online)

Officials' encounter with citizens and civil society actors is seen as an opportunity to start a mutually beneficial discussion: officials can showcase the work done and receive feedback on the actual issues on the ground, while citizens improve their understanding of the work that has (and has not) been done as well as the issues that the municipality faces. This is especially true at the local level, where the geographical proximity of citizens, CSOs and officials enables easier engagement as, simply put, people know each other already.

The development of such tools and spaces is not limited to the physical encounter of citizens and decision-makers: digital platforms that aim to bridge this gap have been proliferating in recent years. They include Nouabook and Alloeco, which create a space where citizens and decision-makers connect around a specific issue. These platforms create direct avenues to present citizens' claims to decision-makers and also reinforce citizens' capacity by providing information on decision-making processes and the framework for citizen action. However, CSOs developing these platforms had to engage in substantial advocacy efforts to secure officials' engagement to participate (civil society actor 6, personal communication, 13 September 2021, in person). Moreover, while such platforms potentially increase authorities' capacity to respond to bottom-up claims (since they are more aware of citizens' demands), this does not mean that authorities are more willing to do so (Peixoto & Fox, 2016).

Raising Awareness of Fellow Citizens

While the creation of tools and spaces for SA enables citizens and CSOs to improve their access to information on certain matters, many organisations directly engage in actions aimed at raising awareness on accountability and citizens' potential role in it. In the eyes of many interviewees, the lack of awareness of the principle and practices of accountability and the limited knowledge of citizens' opportunities to hold officials to account are key barriers to the development of a 'culture of accountability' in Morocco. In other words, access to information is paramount.

Generally speaking, actions aim at raising awareness of how to identify issues related to the lack of accountability (such as corruption, mismanagement of public funds, clientelist practices and void electoral promises) and showcase the opportunities citizens have to resist them. Fundamentally, these actions present SA as a means to concretely improve people's livelihoods. Actions aimed at enhancing the right to access information provide a clear example:

> The idea is to develop the mindset in which access to information [is used] as a tool for advocacy and good governance. We don't want to file access-to-information requests for the sake of it, but we want to have citizens think about their issues and the potential solutions to them. (Civil society actor 5, personal communication, 3 September 2021, in person)

Furthermore, these activities tend to focus on actors that are less engaged in traditional forms of political action (such as youth). This also means that actions' approach needs to be adapted to the specific population they target. This results in the dissemination of notions and practices of accountability through a variety of means, ranging from video clips to theatre pieces. Indeed, art and cultural activities are seen as particularly fit vectors to share these messages. In the words of an interviewee:

> One of the first things we realised is the need to vulgarise [i.e. simplify the jargon around] those things to make sure that the youth is interested. That's when they hear words that are not so technical for them, that it is something that everyone can grasp and that, of course, that it's not something that is way beyond their interests. (Civil society actor 1, personal communication, 11 August 2021, online)

Another interviewee stated: 'We also know that when you package a message in an artistic medium, it gets across much better' (civil society actor 7, personal communication, 16 September 2021, in person).

To sum up, these activities aim at fostering a culture of accountability, engrained in a wider understanding of citizens' rights and materialised in their daily practices. Without this 'reflex' of accountability, it is much more complicated to convince fellow citizens to mobilise to hold power holders to account.

Boosting Pressure: Advocacy, Litigation and Actions in the Public Space

The last mobilisation strategy relates to the variety of tactics that citizens and CSOs deploy to increase pressure on decision-makers with the goal of holding them to account. Advocacy is a key component of mobilisation strategies employed to improve accountability. This research identified two main advocacy strategies: first, some organisations focus their efforts directly on decision-makers and attempt to influence policy-making directly. For example, some civil society actors engage in constant advocacy activities aimed at promoting (and improving) pieces of legislation related to accountability, including regulations on corruption, budget transparency, citizen participation, etc. The development of association networks is also perceived as a useful strategy, as they increase civil society's weight and pressure on political actors. Second, other CSOs aim at identifying responsible stakeholders and accountability mechanisms—or the lack thereof—in an effort to systematically tackle the lack of clarity surrounding policy-making and the implementation of projects. According to an interviewee:

> We must also ensure a reflection, but also an advocacy, to define the roles and responsibilities of public authorities ... What kind of policies are involved in this rendering [of accounts] and questioning by the legislative system? What other policies and projects are not subject to this system and for which there are no accountability measures? So, all of this can also be an advocacy plan by civil society: to point the finger where we can monitor and where there is a total blackout. (Civil society actor 15, personal communication, 15 October 2021, online)

On top of 'pointing the finger' to actors at home, some actors have leveraged international dynamics to hold Moroccan decision-makers to account for their engagements. Specifically, CSOs have called upon Morocco's status as signatory to international covenants concerning human rights as well as other multilateral initiatives, such as the Open Government Partnership (OGP), to pressure the government to uphold its international commitments. For instance, in the framework of the Universal Periodic Reviews (UPRs) by the UN Human Rights Council, local CSOs provide their assessment of the situation on the ground. In this way, the government is put in a situation in which, at the very least, it has to provide an answer to civil society's remarks. The importance of these moments is expressed by an interviewee:

> I just wanted to point out the good practice that human rights associations are doing regarding parallel reports and all that. In the frame of the United Nations Human Rights Council, at the international level, that meet in Geneva to monitor the situation, for example, of the respect of human rights, or the situation of the rights and conditions of children or of women. So that's a way of accountability. It is a moment of social accountability that brings together public authorities and civil society on these and other issues. ... it has become an annual exercise that is essential for civil society. It is an important moment even for the government, which puts a significant effort to answer questions, to respond to various comments and remarks. (Civil society actor 15, personal communication, 15 October 2021, online)

Nonetheless, research participants have highlighted how engagement with international dynamics also has its shortcomings. Notably, international organisations are criticised for being more concerned with formal compliance with a framework than with the actual situation on the ground. Often, they focus on the delivery of outcomes and fail to engage with the underlying political issues and power balances (Gaventa & McGee, 2013, p. 56). In other words, they tend to pay attention 'more to the indicator than to the result' (civil society actor 14, personal communication, 5 October 2021, by telephone). The case of the OGP and the Access to Information Law consolidates this argument. Morocco's engagement in this initiative has greatly accelerated the promulgation of the law, for which civil society had been advocating well before Morocco signed up to the OGP. Indeed, the promulgation of a law on the right to access information was a necessary condition to access the OGP. As soon as the law was passed, Morocco was able to join this initiative. However, as we have seen in Sect. 3.3, civil society has been harshly criticising the text of the law, as its regulatory framework imposes important limitations on the enjoyment of this right.

In other instances, some CSOs manage to mobilise (and sometimes obtain) SA through action in court, opting for a direct confrontation with officials to hold them accountable. This has been the case of corruption cases related to the mismanagement of public funds and property, but also of other cases where the rights of citizens were adversely affected. For instance:

> Sometimes we are active as a civil party in certain cases where corruption is proven. … we recently won a case against the president of a district in Marrakech who had sold a piece of public land for a tenth or a fifteenth of its [market] value in exchange of gifts. So he was punished with a few years in prison, as well as the acolytes who were with him. (Civil society actor 7, personal communication, 16 September 2021, in person; see also El Hourri, 2020)

> We have made protests [against the illegal use of wheel clamps in Tangiers], we have created a Facebook group that now has more than 50,000 members, and we have done a lot of things, a lot of demands, a lot of letters to the *wilāya* [regional government], to the municipality... and at the legal level we have won the trial in the first instance and in the second instance. (Civil society actor 10, personal communication, 24 September 2021; see also Zine, 2018)

As the quotes show, judicial action can bear results in some cases. However, it is also a costly process and thus not accessible to everybody. Even civil society actors find it difficult to engage with this process consistently. In relation to the lack of response to access-to-information requests, an interviewee explains that the financial burden of judiciary procedures is a key obstacle: 'There were some participants that wanted to proceed to the administrative court. However, it became a matter of financial means to recruit a lawyer and we could not proceed further' (civil society actor 5, personal communication, 3 September 2021, in person).

Finally, demonstrations in public space remain a central mobilisation strategy for citizens and civil society actors. In Morocco, the increasing engagement in forms of protest and social movements has been identified as a response to the limitations provided by traditional mechanisms of accountability (Saadi, 2012).

Although a presence on the street is still seen as the most effective strategy to get the attention of authorities, the increasing repression of demonstrations in public spaces means that they are becoming an increasingly risky endeavour. Officially in effect until March 2023, the measures introduced in the framework of the government response to the Covid-19 pandemic further limited the possibility to engage in street-level action. This has contributed to increasing mobilisation on social media, which research participants have identified as a key strategy to foster SA. Social media are valued for their potential to reach fellow citizens beyond one's geographical position, and thus federate a larger number of people around common issues. Another advantage is the relative (legal and physical) protection offered in comparison with street-level mobilisation. As explained by an interviewee:

> You can be anonymous and act digitally. And it's not the same thing when you go out on the street: you are seen and identified, you will be either arrested or prosecuted afterwards. Digital technology ensures this anonymity... this protection, if you can say that. ... Everything that is missing in the real world, you find it online. But the risk [of being identified and prosecuted] is still there... it exists, but at home, it's less compared to the street. (Journalist, personal communication, 9 August 2021, in person)

It is difficult to assess the impact of social media campaigns, as they often provide the 'illusion of participation' (civil society actor 4, personal communication, 2 September 2021, online). There are different examples in which they have been strategic in supporting a mobilisation aimed at achieving accountability. For example, the recent case of sexual harassment at various Moroccan universities (known in the media as 'sex for grades') has been bolstered by the unprecedented number of women who came forward on social media to share the harassment they suffered. This wave of testimony has been supported by different social media campaigns, including by the collective #7chak and the movement Moroccan Outlaws, who have been relaying these messages while ensuring the women's anonymity.

3.4.3 *Response from Authorities*

As is evident from the findings related to mobilisation in public spaces, the choice of strategy is deeply influenced by authorities' responses. The particular stance of local authorities, ranging from national decision-makers to the security apparatus, plays a key role in determining the margin of action for citizens and CSOs.

Beyond the need to acknowledge the multiplicity and diversity of CSOs in Morocco, and thus the plurality of the relationships with authorities, this research uncovered some recurring features in the experiences of actors and organisations engaged in SA initiatives with authorities at different levels. At the same time, the important differences between types of authorities (elected-appointed, local-national, etc.) and their interaction have to be taken into consideration when exploring their response to SA initiatives. On the one hand, there is a contradictory stance: while there is a general sensitivity to these initiatives, as reflected in a dominant government discourse calling for increased citizen participation and engagement, the authorities put in place many serious obstacles to effective citizen engagement, as we have seen. On the other hand, this contradictory stance needs to be nuanced by the important differences between the responses of national and local authorities, the responses in specific localities and the factors that can prompt such responses.

The contradictory stance of Moroccan authorities towards accountability has already been discussed as part of the overall context of accountability in Morocco. While the Constitution and the ensuing institutions seem to provide a promising legal and policy framework for effective accountability, actual results on the ground are disappointing. In turn, the limited efficiency of institutional protocols is attributed to the lack of a political will for strengthened accountability. Research participants highlighted the reality of these contradictions by describing their experiences with securing officials' engagement for their initiatives.

A Complicated Relationship with Civil Society

The generally limited engagement of Moroccan authorities with SA initiatives can be explained by the overall nature of the relationship between authorities and civil society. This relationship is often characterised as antagonistic, as authorities (especially those composed of elected officials) look at CSOs as an opposition force—competing for popular approval and support. Research participants believe that officials avoid engaging directly with CSOs, since their participation could lead to them 'being exposed' for their mismanagement of and misconduct in specific issues as well as their lack of knowledge of the situation on the ground (civil society actor 4, personal communication, 2 September 2021, online; civil society actor 1, personal communication, 11 August September 2021, online). Indeed, the different appreciation of the situation on the ground often fosters such conflict:

> When you bring someone, for example, from the ministry, they present you something official, but they have no idea what's going on in the field. … Civil society actors know exactly what's in the field and so decision-makers

> feel attacked. Usually, it's not a very positive discussion. (Civil society actor 1, personal communication, 11 August 2021, online)

In spite of this underlying tension, research participants observed that it is easier to engage with public officials in smaller towns than in bigger cities. This is also the experience of those implementing projects targeting Morocco as a whole, which shows that officials are more responsive in small cities than in larger urban centres. In smaller localities, the proximity between officials and civil society actors implies a certain degree of collaboration. Not only is civil society closer to the citizenry and has an increased capacity to mobilise, but it also works in closer contact with public officials. Hence, the chances of positive collaboration increase.

Finally, a good relationship with local authorities is sometimes a necessary condition for CSOs to carry out their actions—including SA initiatives. This is especially true for participatory governance initiatives, whose success relies on a certain degree of collaboration. If CSOs want to work directly with municipalities, schools, health centres, etc., they have to develop a good relationship with the authorities that manage these institutions. However, the need for a good relationship goes beyond participatory governance initiatives, and CSOs often depend on such relationships to carry out other initiatives, especially in public space. This need may also impact the overall stance of CSOs towards local authorities, as explained by this interviewee:

> [Local CSOs] try to be as critical as they want, to a certain level, and try to ask for accountability as well. But they would still try to maintain a good relation with the authorities, because they definitely need it to occupy the public space. (Civil society actor 1, personal communication, 11 August 2021, online)

Once again, it is the specific relationship between local authorities and CSOs that structures authorities' collaboration with and participation in CSOs' actions—including in SA initiatives. Authorities tend to participate in CSOs' initiatives when the risk of conflict or exposure is limited, and this happens especially in smaller cities, where proximity binds authorities and civil society to the same locality and thus ensures a certain level of collaboration. This risks being problematic for SA, as attempts to hold local officials to account are in tension with the need to maintain a good relationship with local authorities—implicitly limiting the extent to which local actors can be critical.

Bottom-Up Demands, (Some) Top-Down Responses

Researching authorities' participation in SA initiatives sheds further light on the discretionary nature that characterises Moroccan authorities' approach to accountability. Research participants observed that authorities' engagement is dependent on the specific relations they have with the citizenry and with CSOs. Similar observations emerge in relation to authorities' concrete responses to grassroots initiatives, which are often guided by ad hoc considerations rather than a comprehensive approach to bottom-up demands for accountability.

A key trend is that responses are prioritised when the situation could escalate towards wider demands or increased unrest. Research participants stressed that Moroccan authorities are not oblivious to popular demands. On the contrary, they are able to react promptly where and when needed. For instance, Moroccan authorities are believed to be extremely aware of the differences in terms of mobilisation capacities and propensities in the different regions of the country, allowing them to prioritise responses in specific areas. This is motivated by the potential 'snowball effect' of mobilisation in sensitive contexts: regions that have showed an increased tendency to mobilise, especially where precarious socio-economic conditions could further amplify the intensity of demonstrations, receive a swift response from Moroccan authorities. This interviewee provided some examples:

> When [citizens] react, I think that the state has the means to know, to test, to understand the expectations of these people and finally, if and how it should act … historically, certain areas of the country were much more militant than others, whether during colonialism or during the fight for liberation. … If there is a problem in this or that area, they will react quickly because they know that Casablanca, it's not a joke. When it bursts, it is practically impossible to control … from what I see, you can have the same problem in Jerada and in Ouarzazate, but the state prefers to act quickly in Ouarzazate because it has other issues in that area. The state prefers to respond to that area and according to other criteria rather than accountability itself, showing that other considerations push for this or that choice. (Civil society actor 16, personal communication, 15 October 2021, online)

Besides taking into account the specific situation of different localities, the responsiveness of Moroccan authorities is also associated with the contextual factors of citizens' initiatives for accountability. Here, the relative mediatisation of initiatives plays a key role. Moroccan authorities are believed to be very attentive to public debate (in both traditional and social media): when an issue becomes the concern of public opinion, it is more likely that a response will follow. For example, a draft law aimed at regulating social media was approved by the government some days after proclaiming the state of emergency to deal with the Covid-19 pandemic, but it was rescinded after a wide mobilisation on social media. The impact of contextual factors on this matter was highlighted by this interviewee:

> It was taken off the government agenda, officially. ... It was the effect of social networks, but I think the context contributed to that. The context of lockdown and Covid-19 ... the state needed the minimum of problems and unrest and that's why they withdrew the law. (Journalist, personal communication, 9 August 2021, in person)

To sum up, authorities' responses to SA initiatives depend first and foremost on the specific relations between citizens and civil society actors promoting the initiative on the one hand and the concerned administration on the other. A good relationship can be conducive to a positive response by authorities, but latent frictions between authorities and civil society greatly limit this possibility. In parallel, authorities have showed responsiveness to bottom-up initiatives, but in the form of a 'drip system of accountability' (civil society actor 16, personal communication, 15 October 2021, online) instead of a systematic approach to state–society relations. Such a drip system resembles forms of tokenism, where power holders maintain the discretion to decide which popular demands they will follow up. Instead of structural change, limited top-down concessions are the main form in which Moroccans experience accountability. As an interviewee eloquently put it, 'in Morocco, accountability only happens when the regime decides to dismiss elected officials' (journalist, personal communication, 9 August 2021, in person).

3.4.4 Outcomes

This section concludes the empirical portion of the paper by reviewing the outcomes of SA initiatives. To avoid overlap with the sections above, it will present additional elements to nurture reflection on the conditions that enable SA initiatives to have an impact and on the obstacles that limit them.

What Can Citizens and Civil Society Actually Do?
Perhaps unsurprisingly, the overall feeling is that citizens and civil society alone rarely manage to hold power holders to account through SA initiatives. Specifically, the success of grassroots initiatives is dependent on a number of factors that go beyond the sole action of citizens and CSOs:

> Sometimes it doesn't just depend on [civil society] and on good citizens, it also depends on who is in charge of our context, our environment. Are they listening? Do they respond? Are they attentive or rather not? And how can we use all the means that are available? It is a set of ingredients. (Civil society actor 16, personal communication, 15 October 2021, online)

Institutional shortcomings—in terms of a lack of electoral accountability and the failure of institutional protocols, including the limited impact of institutional mechanisms for citizen participation—give citizens the impression that accountability is neither possible nor desired. SA initiatives manage to reach their expected results only in specific circumstances, when there is a special relationship with a given authority or when contextual factors favour a wide mobilisation. Overall, when efforts are measured against the results obtained, the assessment is rather bleak:

> When you analyse all this, everything that has been considered so far, which was supposed to introduce a number of changes in principles, through reforms… All this for that? All these efforts for that little change? Small, big, or medium actions, in terms of results, we simply aren't there yet. (Scholar, personal communication, 6 September 2021, in person)

Even when the results obtained by SA initiatives are recognised, research participants question the extent to which changes at the micro-level can have an impact at the macro-level, given the resistance by authorities as well as the obstacles for citizens and civil society to scale up and eventually institutionalise their initiatives (civil society actor 14, personal communication, 5 October 2021, by telephone).

Results in the Short Term, Doubts About the Long Term

Another central limitation of the outcomes of SA initiatives is that results cannot easily be reproduced in other contexts, scaled up or even institutionalised.

First and foremost, the lifespan of donor-funded initiatives is often limited to the duration of such funding—especially if local authorities do not engage with them. This has been noted in the case of participatory budgets in Morocco. Goehrs (2017) demonstrates a key difference between cities that financed an initiative through the municipality's budget and those that relied on international funding alone. In the former, continuity was ensured by the will of the municipality (and materialised in its budget support) while in the latter these initiatives ended at the same time as the project.

Moreover, the engagement of national authorities is a key step in scaling up and institutionalising local initiatives. However, citizens and civil society face significant challenges in reaching higher-level decision-makers. On the one hand, the complex and bureaucratic nature of decision-making in Morocco makes it harder to understand who is the right person to talk to (civil society actor 12, personal communication, 5 October 2021, online). This is related not only to overlaps between multiple administration layers but also to a lack of clarity about who occupies which position (civil society actor 13, personal communication, 5 October 2021, online). On the other hand, this lack of clarity is coupled with limited communication with and availability of high-level decision-makers. This is visible on institutional websites: most ministries' websites list hardly any information on who occupies which position. When names are indicated, there are no contact details except the main telephone number of the ministry in Rabat and generic 'contact@' email addresses. This limited information makes one wonder whether this opacity is a deliberate strategy. In sum, civil society rarely manages to get in touch with, and even less meet, decision-makers that could play a role in the institutionalisation of SA initiatives, such as ministers, heads of directorates and other high-level profiles at the level of central administration (civil society actor 12, personal communication, 5 October 2021, online). This limited availability is exacerbated by the highly centralised decision-making system. As eloquently explained by this interviewee:

> Today, the whole architecture is complicated... the decision is not at the local level, but at the national level and the national level has priorities,

> they are looking at policies and big strategies. So today we haven't found the magic formula to connect the dots, how to make [national and local authorities] sit together to make things happen. … There are too many layers for the decision. You have the municipality, the province, the region, then there is the *wālī* [regional governor], then the *wālī* has the Ministry of Interior… there are so many stakeholders. (Civil society actor 2, personal communication, 11 August 2021, in person)

Ultimately, these limitations reinforce doubts about the long-term effects of SA initiatives. If civil society wants to ensure the continuity of its initiatives, it needs to make important efforts to secure the engagement of not only local authorities but also national stakeholders.

Civil Society's Resilience: The Vital Ingredient for Change?

The rather pessimistic outlook that has been presented so far does not necessarily lead to the conclusion that citizens and civil society are not standing their ground. On the contrary, actions of citizens and civil society are seen as the main and potentially last hope for achieving any result:

> There are lawyers' associations, there are consumer protection associations, there are human rights associations that continue to make their voices heard and to hurt. They continue to hurt by bringing complaints, for example, in court, against officials, etc... I think they resist. They do not bow down like politicians or political parties do. Civil society resists. … You even see people who have left political parties to focus on civil society work, because they see that there is an impact. Whether it's with activities on the ground, or doing something through the means that exist now, like petitions and all that, or for advocacy. Advocacy is more effective, and it's heard more than political parties. … To express the same idea, for me, it would be better to do it in the name of the civil society than to do it in the name of a political party: I would have more difficulties to pass the messages with a political position. It is no longer credible. It has been completely discredited. (Journalist, personal communication, 9 August 2021, in person)

As highlighted in this extract, civil society still manages to resist and make its voice heard. Civil society is increasingly occupying the space left by the shrinking role of political parties and trade unions, who have progressively been losing their legitimacy as political intermediaries (Mouna, 2020). In spite of the negative results, actors on the ground are not discouraged:

> Not reaching our goal doesn't mean we're going backwards. We'll always keep going forward and doing what we should be doing. For us, if you're not going to do anything, you're not going to change anything. But if we submit, for example, ten petitions and one goes well, we already won one. If we don't submit anything, we won't win anything. We think like that: we are going to do 100 trials, if we win three that's good, if we win five that's good, if we got one that's good too, but if we don't do any, we will never win anything. (Civil society actor 10, personal communication, 24 September 2021, in person)

Civil society actors' experience that continuous pressure can bear results motivates their persistence and resilience. Most of all, the awareness that 'you cannot undo a system that has been developed in 60 years from one day to another' (civil society actor 4, personal communication, 2 September 2021, online) motivates civil society to continue to exercise such pressure. Be it during years of strategic advocacy aimed at improving the legislative framework or through the contentious actions of grassroots groups to hold decision-makers to account for the respect of their rights, civil society continues to exercise a central role in bringing about change in Morocco.

3.5 Conclusion

In Morocco, the institutional context fundamentally influences how SA initiatives are carried out and the impact they have. First, institutional protocols for accountability are in place but have so far not produced many results. The regime's preference for using extra-institutional avenues coupled with a general lack of political will for accountability substantially reduces the 'bite' of the bodies and institutions formally charged with holding high-level stakeholders to account. At the same time, the institutional mechanisms available to citizens to demand accountability have an ambiguous record: they have been used to demand accountability, and sometimes even achieved concrete results, but the combination of built-in limits to what can be demanded and how, in addition to contextual obstacles, undermines their potential as a systematic tool for bottom-up accountability. This research also found that while citizens and CSOs are aware that they have a role in holding power holders to account, the realisation of this role cannot be taken for granted. Centrally, it depends on the degree to which these actors self-identify as citizens and right-bearers and the degree to which they consider engaging with accountability to be a societal demand. However, the fact that they hardly see accountability applied at the national level substantially reduces their expectations of what they can achieve.

Nonetheless, citizens and CSOs have carried out a plethora of initiatives. They include the development of tools, spaces and digital platforms to connect citizens and decision-makers as well as multiple actions (such as advocacy efforts, strategic litigation and protest) to increase pressure on specific stakeholders and hold them accountable for their actions and decisions. In spite of some positive experiences, the overall response of authorities remains limited. This is due partly to the complicated relationship of authorities with civil society actors—especially with those critical of authorities' work—and partly to the considerations that motivate the response. Specifically, the logic of avoiding escalation prompts sporadic concessions rather than consistent accountability. This has led to overall pessimism regarding what SA initiatives can achieve, especially in terms of scaling up and institutionalising results achieved at the local level. Nonetheless, the perseverance of civil society actors remains central to improving the situation. Civil society acts with the awareness that results may come in the long run and that limited results today should not diminish their will to achieve change—both at the micro-level and the macro-level.

Notes

1. Institutional petitions follow the conditions set out by Organic Law no. 44-14 in relation to national authorities, or the regulation on the right to petition the council of local governments defined in the organic laws on regions (no. 111-14), provinces and prefectures (no. 112-14) and municipalities (no. 113-14).
2. The law also provides for the proactive publication of information by authorities, which has not been mentioned in the text since it does not depend on citizens' initiative. It is nonetheless relevant for its potential contribution to accountability in Morocco.
3. Data retrieved from https://www.eparticipation.ma/, the online portal dedicated to citizens' participation in Morocco (retrieved 24 January 2023).

References

Aspers, P., & Corte, U. (2019). What is qualitative in qualitative research. *Qualitative Sociology, 42*(2), 139–160. https://doi.org/10.1007/s11133-019-9413-7

Belghazi, A. (2014, December 2). Droit d'accès à l'information, le Maroc critiqué au FMDH. *Medias24*. https://medias24.com/2014/12/02/droit-dacces-a-linformation-le-maroc-critique-au-fmdh/

Bendourou, O. (2012). La nouvelle Constitution marocaine du 29 juillet 2011. *Revue Française De Droit Constitutionnel, 91*(3), 511–535. https://doi.org/10.3917/rfdc.091.0511

Berrada, E. (2018, May 17). Maroc: le Parlement rend public un rapport sur les prix des carburants sur fond de boycott commercial. *Jeune Afrique*. https://www.jeuneafrique.com/560340/economie/maroc-le-parlement-rend-public-un-rapport-sur-les-prix-des-carburants-sur-fond-de-boycott-commercial/

CARE International Maroc. (2019). *Evaluation finale du projet LEAD 'Intégration de la Redevabilité Sociale dans l'Education pour le Développement'*. https://www.careevaluations.org/wp-content/uploads/EVALUATION-FINALE-DU-PROJET-LEAD-INTEGRATION-DE-LA-REDEVABILITE-SOCIALE-DANS-L'EDUCATION-POUR-LES-DEVELOPPEMENT.pdf

Colin, F. (2023). Institutional petitions in Morocco: Opportunities and challenges of claiming rights in participatory arenas. *British Journal of Middle Eastern Studies, 50*(2), 486–500. https://doi.org/10.1080/13530194.2021.1981233

Conseil de la Concurrence: La commission ad-hoc livre son rapport sur la gestion du dossier des hydrocarbures. (2021, March 22). *L'Opinion*. https://www.lopinion.ma/Conseil-de-la-Concurrence-La-commission-ad-hoc-livre-son-rapport-sur-la-gestion-du-dossier-des-hydrocarbures_a12874.html

Dalil, R. (2021, 17 September). Gouvernement Akhannouch: argent, pouvoir et paranoïa. *Telquel*. https://telquel.ma/2021/09/17/gouvernement-akhannouch-argent-pouvoir-et-paranoia_1737055

Droit d'accès à l'information. Il faut attendre 2020. (2019, March 6). *LesEco.ma*. https://leseco.ma/maroc/droit-d-acces-a-l-information-il-faut-attendre-2020.html

El Hourri, A. (2020, November 29). Affaire Casino Es Saadi: la condemnation e Abdellatif Abdouh confirmée. *Medias24*. https://medias24.com/2020/11/29/affaire-casino-es-saadi-la-condamnation-de-abdellatif-abdouh-confirmee/

El Hourri, A. (2021a, March 24). Jouahri sur le dossier des hydrocarbures: Circulez, il n'y a rien à voir. *Medias24*. https://medias24.com/2021/03/24/jouahri-sur-le-dossier-des-hydrocarbures-circulez-il-ny-a-rien-a-voir/

El Hourri, A. (2021b, September 20). Conseil de la Concurrence: règlement intérieur modifié, grande réforme attendue. *Medias24*. https://medias24.com/2021/09/20/conseil-de-la-concurrence-reglement-interieur-retoque-grande-reforme-attendue/

Gaventa, J., & McGee, R. (2013). The impact of transparency and accountability initiatives. *Development Policy Review, 31*, s3–s28. https://doi.org/10.1111/dpr.12017

Gaventa, J., & Oswald, K. (2019). *Empowerment and accountability in difficult settings: What are we learning? Key messages emerging from the Action for Empowerment and Accountability Programme*. IDS. https://assets.publishing.service.gov.uk/media/5e5687a886650c53a363f749/A4EA_Synthesis_Report_Phase1_FINAL.pdf

Goehrs, M. (2017). Budgets participatifs: s'approprier la dialectique de la gouvernance participative locale. *L'année Du Maghreb, 16*, 223–244. https://doi.org/10.4000/anneemaghreb.3061

Hickey, S., & King, S. (2016). Understanding social accountability: Politics, power and building new social contracts. *The Journal of Development Studies, 52*(8), 1225–1240. https://doi.org/10.1080/00220388.2015.1134778

Le Conseil de la Concurrence bientôt de retour? (2015, February 23). *Telquel*. https://telquel.ma/2015/02/23/nouvelle-autorite-concurrence-bientot_1435520

Mouna, K. (2020). Civil society versus the state: The case of Morocco. *European Foreign Affairs Review, 25*(Special Issue), 67–86. https://doi.org/10.54648/EERR2020012

Moussalih, A. (2021). Dispositif participatifs à Tiznit: de l'expérience endogène à la méthode procédurale. In A. Iraki & A. Houdret (Eds.), *La participation citoyenne au Maroc: Entre expériences passées et régionalisation avancée* (pp. 189–224). Institut National Aménagement Urbain and German Development Institut.

Peixoto, T., & Fox, J. (2016). When does ICT-enabled citizen voice lead to government responsiveness? *IDS Bulletin, 41*(1), 23–39. https://doi.org/10.19088/1968-2016.104

Saadi, M. S. (2012). Water privatization dynamics in Morocco: A critical assessment of the Casablancan case. *Mediterranean Politics, 17*(3), 376–393. https://doi.org/10.1080/13629395.2012.725302

Shalaby, M., & Bergh, S. I. (2020, September 30). *Power to the people? The right to information law in Morocco*. Sada—Carnegie Endowment for International Peace. https://carnegieendowment.org/sada/82835

Vloeberghs, W. P., & Bergh, S. I. (2021, March 10). *Weapons of discontent? Sketching a research agenda on social accountability in the Arab Middle East and North Africa* (ISS working paper no. 671). https://repub.eur.nl/pub/135292

Zine, G. (2018, December 27). Tanger: Les habitants obtiennent gain de cause contre la pose de sabot. *Yabiladi*. https://www.yabiladi.com/articles/details/72706/tanger-habitants-obtiennent-gain-cause.html

CHAPTER 4

Social Accountability in Tunisia: Processes of Learning in Civic Innovation Between 2011 and 2021

Intissar Kherigi and Tasnim Chirchi

Abstract This chapter explores the different conceptions of social accountability held by Tunisian civil society actors and public officials in the context of the country's transition from authoritarian rule between 2011 and 2021. It analyses the strategies and methods used by civil society actors to engage citizens in demanding accountability, to exact accountability from public officials and to enforce commitments. The chapter draws on qualitative research methods, namely semi-structured interviews, one focus group discussion and three in-depth case studies conducted between April and September 2021. We find that four main factors were important to the success of SA initiatives: first, the need for civil society to build credibility with both citizens and officials over time;

I. Kherigi (✉)
Institut d'Etudes Politiques de Paris (Sciences-Po), Paris, France

Southern Mediterranean University, Tunis, Tunisia

T. Chirchi
Ibn Haldun University, Başakşehir, Turkey

W. Vloeberghs and S. I. Bergh (eds.), *Social Accountability Initiatives in Morocco, Tunisia, and Lebanon*, EADI Global Development Series,
https://doi.org/10.1007/978-3-031-51322-0_4

second, the importance of tackling both ends of the accountability equation by working with citizens and officials to strengthen the commitment of both to accountability; third, the need to build coalitions of CSOs and local–national civil society linkages; and fourth, utilising cooperative as well as confrontational strategies towards officials that involve multiple methods, such as media campaigns, community mobilisation and training for officials. When these factors were present, SA initiatives were seen to advance downward accountability and reshape state–society relations.

Keywords Social accountability · Participation · Civil society · Democratisation · Tunisia · Local governance

4.1 Introduction

This chapter analyses the different conceptions of accountability and social accountability (SA) held by Tunisian civil society actors and public officials. It explores (a) the multiple ways in which local actors understand the word 'accountability', (b) the strategies they use to mobilise fellow citizens and exact accountability from public officials and (c) their perceptions of the value of SA in getting power holders to deliver on commitments. We find that conceptions of accountability cover a wide range of notions, from answerability—the right of citizens to question public officials—through to citizen participation in decision-making.

We find that Tunisian civil society actors and public officials broadly view SA as a set of initiatives undertaken by civil society or citizens aimed at achieving governance based on rule of law, transparency, integrity, citizen participation and inclusive development, and as a means of putting an end to a governance model dominated by corruption, nepotism, legal impunity and exclusionary policies that serve a narrow elite close to power. SA is viewed as a broad set of strategies and tools to *supplement* classical forms of accountability, such as elections and representative institutions, rather than replacing them. Between 2011 and 2021, several advances were made in Tunisia in adopting and enabling legal framework for accountability, including new laws on transparency and access to information, conflicts of interest, declarations of interest rules, etc. However, in the face of continued resistance by some public officials and institutions, as well as interest groups, civil society had to pursue strategies to 'activate' these laws, using various methods to pressure public officials and institutions to adhere to their legal obligations.

In the political opening since the 2011 uprising, the range of SA methods available to citizens significantly expanded. We find that social media in particular provided a cheap and accessible tool for ordinary citizens and civil society groups to expose wrongdoing and pressure officials to respond to public demands. To some extent, the ability to film and broadcast acts by public officials and the existence of free media able to amplify social media posts caused a shift in the traditional relationship between ruler and ruled, making public officials more vigilant about the risks involved in flouting legal standards. In some instances, as we explore below, SA tools were effectively used to force government institutions or individual public officials to account for decisions, reverse specific decisions or adopt changes to government policy.

However, while effective in some cases, SA tools have been of limited value where public officials were able to disregard them without any consequences, and where citizens were unable to apply sufficient pressure to force officeholders to respect the law. For example, access-to-information obligations introduced since 2011 have been flouted by some powerful ministries, which simply refuse to comply with information requests without facing any sanctions. Thus, the ability of SA to deliver results is highly variable. It appears to be most successful when there is a combination of bottom-up pressure from citizens together with responsiveness from allies within public institutions willing to overcome institutional resistance and give SA 'teeth'.

We also observe that civil society actors' efforts to exact accountability using SA tools are frustrated by short-term, project-based approaches. Civil society organisations (CSOs) that depend on international donor funding complain that accountability cannot be built through projects of one to two years requiring immediate, demonstrable results. Instead, SA is seen as involving long-term, iterative processes, where CSOs can experiment with different strategies, learn from failures and build up social capital in the form of engaged citizens, organisational credibility and experience. This effort is undermined by the project-based approach of most international donor support, which typically requires CSOs to focus on short-term aims and demonstrate measurable short-term results.

Finally, the findings show that all the civil society actors involved in the SA initiatives covered by the study concluded, through a process of experimentation, that SA tools are most effective where they use both collaborative and confrontational strategies to exacting accountability. Many of the SA initiatives examined began by using confrontational methods alone when seeking to forcing public institutions to be accountable. However, over time, they developed more collaborative approaches that involved cooperating with public institutions and identifying allies within them who could help them achieve their demands. Through a process of learning, civil society actors shifted towards SA approaches that worked on building alliances with reformers within public institutions while also placing pressure when needed, in order to overcome resistance. Through iterative processes, civil society actors learned how to analyse institutional dynamics, negotiate with officials and develop strategies using a mixture of confrontation and collaboration to pressure, persuade and cajole public institutions to account for their actions and respond to the needs of ordinary citizens.

The chapter is structured as follows. Section 4.2 sets out the methodology used in the study. Section 4.3 provides a background to the political and institutional context in Tunisia, with a focus on changes following the 2011 uprising. It also describes the legal framework on SA in Tunisia at the time that the initial phase of research was conducted (April–June 2021). Finally, it examines the emergence of SA as a concept since 2011, providing examples of SA initiatives involving state institutions and civil society actors identified through the mapping phase. Using Hickey and King's (2016) typology of SA initiatives, these were categorised into three groups: (a) *transparency* initiatives aimed at increasing citizens' access to information on public decisions; (b) *contentious actions*, such as public demonstrations, public campaigns and public interest litigation; and (c) *participatory governance* initiatives, aimed at involving citizens in decision-making processes. Sections 4.4–4.7 constitute the main body of the chapter and seek to answer the main research questions in the study, as set out above. The chapter ends with a section setting out key themes and conclusions.

4.2 Methodology

The chapter draws on a range of qualitative research methods, namely semi-structured interviews, a focus group discussion (FGD) and in-depth case studies conducted between April and September 2021. The first phase involved desk research, through which we mapped SA initiatives in Tunisia based on an Arabic-language online search using Google, the official civil society database IFEDA (Centre d'Information, de Formation d'Études et de Documentation sur les Associations), civil society platform Jamaity and Facebook, the most popular social media platform for Tunisian CSOs.

The mapping exercise identified a number of documents on SA, which include annual reports of CSOs, assessments, charters, government and UN reports. This exercise helped identify the main actors in the SA field. Since the research questions focused on how *local* actors view SA, the choice was made to focus on domestic actors, specifically Tunisian CSOs, as the primary actors leading SA initiatives. In addition, we decided to include a small number of Tunisian government officials in the FGD, given that state institutions are involved in SA initiatives. The discussion thus provided an opportunity to juxtapose the differing conceptions of SA that civil society and governmental actors hold and the interaction between these two groups in the context of SA initiatives.

We organised the SA initiatives identified through the mapping according to (a) the type of lead actor (state institution, national or local CSO, bi- or multilateral organisation) and (b) the type of SA initiative, based on Hickey and King's (2016) categorisation, as set out in Sect. 4.3.2. An interview list was prepared that sought to cover all three types of lead actors and the three types of SA initiative (transparency initiatives, contentious action and participatory governance initiatives). Thirteen semi-structured interviews were conducted with 12 representatives of Tunisian CSOs and one expert on SA initiatives (Table 4.1).

Table 4.1 Interview sample categorised by type of SA initiative

Transparency initiatives	Al Bawsala ATIDE Pole Civile Min Hakki Nsaalek Network
Contentious action initiatives	El Comita I Watch Tunisia Green Network
Participatory governance initiatives	Action Associative iChange Jasmine Foundation National Federation of Tunisian Municipalities WeStart

Based on the sampling, a hybrid FGD was organised with 14 participants—four public officials (one elected municipal official, one national-level bureaucrat and two municipal bureaucrats) and 10 civil society representatives. A gender balance was sought, with eight male and six female participants attending.

The initial research plan included a third phase of case studies involving participant observation of three SA initiatives. However, due to Covid-19 health restrictions imposed in May–July 2021 the research plan was modified. Instead, interviews were carried out within the Tunis area with representatives of three CSOs that were leading SA initiatives. The selection drew on the initiatives identified in the mapping, interviews and FGD and was designed to compare SA initiatives according to the typology of the three different approaches to exacting accountability developed by Hickey and King—one transparency initiative, one contentious action initiative and one participatory governance initiative. All interviews and the FGD were conducted in Tunisian Arabic dialect. They were recorded, transcribed and analysed manually.

4.3 Accountability in the Tunisian Context

After its 2010–2011 uprising, Tunisia underwent significant political and constitutional change, including holding free and fair elections, greater competition in political life and a significant growth in civil society activity. Street protests, strikes and other forms of social contestation increased significantly across the country (Forum Tunisien de Droits Economiques et Sociaux n.d.). The number of registered CSOs rose from approximately 9,000 in 2011 to 23,700 in 2020, with particular growth in associations working on election monitoring, rule of law, citizen participation and a range of themes related to institutional reforms, as well as development (IFEDA, 2021). The political transition also brought about an influx of international organisations and donor funding.

Successive governments between 2011 and 2021 adopted an agenda of 'good governance' reforms. Tunisia joined the Open Government Partnership in 2014 and made a range of 'open gov' commitments relating to access to information, promoting public participation and combating corruption (Open Government Partnership Tunisia n.d.-a). Numerous 'good governance' initiatives were launched, such as the creation of a national anti-corruption agency (Law no. 59, 2017, on the Good Governance and Anti-Corruption Authority); a national good governance and anti-corruption strategy; an online platform to promote transparency in procurement processes (2013); a code of conduct for public officials (2014); a new governmental decree on public procurement designed to strengthen transparency and complaints mechanisms (2014); the creation of Governance Units within all ministries, governorates, large municipalities and state-owned enterprises to implement good governance principles (Decree no. 1158, 2016, on Establishing Governance Units in Public Institutions); the creation of the position of coordinator for relations with civil society and citizens in most ministries, the presidency and Parliament, tasked with responding to and managing relations with civil society and citizens; the adoption of a law on the right to access to information (Law no. 22 of 2016) and a law protecting whistle-blowers (Law no. 10, 2017, on Reporting Corruption and Protection of Whistle-Blowers); the introduction of an obligation to introduce a citizen charter for all public authorities in direct contact with the public (2018); and legislation on declarations of assets and conflicts of interest for all public officials (Law no. 46, 2018, on Declaration of Assets and Interests and Combatting Illicit Enrichment and Conflicts of Interest), among others.

The Constitution adopted in January 2014 set out a number of principles to guide the work of public authorities, including 'transparency, integrity, efficiency and accountability' (article 15, see Constitute Project, n.d.). It also stipulated the creation of a number of independent constitutional bodies to oversee the protection and promotion of good governance, anti-corruption, media freedoms and human rights. Chapter 7 of the 2014 Constitution also introduced an obligation for local authorities to ensure citizen participation in decision-making (article 139).

While the legal framework is largely praised by civil society activists, implementation leaves much to be desired, as discussed below. According to the Organisation for Economic Co-operation and Development (OECD, 2019), corruption costs represent 54% of Tunisia's GDP. Public opinion points to high levels of dissatisfaction with governance, with 67% of Tunisians believing corruption had increased in a 2017 poll (OECD, 2019). Institutional reforms to strengthen accountability and combat corruption have run into obstacles, with independent bodies such as the National Anti-Corruption Authority (Instance nationale de lutte contre la corruption, INLUCC) and Truth and Justice Commission complaining of having their work obstructed by other state institutions (Amnesty International, 2018).

Within the context of accountability initiatives, both the national government and international donors have emphasised civil society's role in pushing for the implementation of legal and institutional frameworks that promote accountability. Since 2011, legal restrictions on civil society have been lifted and it has significantly expanded, in terms of both the number of CSOs and their areas of work, from election monitoring, judicial reform, women's rights, transitional justice and human rights to development and job creation. A number of national organisations have emerged that enjoy significant visibility and regularly appear in the media to comment on public affairs. The status and credibility of civil society have also been enhanced through the involvement of CSOs in shaping key laws and brokering dialogue, such as the 2013–2014 National Dialogue Quartet, which was awarded the Nobel Peace Prize. This international recognition reinforced the legitimacy of civil society and its role as a countervailing force and check against abuses of power (Kherigi, 2020).

This chapter considers the period from March 2011 until September 2021, when fieldwork was completed. It should be noted that during the fieldwork, significant political changes occurred following the declaration of a state of emergency on 25 July 2021 by the President of the Republic Kais Saied. This included freezing Parliament, dismissing the prime minister and government, dissolving the Supreme Judicial Council and suspending the INLUCC. This had significant implications for the context in which CSOs were operating. Presidential decree No. 117 issued on 22 September 2021 suspended the Parliament and transferred all legislative powers to the president, as well as placing all presidential decisions above any judicial scrutiny. Decree 117 suspended large parts of the 2014 Constitution, which had been drafted by an elected constituent assembly between 2011 and 2014, and granted the president virtually all executive and legislative powers, deepening concerns about rights and freedoms (Human Rights Watch, 2021).

Following these steps, the president appointed an advisory committee to draft a new constitution to replace the 2014 Constitution. The constitution-drafting process was swift and largely opaque. The public referendum on the draft text, held on 25 July 2022, witnessed very low levels of public participation, leading to questions being raised about the legitimacy and credibility of the new text (Venice Commission 2022). Nevertheless, it was officially promulgated in 2022, thus replacing the 2014 Constitution. Civic space has also been under threat, with the promulgation of new laws such as Decree-law No. 54 of 2022. This decree and other legislation such as the counter-terrorism law have been widely used to prosecute political and human rights activists and ordinary citizens for making statements that are critical of the government or president. Decree 54 has been met with widespread criticism by civil society organisations such as the journalists' union, whose president described the decree as '*a clear and deliberate political manoeuvre to suppress press freedom, restrict media operations, and hinder the defence of rights and freedoms*' (Ben Ismail, 2023). Government repression has intensified since February 2023, with the arrest and imprisonment of dozens of opposition figures (Amnesty 2023).

In the light of these restrictions, CSOs have had to adapt their strategies to take account of these changes. Initiatives involving local government have also faced challenges, as it seemed that Saied might dissolve all elected municipal councils after accusing them of being 'states within a state' (Reuters, 2023). The municipal councils continued functioning in a climate of uncertainty for approximately a year and a half until they were abruptly dissolved by decree in March 2023. This has had implications for SA initiatives, as CSOs have been forced to adapt to a shifting institutional context.

4.3.1 Social Accountability in the 2014 Constitution

Between 2011 and 2021, the legal framework on public authorities' obligations to account for their actions was generally an enabling factor for SA initiatives in Tunisia. The 2014 Constitution (still in force at the time fieldwork was conducted) set out key principles and obligations related to the accountability of public officials and institutions. The Preamble refers to a 'democratic and participatory system' and a civil state that

> guarantees freedom of association in conformity with the principles of pluralism, an impartial administration, and good governance, which are the foundations of political competition, where the state guarantees the supremacy of the law and the respect for freedoms and human rights, the independence of the judiciary, the equality of rights and duties between all citizens, male and female, and equality between all regions. (Constitute Project, n.d.)

Article 15, cited by a number of civil society actors interviewed in this study, also refers specifically to *musāʾala* (accountability). Despite the difficulties in implementing these provisions, as cited above, civil society actors interviewed found these provisions useful to draw on to justify their accountability efforts when challenged by officials.

The articles of the 2014 Constitution most frequently cited by civil society actors when discussing SA were the following:

- Article 10: 'The state shall ensure the proper use of public funds and take the necessary measures to spend it [sic] according to the priorities of the national economy, and prevents corruption and all that can threaten national resources and sovereignty.'
- Article 11: 'All those who assume the roles of President of the Republic, Head of Government, member of the Council of Ministers, or member of the Assembly of the Representatives of the People, or member of any of the independent constitutional bodies or any senior public position, must declare their assets according to the provisions of the law.'
- Article 15: 'Public administration is at the service of the citizens and the common good. It is organized and operates in accordance with the principles of impartiality, equality and the continuity of public services, and in conformity with the rules of transparency, integrity, efficiency and accountability.'
- Article 32: 'The state guarantees the right to information and the right of access to information and communication networks.'
- Article 137: 'Local authorities shall have the freedom to manage their resources freely within the budget that is allocated to them, in accordance with the principles of good governance and under the supervision of the financial judiciary.'
- Article 139: 'Local authorities shall adopt the mechanisms of participatory democracy and the principles of open governance to ensure the broadest participation of citizens and of civil society in the preparation of development programmes and land use planning, and follow up on their implementation, in conformity with the law.'

Civil society actors and officials cited these provisions as important principles that provided a legal basis for their work and for persuading public institutions to involve citizens in public decision-making. In addition, the 2014 Constitution guaranteed the right to participate in public affairs, political pluralism, free and fair elections, freedom of expression, freedom of association, media freedoms and access to information, among others. *Decree*-Law No. *88 of 2011, the main legal text that regulates the creation and functioning of CSOs since 2011 (still in force as of writing),* is also described by civil society as enabling their accountability efforts, as it largely simplifies and facilitates the creation of an association (although CSOs interviewed did complain of administrative obstacles in practice). These findings are confirmed by a 2020 survey by the Arab Network for Social Accountability (ANSA), which found that CSOs participating in the survey found that the legal framework in Tunisia enabled the exercise of SA (ANSA 2021).

4.3.2 The Emergence of the Concept of Social Accountability

The term 'accountability' (*musāʾala*) features several times in the 2014 Constitution, the constitutional framework in force at the time the study was conducted. Article 15 states that '[p]ublic administration ... is organized and operates ... in conformity with the rules of transparency, integrity, efficiency and accountability'. Article 103 refers to the judiciary's accountability for any violations of professional standards, and article 130 sets out the mandate of the Authority for Good Governance and the Fight Against Corruption, which includes 'strengthening the principles of transparency, integrity and accountability'. However, accountability has no official definition under Tunisian law. The term is used in the 2014 Constitution in a number of different ways and often in conjunction with transparency, integrity, good governance, open governance and participation. It is also frequently used in relation to the role of Parliament in questioning members of government through special sessions known as *jalsāt musāʾala* (accountability sessions, see ʿAmārī, 2021).

However, the term 'social accountability', or *al-musāʾala al-ijtimaʿiyya*, makes no appearance in Tunisian law and is less common in civil society and public discourse. It does not appear to have been used at all before 2011, due to the absence of freedoms and the restrictive institutional and legal environment for civil society actors (ANSA 2021). After 2011, a large number of civil society initiatives were launched that centred on the themes of public participation, monitoring of public institutions, transparency and combating corruption. Few of these used the term 'social accountability', although they would fall under the broad definition of SA as 'any citizen-led action beyond elections that aims to enhance the accountability of state actors' (Vloeberghs and Bergh, 2021, p. 8).

Below, we draw on Hickey and King's (2016) useful categorisation of SA initiatives into three main types: *transparency* initiatives aimed at increasing citizens' access to information on public decisions; *contentious actions*, such as public demonstrations, public campaigns and public interest litigation; and *participatory governance* initiatives, aimed at involving citizens in decision-making processes. We provide examples of SA initiatives involving state institutions and civil society actors identified through the mapping, although this list is not intended to be exhaustive.

Transparency Initiatives—Increasing Citizens' Access to Information

- Open Gov partnership: in 2014, Tunisia signed up to the Open Government Partnership (OGP), which promotes transparency and the use of new technologies to strengthen good governance (http://www.ogptunisie.gov.tn/en/). Civil society representatives sit on the national steering committee alongside government representatives and monitor the implementation of the National Action Plan.
- Platforms that enable citizens to monitor their elected representatives, such as Marsad Majles by Al Bawsala (https://majles.marsad.tn/fr/).
- Initiatives that promote dialogue between elected officials and civil society, such as Parliament's online platform for civil society (United Nations Development Programme [UNDP], 2018) and the Eselni platform for parliamentarians, municipal officials and civil society by the Action Positive association (US Embassy in Tunisia 2021).
- Publishing information on public policies and decisions, including the Jasmine Foundation's Nebni project, which promotes local government transparency using various tools, such as citizen bulletins on municipal government decisions and budgets (Jasmine Foundation n.d.); Al Bawsala's Marsad Baladia, an online platform to publish data on municipalities (https://baladia.marsad.tn); and the Open Baladiati platform to publish data relating to municipalities, an initiative by Onshor association (http://openbaladiati.tn).
- Online platforms to help the public submit access-to-information requests, such as the Informini platform by the Onshor association in partnership with the Tunisian Association of Public Auditors (Association Tunisienne des Contrôleurs Publics, ATCP) (https://www.informini.org).

- Online platforms to monitor public investment projects, for example the Cabrane platform by the ATCP (http://www.cabrane.com).
- Publication of citizen guides on monitoring public investment projects, such as those published by the ATCP (n.d.).
- Transparency indices that evaluate the transparency of public bodies, including those by Al Bawsala (such as its ranking of municipalities, see Al Bawsala, n.d.-b) and ATCP (in relation to state-owned enterprises, see ATCP, 2016).
- Citizen monitoring of public services, such as Mourakiboun's Primary Health Care (PHC) Monitoring Initiative, which deployed citizen monitors to health centres to measure the quality of medical services and provide data to decision-makers and advocates to make improvements (La Presse, 2017).
- Citizen monitoring of the extractive sector, such as the Tunisian Network for Transparency in Energy and Mines. This network is composed of 13 organisations that promote transparency in the extractive sector, including advocating for the government to adopt laws on transparency in the extractive sector (RTTEM, n.d.)

Contentious Actions

- Winou el Petrole, 2015: online and street campaign demanding transparency on Tunisia's natural resources management.
- Manich Msemeh, 2017: protest movement against a proposed amnesty for bureaucrats and businessmen accused of corruption under the former regime.
- El Kamour, 2017: sit-in at an oil and gas facility in Southern Tunisia to demand jobs and development and a review of oil and gas contracts.
- Public interest litigation: legal challenges to government decisions, such as I Watch's legal challenges to ministerial decisions (e.g. legal action against former Prime Minister Youssef Chahed and former Prime Minister Elyes Fakhfakh for financial corruption, see Webdo.tn 19; Webdo.tn, 2020) and the Tunisian Green Network's challenge to a government decree on the use of plastic packaging in the concrete industry.

Participatory Governance

- Public consultations: the creation of a governmental online platform for consultations related to draft statutes and decrees (Tunisian Republic, n.d.).
- Parliamentary liaison with civil society and the public: between 2011 and 2021, the Parliament had a dedicated contact point for civil society and citizens.
- Participatory budgeting: an initiative involving citizens in deciding how to spend a portion of the municipal budget, first launched by the association Action Associative (n.d.).
- Participatory annual development plan: a programme led by the Ministry of Local Affairs requiring all municipalities to include participatory mechanisms in their annual investment planning process (Ministère de l'Interieur, 2016).
- Citizen charters used by various Tunisian CSOs such as Jamaity, the ATCP and the Jasmine Foundation.
- Citizen score cards, community score cards and other participatory tools for monitoring and evaluating public services, used by International Alert (health sector, see International Alert, 2021); the Jasmine Foundation (municipalities and local development, see Jasmine Foundation 2017); the Tunisian General Labour Union (Union Générale Tunisienne du Travail, UGTT), Tunisia's largest trade union federation funded by the Global Partnership on Social Accountability (GPSA); and article 19, also funded by the GPSA, on citizen participation in monitoring and evaluating public health and education investments (see ARTICLE19, 2014).

While the term 'accountability' is commonly used in government documents, public debate and the civil society arena, the term 'social accountability' is used less frequently (see, for example, INLUCC, 2020b; Al Bawsala, n.d.-a; Instance d'Accès à l'Information [INAI], n.d.; "Al-Siyāsa", 2001). Its earliest visible uses in the Tunisian context can be back traced to the World Bank's Programme d'Appui à la Relance Économique (PARE) in 2011–2013, which introduced various mechanisms for participatory citizen evaluation of public services, as well as the issuing of governmental decrees on participatory monitoring,[1] making Tunisia 'the first country in the region ... to adopt an official policy on the performances of public services' (Espace Manager, 2013).

However, this programme was not cited by any of the research participants, which suggests that it was not significant in popularising the concept of SA. Instead, several civil society actors stated that SA became a concept of relevance to Tunisian civil society with the launch of the Tamkeen project by the United Nations Development Programme (UNDP, n.d.) in 2015. As one public finance expert who worked on the programme explained, 'There were many [SA] experiences like participatory budgeting before 2014 but they didn't specifically refer to social accountability. They mainly focused on participation because people had been excluded from so long from decision-making' (expert consultant to the UNDP on social accountability, personal communication, 16 August 2021, online).

The Tamkeen programme's declared objectives centre on building civil society capacity, with the second objective being to 'give [CSOs] the necessary skills for their active participation in the domain of social accountability [*redevabilité sociale*] and the fight against corruption' by 'finalising the implementation of the legal and institutional framework' and creating 'islands of integrity at the local or sectoral level' (UNDP, n.d.). The programme refers to SA in association with 'the fight against corruption' and development, with these three being linked repeatedly throughout programme documents. The programme focused largely on the demand side of governance by strengthening the role of civil society in activating legal and institutional frameworks through monitoring, awareness-raising and engaging citizens in decision-making. However, it also worked on the supply side of accountability by seeking to strengthen institutional and legal frameworks on combating corruption. As the first large-scale programme on SA, it is seen as having introduced the term to the Tunisian context and popularised its usage among civil society actors and officials.

4.4 Meanings: From Constitutional Ideal to Applied Concept

Social accountability (*al-musāʾala al-ijtimāʿiyya*) lends itself to multiple meanings. The term contains the word *musāʾala* (accountability), which is interpreted in different ways. As several interviewees mentioned, the term occurs in the 2014 Tunisian Constitution, but no national definition exists. There is confusion among officials, civil society actors and ordinary citizens about what *musāʾala* entails. Often, there is an overlap between the use of *musāʾala*, which carries the notion of answerability—being questioned and required to provide answers—and *muḥāsaba*, which means being held liable and carries more punitive connotations. In Arabic, *muḥāsaba* is etymologically linked to *muḥāsabāt* (financial accounting) and is used to refer to bodies that carry out legal and financial accountability, such as the Court of Auditors (*dāʾirat al-muḥāsabāt*). *Musāʾala* and *muḥāsaba* are often used interchangeably, both in official documents and among CSO officers. As one civil society activist noted, 'Political officials are scared of the term *musāʾala*, as if we will judge them. It doesn't necessarily mean the citizen will judge you, that if they monitor your work, they will sanction you or place pressure on you' (representative of ANSA, FGD, 23 June 2021).

Here is a selection of the definitions put forward by civil society activists when discussing accountability and SA:

- 'Accountability is about two things – about state institutions' respect for the law and their performance … meaning delivering for citizens' (project coordinator I Watch, 21 June 2021, in person).
- 'A set of tools that citizens can use to influence decisions and improve public services and policies' (project coordinator Jasmine Foundation, 2 September 2021, online).
- 'Social accountability is any accountability initiative initiated outside state institutions' (project coordinator I Watch, personal communication, 21 June 2021, in person).
- 'Social accountability is the bridge that will take us to transparency … and fighting corruption' (representative of ANSA, FGD).
- 'Accountability … is when the ordinary citizen is able to ask the state, whatever their rank, to account for their actions, whether the prime minister, head of state, judge, no matter what, they are all subject to accountability of all kinds' (lawyer and co-founder of Tunisia Green Network, personal communication, 29 June 2021, in person).
- 'Accountability is a type of support for officials – having a citizen who is aware, who has the right mechanisms of accountability, who knows how to deal with a problem or issue' (Access to Information Authority [INAI] ambassador for Freedom of Information, FGD).

Meanwhile, definitions proposed by government officials tended to focus on accountability as a means to make governmental action more effective and facilitate the work of public institutions:

- 'The decision-maker has a duty to respond to the demand for justification of the decisions taken or decisions not taken – why did/didn't you decide this? ... Today to ensure we can attract investors and bring investment, we need to emphasise this kind of governance ... All economies have to guarantee this governance ... alongside participation, efficiency, transparency, etc.' (director General of the Ministry of Local Affairs, FGD).
- 'The aim is to build a relationship of transparency between institution and citizen. The more transparent it is, the more citizens reduce their questions' (board member, Action Positive, Tunisia Accountability in Politics Programme, FGD).

4.4.1 *The Multiple Meanings of Accountability*

Below, we distinguish further between local actors' understanding of accountability. In particular, we explore the various understandings of SA encountered during our fieldwork. We detail the main elements that feature in local actors' discourse on accountability and SA, organised in the order in which they were most frequently cited in the FGD.

Led by Civil Society and/or Citizens

The main common element that distinguishes SA from other forms of accountability, as viewed by research participants, is that it is led by civil society and citizens. SA depends primarily on civic engagement, unlike other forms of accountability such as political or legal accountability, which are implemented and led by official institutions, such as parliamentary oversight of government, as a form of political accountability, or the role of public audit bodies and courts, as a form of legal accountability. Notably, SA is also a term used more commonly by civil society than officials. While the term 'social accountability' appeared in the discourse of civil society actors—both among those interviewed and in the civil society documentation reviewed during the desk research—government documents do not use the term 'social accountability' but rather refer to 'transparency', 'open governance' and other, related terms (see, for example, INLUCC, 2020a; Open Government Partnership Tunisia, n.d.-b).

Targeted at Public Institutions
Secondly, SA is seen as being focused on the accountability of *state* institutions, rather than non-state actors, such as the private sector. All the examples of SA given by research participants centred around efforts to bring about accountability by public bodies or officials. This raises the question of whether and how citizens can hold private companies accountable, for example, for environmental harm or failure to respect their legal obligations where the state does not take action.

SA initiatives in Tunisia in 2011–2021 focused on a very wide range of public institutions. Our research revealed two trends. First, a strong focus on local state institutions, particularly municipalities. A vast number of SA initiatives targeted municipalities, such as participatory budgeting, citizen score cards, town hall meetings, online information platforms, etc. This appears to be due to the proximity of local government and ease of access to it. As activists explained, municipalities are more easily accessed because of dense social ties at the local level and the proximity of local officials. Local decisions, programmes and budgets can also be more easily monitored given their proximity and visibility, e.g. spending on local infrastructure projects. In contrast, civil society actors found it more difficult to locate points of access in central ministries, which are seen as more opaque and harder to access. In addition, the political settlements—or 'balance or distribution of power between contending social groups and social classes' (Di John & Putzel, 2009, p. 4)—that regulate local government institutions appear to be easier to shift than those in other sectors.[2] Finally, it is easier for CSOs to create public pressure on officials at the local level using relatively simple and cheap means, such as local Facebook groups, local radio and public protests.

Second, SA initiatives in Tunisia in 2011–2021 appeared to be mainly focused on elected officials but less so on bureaucrats. This may be because bureaucratic officials are more difficult to access and engage with, or because they are not seen as the real decision-makers. However, civil society actors appeared to have begun shifting their strategies to focus more on engaging the public administration. This is particularly the case for SA initiatives at the local level, which are increasingly engaging with municipal general secretaries (chief executives). As one former civil society activist (who was an elected municipal councillor at the time of the study) noted,

> A very important point … is that we didn't involve and develop the local administration. Today we're talking about open data, open gov, social accountability, we're working on this in civil society. But elected officials are not the implementors, we set strategies and policies. Implementation is the role of the administration. Thus, we need to work on the administration … Progress needs to go in parallel between municipal officials and administration, so that they go in the same direction and not in conflict'. (representative of ANSA, FGD)

Accountability as the Duty to Give Answers

A third common element in civil society's and officials' conceptions of accountability is that accountability essentially means requiring officials to *answer for their actions*. It is seen as the right of citizens to demand explanations regarding public decision-making and the corresponding obligation of officials to provide these. Research participants described accountability as being about 'citizens asking questions', 'seeking information' and 'requesting officials to explain' (FGD participants). As one civil society activist explained, 'When we said we would hold the mayor to account [*sāʾil*] … [he thought] we were going to try him! We just want to clarify things for public opinion, sit with you and clarify things for people. That's all' (INAI ambassador for Freedom of Information, FGD).

However, as the accountability literature highlights, accountability is composed of two components: *answerability*, 'making power holders explain and give reasons for their actions', and *enforcement*, 'ensuring that poor or immoral performance is punished in some way' (Hickey & Mohan, 2008, p. 236). While research participants frequently mentioned answerability, there was little mention of enforcement. Overall, there were three different ways of thinking about how SA relates to the enforceability of legal obligations.

The first approach sees SA mechanisms as *alternative mechanisms* to obtain compliance with legal frameworks *without imposing legal sanctions*. For example, a large CSO working on access to information at the municipal level at first used litigation as a central plank of its strategy. However, it soon concluded that the legal route was lengthy, expensive and ineffective, after INAI's decisions in its favour were ignored by some public bodies.[3] The association shifted its efforts from applying legal pressure to applying reputational pressure, creating a national transparency index that rated municipalities' level of transparency. This was found to be a far more effective tool for enforcing access-to-information laws than litigation, since it exposed municipalities to reputational pressure. Thus, CSOs pursue SA as a shorter and more effective means to exact accountability through *informal* sanctions, such as public disaffection and reputational pressure, while abandoning the idea of obtaining compliance through legal sanctions, seeing the latter as implausible or ineffective. Here, SA tools operate *in parallel with* traditional accountability mechanisms.

A second way of thinking about how SA relates to enforceability of legal obligations is to see it as *a means to implement legal frameworks* and enforce legal sanctions. Thus, the role of SA here is to reinforce and activate legal mechanisms, rather than bypassing or despairing of them altogether. Peruzzotti and Smulovitz define SA in the following terms, 'Social mechanisms constitute an alternative mechanism for imposing costs on political actors *and are a necessary condition for the operation of those institutional mechanisms that have mandatory sanctioning capacities*' (2006, p. 26, our emphasis). This understanding is adopted by, for example, Tunisian whistle-blower associations such as I Watch (www.iwatch.tn/ar), which use accountability tools—such as litigation, investigative reports, monitoring of natural resource contracts and social media campaigns—as a means of pressuring the state to *enforce* legal frameworks and impose sanctions on individuals or institutions. Thus, some civil society actors framed SA as a method for 'activating' the implementation of laws and sanctions. Here, SA tools operate as a way to help *enforce* traditional accountability mechanisms.

A third way is to see SA as being *distinct from but complementary to legal sanctions*. In this view, SA tools can be utilised alongside other tools involving legally enforceable sanctions. SA mechanisms here are seen as helping 'enrich and support the effectiveness of legal sanctions', where 'legal mechanisms and social accountability mechanisms can provide different tools in the toolbox of activists to help get state institutions to deliver on their promises and obligations' (expert consultant to the UNDP on social accountability, personal communication, 16 August 2021, online). Here, SA tools operate *to reinforce* traditional accountability mechanisms.

Accountability as Citizens' Access to and Participation in Decision-Making

A fourth common element in discussions on accountability was the notion that citizen participation is key to accountability. When asked how they understood accountability, both civil society actors and officials at the local and national levels focused on citizens' right to be consulted by decision-makers and effectively participate in decision-making by putting forward their needs and demands, proposing solutions and monitoring the implementation of decisions. In the context of a transition from an authoritarian system in which there were few institutional spaces for ordinary citizens to express demands freely and seek to influence public policies, the post-revolution period saw citizens and civil society demand to be included in decision-making through a variety of forms, from street protests and sit-ins to media and online campaigns. In addition, in a context in which institutional mechanisms for accountability and levels of trust in state institutions were weak, the role of the citizen in holding public institutions to account becomes even more central. Accountability, thus, requires citizens to be active agents throughout public decision-making processes. As one research participant stated,

> Accountability is the process of moving from a situation where the citizen isn't exercising influence or oversight, isn't represented or participating, or aware of public policies and their implementation to a citizen who is following, participating, influencing positively, understanding. It means moving from a dictatorship where the citizen is just a statistic to a system where the citizen influences public policies at all stages. (project coordinator Nebni Local Citizens' Observatory, Bizerte, FGD)

Participation is thus a central element of SA initiatives by national and international NGOs working in Tunisia in 2011–2021. Participatory budgeting by organisations such as Action Associative, for example, involved citizens in holding local governments to account and setting priorities for local public spending through a process of public deliberation. Organisations such as International Alert used SA methods such as citizen evaluations of public services as tools for highlighting inequalities in access to public services and placing citizens at the centre of public decision-making. International Alert's citizen evaluation of public healthcare in the Southern region of Tataouine defines SA as 'genuine societal participation in all the stages of decision-making and implementation' (2019, p. 18). Similarly, ANSA states that '[s]ocial accountability goes beyond [public institutions] simply justifying activities, actions and outcomes and takes into account citizens' participation and especially the monitoring of local public authorities by citizens' (2021, p. 4).

In discussions with civil society actors, SA is seen as key to building a new relationship of trust between the state and citizens through participation, enabling citizens to monitor and take part in decision-making processes. This, in turn, is closely tied to the idea of generating a sense of public ownership of public decisions and policies and, ultimately, of the state itself. By opening up decision-making processes to citizens, SA initiatives that focus on citizen participation are seen as providing part of the solution to the crisis in trust between citizens and the state, which is so profound that it undermines the notion of citizenship and belonging. As one anti-corruption activist put it,

> When you feel a sense of injustice, when you have no mechanisms for obtaining your rights, you do not feel you belong to the state. You no longer feel belonging to that state, and this is what makes many people say, why do our youth leave? Simply because they do not feel a sense of belonging, of ownership of this country, of this earth, and they no longer feel any social solidarity. (lawyer and co-founder of Tunisia Green Network, personal communication, 29 June 2021, in person)

Accountability as Transparency

The fifth common element in defining accountability is transparency. When discussing accountability, civil society actors frequently referred to three related elements:

- Access to information (*nafādh lil maʿlūma*): accountability is obtained through citizens having access to information on how public decisions are made and how public funds are spent.
- Monitoring (*raqāba*): accountability is obtained through citizens' continuous monitoring of decision-making processes in order to hold officials responsible for decisions and their outcomes, and to expose wrongdoing.
- Transparency (*shafāfiyya*): citizens' ability to access information on decisions by the government and state institutions and the creation of channels of communication between the government and citizens.

Here, accountability is seen as requiring the state to divulge information to citizens and enable them to have access to decision-making processes. The three elements outlined above were all mentioned in relation to the fight against corruption, an issue that dominates public debate in Tunisia. In this context, the widespread nature of corruption calls for transparency as a first step to exacting accountability. When discussing accountability, civil society actors frequently returned to the idea of SA as a set of tools or mechanisms for *monitoring* public decision-making in order to prevent the misuse of public authority, such as corruption in public procurement, demands for bribes when accessing public services and the awarding of public jobs based on personal relations or bribes. As mentioned above, it is the inability of traditional accountability mechanisms—e.g. legal frameworks, internal regulations, financial controls, judicial processes, elections, etc.—to ensure that public institutions behave in a fair and honest way that makes SA mechanisms necessary. As one civil society activist stated, 'Social accountability is the bridge that will take us to transparency ... and fighting corruption' (representative of ANSA, FGD).

Accountability as the Rule of Law

A sixth element used to define accountability is the concept of the rule of law. Accountability is often described by civil society actors as a central element of a system of government based on the rule of law (*dawlat al-qanūn*). In the aftermath of a revolution that was driven by anger at vast inequalities and the usurpation of state resources by regime allies, it is unsurprising that *dawlat al-qanūn* is primarily defined by civil society actors as equality before the law: state institutions, public officials and ordinary citizens are all subject to the law, and the law is implemented equally, regardless of status. As one civil society activist stated,

> You cannot talk about a state based on the rule of law and its institutions without accountability ... a state that respects the hierarchy of legal texts in form and content respects the Constitution's supremacy in form and content, where the one who has the authority to do something does it, and the one who does not have the authority to do something doesn't do it, and everyone who exceeds these powers must be held accountable. (lawyer and co-founder of Tunisia Green Network, personal communication, 29 June 2021, in person)

Accountability as Decent Public Service Provision

An alternative conception of accountability held by some civil society actors is accountability as a *means* to improve public service provision and make it more just. Both civil society actors and public officials defined accountability as being key to achieving public services that meet citizens' needs. Accordingly, SA was seen as 'a set of tools that citizens can use to improve public services and policies in line with their needs and demands' (project coordinator Jasmine Foundation, personal communication, 2 September 2021, online). In this sense, accountability is seen to improve several aspects of service provision, including:

- Equality: accountability as a means to ensure equal access to public service provision for all citizens, without discrimination or privilege.
- Quality: accountability as a means to improve the quality of public services by monitoring the use of public funds and the management of public services and infrastructure, thus reducing corruption and fraud.
- Responsiveness: accountability as a means to direct public institutions to respond to the demands and changing needs of citizens. As one activist noted, 'When it comes to accountability, we want to help with the efficiency of the political process. In the end it's about how to ensure our budget of one million [dinars] or whatever we have goes to priorities. This is what it's about' (project coordinator Al Bawsala, FGD).
- Effectiveness: accountability as a set of mechanisms to help inform decision-making so that policies will reflect real needs, as opposed to decisions imposed from above, which fail to solve problems or are not accepted by the public.
- Efficiency: accountability as a means of achieving greater efficiency in the provision of services or the implementation of policies by identifying problems in the design and delivery of services and enabling the timely adjustment of services or policies to citizens' needs. As one administrative official explained,

  > We municipalities … try to make participatory sessions succeed because through them we can achieve an efficient and effective programme. There is no point proposing non-effective projects that get stuck later in implementation with citizens … When we have participation from the beginning, we target what the citizen wants …

and we don't get stuck later in implementation, because the citizen accepts it'. (board member Action Positive, Tunisia Accountability in Politics Programme, FGD)

4.5 Mobilisation Methods: Civil Society Strategies to Move From Concept to Action

This section analyses the strategies used by citizens and civil society groups to exact accountability, organised in the order in which they were most frequently cited in the focus group. It examines the strategies used to engage other citizens, mobilise officials and ensure the latter's fulfilment of their commitments.

4.5.1 Mobilising Officials

Between 2011 and 2021, civil society actors used a variety of different strategies to engage officials, which changed over time through iterative processes of learning. Civil society groups used a range of (a) persuasive and (b) coercive methods. They deployed these methods in different ways according to the nature of the local context in which they were operating and the official or institution in question. They also differed in their approach: some adopted a 'friendly' approach, relying purely on persuasive methods, some used coercive methods, while others used a combination of the two, depending on the response of public officials.

While the choice of mobilisation methods is important, civil society actors also emphasised the importance of the existence of political will to engage on the part of public officials. The presence of individual officials within public institutions who were receptive to civic initiatives was seen as an important condition to the success and sustainability of accountability initiatives. While civic initiatives were occasionally able to force a change in government policy through coercive methods, sustainable change towards greater accountability was seen to require identifying and cooperating with public officials who were supportive of change. An example of this is access-to-information requests. An association that worked on submitting access-to-information requests to public institutions and tracking compliance with the legal obligation to respond to these requests found that many institutions did not comply and that simply highlighting failure was not sufficient to bring about compliance.

The association found that when it shifted its approach to working with officials within these institutions to identify reasons for failure to comply with access-to-information requests and developing strategies to remedy these failures, these institutions were subsequently more likely to comply with such requests. This also required civil society actors to understand the political economy of specific public institutions, identify and engage allies, and develop strategies to overcome resistance or other obstacles to accountability.

Why some officials cooperate with SA initiatives and some do not was largely seen as being a question of individual values. Civil society actors described their allies within public institutions as being motivated by a personal commitment to accountability, rather than simply interests or incentives. This was expressed in various instances through officials' efforts to promote accountability even at the expense of their material interests. This echoes findings in the literature, which has moved away from a focus on 'incentives' to one on the role of ideas in shaping elite behaviour (Hickey, 2013). This led many associations to adopt a 'go with the grain' approach of working primarily with officials or institutions where political will already existed. This supports the notion of 'a sandwich strategy' formulated by Fox, which argues that in order to break 'low-accountability traps' and overcome resistance to accountability, pro-change actors in society need to empower pro-change actors within the state, 'thereby triggering a virtuous circle … of mutual empowerment' (Fox, 2015, p. 356). However, other associations engaged using both persuasive and coercive methods, as discussed below.

Persuasion

While civil society actors in Tunisia insist on their right to demand accountability and use a range of methods to do so, many of those involved in the study argued that purely 'hostile' tactics are less effective at exacting accountability. Several noted that when they first began working on accountability, they had adopted a confrontational approach but soon realised this would not be effective. As one community organiser noted,

> The methodology [in the beginning] assumed a confrontational relationship. We see the citizen as having rights over state institutions. The citizen is above the institutions of the state … This is how we started off but little by little, we realised that, to be honest, we are in the Tunisian context, it

> is not the French, Canadian or American context. We noticed many times that when we go with a logic of confrontation and force, officials don't engage. It's a logic of power and status, they want to show, 'I'm stronger than you'. (board member El Comita, personal communication, 19 August 2021, online)

Even organisations that used largely 'hostile' methods such as public litigation say that they also used persuasive methods when, for instance, they found that public officials or institutions actually wanted to comply with their legal obligations but were unable to due to lack of resources. As one activist from the organisation I Watch, known for its frequent litigation against public officials and institutions, explained:

> We used to use very confrontational methods, which we're known for. But then we found that this isn't a solution. You can't get into a fight with a municipality in Tataouine, for instance, because it did something wrong. I should show it how to do it right, how to write their internal rules of procedure, how to do a public tender. Instead of reporting them for not having a website and respecting access-to-information rules, I can create a website for them. So, we have a new approach since 2019, which is to build partnerships with institutions ... focused on training for their personnel, etc. ... So we moved from confrontation to support [*accompagnement*]. (project coordinator I Watch, personal communication, 21 June 2021, online)

The following are the persuasive methods CSOs used to engage officials (organised according to the frequency with which they were mentioned in the focus group discussion):

Drawing on Personal Relations. Civil society actors noted that engagement with officials is usually mediated through personal relationships based on friendship, ideological or partisan affinity, regional belonging or kinship ties. For instance, one civil society activist from a network of associations noted that it is important for any association to be composed of activists from a range of ideological backgrounds so that they can mobilise officials from their own political orientation through personal relationships. However, while recognising the highly personalist and, in many cases, clientelist nature of relations between officials and citizens, civil society actors were also critical of these modes of interaction as ultimately being counterproductive to accountability. As one civil society activist noted, 'I'm not sure we can say we succeeded in social accountability because our cooperation [with state officials] became through personal friendships [*muḥābbāt*] so the people we got used to seeing always came because they knew us' (co-founder Min Hakki Nsaalek accountability network of NGOs, FGD).

Emphasising the Benefits of Cooperation. Both civil society actors and officials pointed to the need to look at the interaction between officials and citizens or civil society as a win-win situation or exchange. When seeking to engage officials in SA initiatives, many activists frame their discourse around the benefits it could bring, such as helping officials find solutions to problems, strengthening public ownership of decisions, making implementation of decisions easier and more efficient and building trust. As one local official explained, 'Officials want to solve problems, that's their objective … If you will accompany me and stay with me until I solve my problem, I will extend my hand to you' (municipal administrator El Mourouj municipality, FGD). State institutions are perceived as needing civil society support due to their lack of resources. In a context of economic crisis, civil society is able to 'offer a product or a service that is free' for under-resourced state institutions (project coordinator I Watch, personal communication, 21 June 2021, online). These resources include providing training for officials, hiring experts to provide expertise to public institutions, designing websites and other communication tools, facilitating participatory processes and observing public procurement and recruitment processes to give them more legitimacy in the eyes of the public.

Some civil society groups have thus shifted their discourse to framing SA as a source of assistance to officials. As one activist noted,

> Accountability is a process of support [*accompagnement*]. In our project with parliamentarians and mayors, that's what we called it. There was a conflict in the beginning with them, there was that mentality that we are seeking to sanction them [*muḥāsaba*]. We said no, it's accountability, it is about supporting you. As a decision-maker, you can't know everything. We give you information. (project coordinator Al Bawsala, FGD)

This more 'supportive' approach to engaging officials was also emphasised by a number of civil society activists, who concluded from their experience that a persuasive approach was conducive to exacting accountability:

> You need as a civil society representative to make the official feel comfortable, that you're not coming to sanction them at all. On the contrary. You need to make them feel … that you're going to reduce the pressure on them and [help them deal with] all those people shouting outside their door … In the beginning, officials closed the door to civil society but when they found many problems, they reopened the door. They realised we can help them … We need to not accuse them. We have nothing against officials (project coordinator Munadhara Initiative, FGD)

Signing Partnership Agreements. Establishing official agreements with public institutions was also an important means of securing commitment by public institutions to engage with SA initiatives a period of time (see, for example, INAI, 2019). Such agreements bring benefits to both sides. Public officials can use them to improve their public image and demonstrate to the public their commitment to 'good governance' and citizen participation. For civil society groups, they provide access to public institutions and a way to institutionalise the relationship by setting out each side's obligations and procedures for cooperation (see Sect. 4.8.5 for more details).

Building Credibility. An important factor in whether officials engage with a CSO or not is its credibility. Having a strong public reputation, media visibility or partnerships with international donors are all factors that help civil society secure official engagement. As one activist noted, 'The first question an official asks when you invite them is, who are you? So, your team needs to have strong capacity, skills to engage in dialogue with officials and understand the topic well and have clear messages or demands' (co-founder of Min Hakki Nsaalek accountability network of NGOs, FGD). Another strategy is to form civil society coalitions centred on common initiatives in order to give them greater weight when engaging officials. As one civil society activist stated, 'If you're alone, your impact is weaker. If you work together, as a number of associations … this makes the official take you seriously and continue working with you' (ibid.).

Training. Civil society groups also seek to demonstrate to officials the benefits of cooperating with them by offering training on technical issues (public finance rules, planning processes, etc.) and 'soft skills' such as communication and conflict resolution. This is particularly common at the local level, where civil society have trained newly elected municipal councils, given their lack of experience.

Coercion

Civil society actors also resorted to more coercive methods to put pressure on officials to cooperate with SA initiatives. These include the following:

Mobilising Legal Arguments. One tactic is to draw on the legal framework to remind officials of their legal obligations to engage with civil society and account for their actions. As one activist explained, 'We have a constitution and laws that allow citizens to defend their rights and we often start with that' (project coordinator Nebni Local Citizens' Observatory, Bizerte, FGD). Being familiar with the legal framework and having access to legal expertise is thus an important resource for civil society actors.

Mainstream Media. Civil society groups frequently use mainstream media, both local and national, to put pressure on officials to engage with civil society or fulfil commitments. Methods include press releases, press conferences, open letters, media interviews and hiring communications companies to help them with media outreach.

Social Media. Social media constitutes one of the most important methods used by citizens to put pressure on officials. Ordinary citizens and civil society groups use Facebook, in particular, to engage directly with officials and demand accountability. Many public institutions have Facebook pages where they post news and developments. This provides citizens with a platform to pose questions. Elected and administrative officials often publicly respond, particularly at the municipal level, given that these platforms have a large audience.

Petitions. Civil society groups and citizens frequently used petitions to create pressure on officials to respond to their demands. Citizens and civil society groups often create informal online public or written petitions with the aim of pressuring public officials to meet with them and engage with their demands. Petition campaigns often began with mobilising around a specific issue on social media or in public spaces such as cafes, before launching a petition on the issue, then using the pressure created by the petition to secure a meeting with an official to negotiate demands. These kinds of methods were frequently used to raise issues at municipal level, such as demands or grievances around infrastructure, public hygiene and environmental issues.

Street Mobilisation. Citizens and civil society groups frequently used protests and sit-ins as a means to apply public pressure. This was seen to be easier at the regional and local than at the national level because of the proximity and accessibility of regional and local officials. However, where social mobilisation was large enough, it has been able to shift national policies to some extent, such as the El Kamour protests in 2017–2020 (Cherif, 2017; Lassoued, 2020) and Manich Msemeh protests in 2016–2017 (Riahi, 2018).

Mobilising more Senior Officials. One method used by CSOs when officials were unresponsive was to enlist the help of officials more senior in their hierarchy, whether within a public institution (e.g. a minister in relation to a mayor) or within the official's party. This is seen as an effective tool to pressure officials to cooperate.

Mobilising Donor Relations. Some civil society groups utilised their relationships with international donor by asking them to raise an issue with officials in order to get the latter to engage with their demands.

Litigation. This is a central strategy for some organisations but is used by only a minority of the organisations interviewed—three out of 10—due to the complexity of legal procedures, the costs involved and the perception that litigation is slow and ineffective or less effective than other methods.

4.5.2 Mobilising Citizens

The public participation literature suggests that how opportunities for participation are communicated and publicised to citizens is critical to the success of participatory initiatives (Hickey & King, 2016). Civil society actors interviewed described using a range of methods that are selected depending on who is being mobilised, since 'each audience has its own tool' (board member El Comita, Sidi Hssine, FGD). The methods used by civil society to mobilise citizens are summarised below.

Mobilising Key Individuals. According to activists, effective mobilisation depends greatly on the social capital of the individuals doing the mobilising. Being able to mobilise others to act to demand accountability is seen to require skills to mobilise—for instance, gained through past experiences of activism—reputational resources and the ability to draw on strong social ties. These resources can derive from the individual's professional status, family ties, organisational ties or record of past civic activism, among others. As a civil society activist noted,

> The charisma of the person who mobilises is very important ... Each area has figures who have status and who, when they write any post, are followed by people in the area. It is those people who can mobilise others and put pressure on officials to change their decisions (project coordinator Munadhara Initiative, FGD)

In some instances, possessing bridging capital—the ability to access people and networks across different cleavages (e.g. social, ideological, etc.) that may exist in a locality—is seen as being important for mobilising citizens. As a civil society activist noted,

> How we choose our local observers depends on a number of factors. They have to have a number of years of activism in local civil society. This is the most important, so that they have experience and networks. Political impartiality is also important – at the local level, this is a very sensitive issue, because people know each other locally. So you need to work with someone who is able to talk to and engage everyone. (project coordinator Al Bawsala, personal communication, 31 August 2021, online)

Longevity. Time also emerged as an important factor in the success of SA initiatives. In order to mobilise citizens, civil society organisations need to build credibility with citizens by establishing a steady presence, building their expertise on specific themes and demonstrating visible achievements. In the light of the explosion in the number of civil society organisations and civic initiatives after the revolution, civil society organisations report that citizens have become more selective when engaging with civic initiatives. After an initial period of enthusiasm for all that was related to citizen participation, the allure of participatory mechanisms appears to have worn off. The continued deep distrust of the state and the resilience of authoritarian structures and mechanisms demonstrate that SA needs to be seen as a long-term process rather than a set of short-term interventions. As the president of one organisation observed,

> There are still deep effects from decades of dictatorship. We are still working on rebuilding citizens' trust even in their own power to change something ... So, you have to work on the psychological and social levels to build a belief in the power of collective action (board member El Comita, personal communication, 19 August 2021, online)

However, a key obstacle frequently mentioned by civil society actors is the project-based funding model, which does not permit the sort of long-term community engagement and social mobilisation needed to build accountability.

Achieving Concrete Wins for Local Communities. An important method to engage citizens is showing concrete wins. In areas and neighbourhoods without strong CSOs, it is particularly important to show citizens who have little direct experience of collective action that it can achieve results. Results, even if small, can thus have a snowball effect and help activists engage the public beyond a small core of activists. As one activist explained,

> At first when we started to work, citizens were apathetic, but then when they see victories and results, they become more interested, start to demand and participate more. This strengthens a reflex of accountability because it's not a theoretical concept, it's something they can see. (board member Min Hakki Nsaalek accountability network of NGOs, FGD)

Social Media. Social media is a central part of civil society groups' outreach strategy to citizens. The most widely used tool by far is Facebook, used by nearly 70% of the Tunisian population (Kemp, 2021). Social media may be used as a standalone tool or as a pathway to gaining coverage in mainstream media. As one activist explained,

> The most frequent tool we use is Facebook. We post on Facebook pages with a large reach. When you raise an issue or a problem, and this happened many times, local radios pick it up and invite you to a talk show, and this gets citizens' attention (project coordinator Munadhara Initiative, FGD)

Direct Engagement in Public Spaces. Activists also emphasise the importance of face-to-face engagement, particularly with certain groups like older people and in working-class neighbourhoods where there is a higher population density. The most popular techniques include inviting citizens to events using loudspeakers in busy public spaces, speaking to people in cafes and conducting 'micro-trottoirs' (street interviews) to gather people's views on a specific issue. Many organisations cite these as a useful means of making themselves known to the public, getting people engaged in specific issues, informing them about a particular event such as a town hall meeting and collecting contact details for future activities.

Maintaining Momentum. In addition to results, another important factor in citizen engagement is returning to citizens to report on progress and explain whether and how their initial participation has led to change. Such dialogue is seen as critical to strengthening trust between citizens and CSOs, especially in a context of a lack of trust.

4.6 Responses: Reactions from Authorities to Social Accountability Initiatives

The proliferation of SA initiatives to make state officials and institutions more responsive raises the question of how state representatives have responded to such efforts. One obvious question is to what extent accountability has been institutionalised. However, determining the degree to which SA mechanisms have been institutionalised is tricky. The sheer array of initiatives and the speed at which new mechanisms emerged in the Tunisian context in 2011–2021 make it challenging to evaluate their impact and institutionalise them through laws and policies.

However, a number of important examples of the institutionalisation of SA between 2011 and 2021 so exist, particularly in the shape of new laws. Perhaps the biggest success in this area is the introduction of new legislation to strengthen accountability. Civil society groups focused their efforts on pushing for and shaping legislation to advance accountability and found a corresponding readiness among some officials, particularly parliamentarians, to adopt such legislation. This combination of civil society activism and political will led to significant advances in establishing legal obligations and mechanisms on accountability between 2011 and 2021. For example, activists cited their work to secure the adoption of article 139 of the 2014 Constitution (on participatory democracy), the Access to Information Law and the Local Authorities Code (Law no. 29, dated

9 May 2018), among others. The latter introduces obligations for local authorities regarding transparency and participation. Provisions included due to strong civil society advocacy are, for example, article 78—which requires local authorities to create committees to monitor the management of local public facilities, composed of local officials and civil society representatives—and article 29, which obliges local authorities to adopt mechanisms to ensure 'genuine participation for all residents and civil society at all stages of the preparation, implementation and evaluation' of local planning.

Civil society actors and public officials gave other examples of the institutionalisation of SA initiatives. For example, agreements between state institutions and CSOs became a common practice used by most organisations covered by the study between 2011 and 2021 (see Sect. 4.5.1.1). These agreements created new pathways for exacting accountability by establishing concrete mechanisms for engagement between authorities, citizens and civil society. These agreements do not carry any formal sanctions but encourage compliance by creating informal sanctions: when officials violate agreements, civil society can apply popular pressure using the methods analysed above. Another common mechanism is to establish steering committees composed of public officials and civil society representatives to follow up on the implementation of commitments made during SA initiatives.

However, despite these advances in the legal framework, civil society activists continue to have deep concerns about the sustainability of their initiatives. Many larger associations rely on international donor funding and are unable to find other sources of financing. The project-based approach used by international donors is seen to undermine the ability to maintain and strengthen local mobilisation for accountability. As one activist explained, 'Each time a project finishes, we just move on to the next event or project. This is a big weakness of social accountability as we are doing it' (board member El Comita, Sidi Hssinem, FGD).

There is also ambivalence on the part of civil society regarding the institutionalisation of SA initiatives in the form of legal instruments. While enshrining SA mechanisms in the law could help institutionalise practices and scale them up, this also risks allowing authorities to shape SA mechanisms and water them down in order to undermine accountability. For instance, a CSO that worked on the Local Authorities Code highlighted that the code, while enshrining the right of local residents to present petitions and request a town hall meeting, imposes such high thresholds that it effectively renders these mechanisms 'meaningless', thus 'giving the right to participation with one hand and taking it away with the other' (project coordinator Al Bawsala, personal communication, 31 August 2021, online).[4]

4.6.1 Problematic Aspects of Social Accountability

While research participants were generally supportive of SA as a means to exact accountability from public institutions, some raised concerns regarding its effectiveness and its relationship with traditional modes of accountability.

Lack of 'Teeth'

SA mechanisms alone are often insufficient for bringing about accountability, given that those who lead SA initiatives, usually civil society actors, lack enforcement powers. This raises the question of how SA can be accompanied by, or lead to, legal accountability (*muḥāsaba*), a question also posed by Fox (2015).

Lack of Evaluation

A common theme that emerged from the research is the lack of evidence regarding SA initiatives in Tunisia and their impact. Associations working in different localities had few methods for evaluating how and why an SA mechanism produced different results in different localities. There is a strong desire among civil society actors to spend more time reflecting on and evaluating their own experiences to develop more effective strategies. This included a desire to move away from looking at the experiences of other countries as 'templates' for action and instead create more fora for civil society actors to come together to compare domestic experiences and develop new approaches.

The Role of Civil Society

The proliferation of SA initiatives also raises questions regarding the relationship between participatory and representative democracy, and the appropriate line to draw between the roles and powers of elected officials and those of civil society actors who seek to hold them to account (discussed below, Sect. 4.6.1.4). The use of participatory mechanisms, in particular, such as participatory planning and budgeting has provoked a debate over the extent to which civil society actors are 'usurping' the decision-making powers of public officials. Conversely, some civil society actors are also critical of elements of the participatory democracy discourse for distracting attention away from the state's responsibilities. They also critique SA initiatives that focus on participation as a means to building trust between state and citizens for overlooking the importance of more inclusive and just *provision* of public goods and services as an essential condition to strengthening public trust in state institutions.

In addition, some research participants questioned civil society's capacity to play an effective role in calling to account public officials due to its internal divisions, deep polarisation and competitiveness, weakening civil society vis-à-vis public authorities.

Who Participates and How?

As the participation and SA literatures highlight, citizen participation can reflect and deepen socio-economic inequalities (Cleaver, 2005; Corbridge et al., 2005). Civil society activists emphasised the need to design SA initiatives in ways that do not further marginalise already marginalised groups.

Furthermore, after decades of living under a dictatorship in which an 'official' civil society existed and was used by the regime as *décor*, Tunisian civil society actors are wary of the government exploiting civil society and participatory mechanisms to improve the image of those in power while doing little to deepen accountability. As International Alert notes in its report on the evaluation of health services, participation 'should not just be used with the aim of giving legitimacy to decisions' (2019, p. 18). Participatory mechanisms can be manipulated to involve only those close to officials or those who will say what officials want to hear, a key concern for civil society activists. Donor-supported initiatives, given the significant funds involved, are particularly vulnerable to misuse for the purpose of creating or consolidating clientelist networks through the distribution of resources. These factors all contribute to a wariness on the part of civil society when designing SA initiatives to ensure that they are not exploited for the purposes of strengthening clientelist networks and practices rather than achieving greater accountability to the public.

4.7 Outcomes: Net Effects of Civic Innovation

Civil society actors referred to a number of perceived successes that can be categorised into four types: (a) legislative reform, (b) policy changes, (c) normative or behavioural change and (d) the building of trust between state and citizens.

The most frequent successes civil society actors pointed to were legislative changes, perhaps because such change is more easily identified than other forms of change. Tunisian civil society has shaped legislation in a number of areas related to accountability, including article 139 of the Constitution mandating public participation at the subnational level, which has become the basis for many participatory programmes. For instance, one activist involved in the Min Hakki Nsaalek (It's My Right to Hold You to Account) network, which advocated for guaranteeing youth participation in elections, reported that 60% of the network's proposals had been incorporated into the 2017 Election Law (board member Pole Civile, personal communication, 19 June 2021, in person). Another activist from Al Bawsala highlighted successes in shaping legislation, stating that the organisation had seen 50% of its proposed amendments to the Local Authorities Code incorporated by legislators (project coordinator Al Bawsala, personal communication, 31 August 2021, online).

To illustrate the diversity in meanings, mobilisation methods and responses by authorities and to better understand the variety in outcomes of SA initiatives in Tunisia, we present three case studies of three CSOs that have led SA initiatives, based on in-depth interviews with their members.

4.7.1 *The Participatory Approach: Action Associative (Case #1)*

Action Associative is a Tunisian CSO set up in March 2012 with the objective of promoting citizenship and human rights. The association is best known for its work on participatory budgeting, which it pioneered in 2013 with a grant from the German Development Cooperation (GIZ by its German acronym). The association adopts a cooperative approach to promoting accountability that aims to build trust between state and citizens (Association Associative, n.d.). Accountability is seen as a virtuous cycle, in which citizen participation at the local level leads to accountability, which leads to increased trust in the state, which leads to better policies and increased willingness to pay taxes, which in turn enables local government to deliver better services. For the association, improving local services is key to addressing one of Tunisia's greatest challenges—regional inequalities and the 'rural exodus' that contributes to over-burdened cities unable to provide decent services and a decent quality of life.

However, popular participation does not mean the end of representative democracy. Rather, it requires the creation of mechanisms that combine public participation with the technical expertise of public administration while 'allowing elected officials to fulfil their electoral promises' (board member Action Associative, personal communication, 18 August 2021, online). Thus, while participatory budgeting might be suitable for certain policy areas, such as roads or lighting, the association states that this might not be suitable for other areas, such as economic policy or cultural policy where public participation might sideline needed technical expertise and lead to 'the dangerous route of populism' (ibid.).

In 2014, the association became aware that a new programme was being designed by the Tunisian government, in partnership with the World Bank, to reform the municipal grant system. The association's relations with international donors enabled it to persuade the World Bank to insert conditions on citizen participation for all municipal investment grants under the programme. However, the participatory element of the programme was not what the association had in mind. According to a board member of the association, the annual participatory investment programme (PAI) imposed on all municipalities under the new grant system was designed by the Ministry of Interior in a way that removed all elements of accountability:

> They [the Ministry of Interior] sent a document to municipalities banning the application of participatory budgeting in municipalities, explicitly telling them that the municipality that uses participatory budgeting would not be given any grants or assistance. This is a huge abuse of power. (ibid.)

The association contacted the World Bank, mobilised its network of associations and issued press releases to apply pressure on the Ministry to withdraw the document, which it did.

While using the discourse of participation, the PAI programme waters down its substance by limiting the role and powers of elected delegates who, in participatory budgeting, are normally given abilities to monitor the fulfilment of municipal commitments and have access to certain documents and decision-making processes. As the association's representative explained,

> One of the conditions for building trust through participation is accountability. The PAI takes participatory budgeting but removes all the elements of accountability. In participatory budgeting, accountability is ensured through the role of elected delegates who follow the execution of projects that were selected. They have clear roles and powers. In the PAI, the delegates have no role or powers. They [the Ministry of Interior] don't want transparency. The fight against corruption doesn't suit them. (ibid.)

This also illustrates the risks of institutionalising SA mechanisms by imposing a single official SA mechanism that empties SA of its substance, reduces the space for civil society to innovate and further deepens distrust between state and citizens.

4.7.2 The Transparency Approach: Al Bawsala (Case #2)

Al Bawsala is a Tunisian CSO active since 2011. The association's work focuses on providing information on the activities of elected officials, advocacy aimed at 'establishing good governance and political ethics' and defending 'social progress and citizen emancipation' (Jamaity, 2020). The association has two main projects on accountability: Marsad Majles (literally: Observatory of the Council), which monitors the work of Parliament, and Marsad Baladia, which monitors municipalities. Both projects extract and publish information on the work of elected bodies through various means, such as information requests, litigation, advocacy campaigns, reporting and media outreach.

The association adopts a more adversarial approach to accountability than Action Associative. Its Marsad Baladia project, which began in 2014 and is funded by the European Union and Oxfam, is a transparency initiative that seeks to 'observe the activity of municipalities through access to information, and communicate it in a clear and updated way' (project coordinator Al Bawsala, personal communication, 31 August 2021, online). The project's theory of change focuses on 'obtaining the maximum amount of information … and putting it at the service of citizens to access information using technology' (project coordinator Al Bawsala, personal communication, 31 August 2021, online).

The project began with a strategy to obtain information by submitting information requests to municipalities under the 2016 Access to Information Law and litigating against municipalities that refused to respond. Over time, the association moved away from litigation towards other methods, specifically the creation of a local observers' network, a transparency index and an annual report based on this index. As a former project coordinator explained,

> We submitted cases to the administrative court and then the Authority on Access to Information once it was created, and we followed the legal process. To be honest, it wasn't very effective. The Authority takes a long time to issue decisions. Even then, the Authority doesn't have the power to impose sanctions. I don't know of any municipality that was sanctioned because it didn't respect these obligations (ibid.)

In contrast, the association found that its transparency index was highly effective in bringing about behavioural change among municipalities. The index ranks all 350 Tunisian municipalities according to indicators on their compliance with access-to-information rules. The four-year grant received by the project enabled comparisons over time to reflect changes in municipal responsiveness. The association found that the best-ranked municipalities were those where both the mayor and the general secretary were willing to provide information and those that had the internal capacity to process and respond to requests for information within the deadline. Over time, the project shifted towards organising visits to the lowest-ranked municipalities to provide advice on how to improve their transparency processes.

Marsad Baladia's shift in strategy from litigation to a more 'supportive' approach illustrates the evolution in civil society actors' strategies towards combining adversarial techniques with cooperation.

4.7.3 The Advocacy Approach: El Comita (Case #3)

El Comita is a Tunisian CSO that works on community organising. The association emerged from a project in 2018 in partnership with French community-organising association Alliance Citoyenne, funded by the Institut Français and later the Open Society Foundation. The association applies the community-organising methodology first developed in the US and has community organisers in seven deprived neighbourhoods of Greater Tunis. Community organising has a particular methodology that seeks to engage and empower ordinary citizens by organising them in collective action. Its philosophy centres on developing the capacities of under-represented groups to influence decision-making. The methodology emphasises the importance of understanding the nature of power, developing indigenous leadership through continuous training, establishing democratic decision-making within communities (through the use of general assemblies, voting and other methods), strengthening social ties, using conflict strategies and securing 'small wins'.

El Comita's approach to accountability differs significantly from the participatory approach of Action Associative and the transparency watchdog approach of Al Bawsala. First, the association strongly rejects the project-based approach to accountability, emphasising instead the importance of long-term movement-building. Rather than working at the national or municipal level, the association adopts a 'micro-local' approach of working in specific neighbourhoods over long periods. Second, the association adopts a confrontational approach to demanding accountability, on the premise that change involves conflict. The main method used is non-violent social mobilisation such as sit-ins, pickets, petitions and street campaigns.

Third, the association eschews most of the language of 'good governance' and 'transparency' and focuses instead on securing tangible public goods and access to services as concrete results that can be enjoyed by citizens. For instance, in 2019–2021, the association mobilised 3,925 households through local campaigns on specific issues. These succeeded in securing access to electricity for 233 households in a poor neighbourhood that was excluded from the electricity network, obtaining changes to traffic rules outside a school to protect pupil safety, persuading the municipality to suspend rent payments for small businesses during the Covid-19 crisis and obtaining a free municipal space for local artisans to sell their goods (board member El Comita, personal communication, 19 August 2021, online). Accountability is thus framed around access to rights for ordinary citizens and to better public services.

The association's strategy is strongly focused on developing local leadership and obtaining commitments by officials through cycles of training, collective mobilisation and negotiation with state institutions. However, it faces challenges in transferring knowledge between micro-local actions and translating this into large-scale policy changes. The association is considering the next steps in its evolution: establish inter-neighbourhood committees to enable exchange and create two national observatories (on the environment and on access to social rights) to formulate and advocate for policy recommendations. The role of these observatories is to use the learning gained from its micro-local campaigns to shape national or local decision-making.

El Comita's first organisers were taught the community-organising methodology used in the US and France. They were asked to implement it exactly as transmitted but insisted on tweaking it to fit their post-authoritarian context. This meant, for example, adopting a more diplomatic approach to engaging with officials, as discussed above. These adaptations also required developing strategies for dealing with the politics of patronage that characterise state–society relations. El Comita's approach self-consciously seeks to build a rights-based discourse with officials that escapes patronage-based logics. Its organisers recalled that when mobilising officials, they deliberately sought to avoid leveraging personal relations with them. As the head of the organisation explained,

> We reject this way of dealing with citizens as if it is a 'favour'. When I come to an official, I am not asking for a favour, I am asking for my right. But if as an activist I come to him through personal connections, or I ask him to come to a general assembly and he does it because I contacted him through a friend, then he will see it as a favour to me and not as his duty to citizens, and this changes the whole dynamic of the interaction. That is not the relationship we want. (board member El Comita, personal communication, 19 August 2021, online)

Accordingly, the organisation trains its members to approach officials through institutional mechanisms in order to discourage the personalisation of relations. It also put in place mechanisms to avoid the development of clientelist relations between its organisers and officials by, for example, banning organisers from working in their own neighbourhoods and moving organisers around different neighbourhoods to avoid the building of patron–client relations between organisers and officials or ordinary citizens over time. The association's mobilisation strategy highlights the importance of building strong relations between citizens over time and of building social capital as citizens are trained in grassroots mobilisation. Community organising's funding model of relying on membership fees may provide an alternative to the project-based approach of donor-funded initiatives, although the association has yet to move towards this model.

4.8 Lessons on Social Accountability in Tunisia

4.8.1 Formal vs. Informal Institutions

A frequently recurring theme in discussions with civil society actors and officials regarding the 2011–2021 political transition is the tension between formal and informal institutions when it comes to accountability. While all actors stated that Tunisia put in place a relatively good legal framework that promoted accountability, there was deep frustration that successive legal reforms and advances were not fully implemented due to the continuing operation of informal rules that governed the conduct of public officials and institutions.

It is notable that many civil society actors focused their efforts on amending formal rules. When asked about their biggest successes, many cited the adoption of laws and their role in influencing legal provisions, such as the Access to Information Law and the Local Authorities Code. It appears that large national CSOs focused their efforts on the adoption of laws, given the relative accessibility and openness of Parliament as opposed to the government and the central administration. In contrast, while influencing legislation proved to be relatively straightforward between 2011 and 2021, reforming institutional cultures and practices was more of a challenge. This created a debate on how civil society could 'activate' laws when they remained largely on paper. It illustrates the need to shift the debate from a legal one focused on how to enforce laws against individuals or institutions to a more sociological one focused on how to shift organisational culture and change organisational behaviour.

4.8.2 Demand Side vs. Supply Side

Many of the SA initiatives studied appear to focus on educating and engaging citizens. Many CSOs worked on raising citizen awareness as a first step towards holding state institutions accountable. They cited many challenges to this, such as prevailing norms and attitudes carried over from decades of authoritarian rule: a lack of trust in state institutions, of a 'reflex' to hold institutions accountable and of a notion of public interest as well as a fear of engagement in collective action. This focus on so-called demand-side initiatives assumes that changing citizens' attitudes and behaviour to achieve greater public participation will strengthen accountability.

Meanwhile, fewer SA initiatives focused on educating officials (both administration and politicians) to strengthen their commitment to participatory mechanisms and engagement with citizens. Our case studies highlight that bottom-up accountability initiatives should be coupled with a focus on the supply side of accountability, that is, strengthening the ability of state institutions to respond. For instance, the Al Bawsala case study highlights the need for civil society actors to work with public authorities to help them understand how to respond to access-to-information requests. Where political will exists to engage with citizens, public institutions may nevertheless lack the ability to do so. In this case, Al Bawsala discovered that in many instances, its access-to-information requests to municipalities went unanswered because institutions did not have internal procedures for managing these requests, were not even aware of receiving them, did not understand legal requirements or lacked the human resources to respond. Thus, failures to respond to requests were not always indicative of a refusal to be accountable. This illustrates the need to understand dynamics within public institutions and the causes behind a lack of accountability in order to develop more nuanced strategies for exacting accountability.

This echoes the shift in SA literature towards a focus on the need to couple bottom-up accountability initiatives (the 'demand side') with efforts to develop the ability of public institutions to respond to such demand (the 'supply side' of accountability) (Brett, 2003). It also echoes findings in the accountability literature that successful accountability initiatives involve building coalitions of reformers in both the state and civil society, who work collectively to change organisational behaviour (Booth, 2012; Fox, 2007, 2015).

4.8.3 The Tensions Between Representative and Participatory Democracy

Many civil society actors and officials argued that elected officials see themselves as enjoying exclusive decision-making authority and see participatory initiatives as an obstacle to exercising this authority. This points to the wider question of the relationship between representative and participatory democracy (Landemore, 2020). Some officials see participatory mechanisms such as the PAI as creating problems for them and as usurping their legitimacy and powers as elected representatives who aim to implement their electoral programme. Some civil society actors themselves emphasised the need to establish clear mechanisms and rules when it comes to public participation to ensure that representative democracy and participatory democracy are compatible and mutually reinforcing and that representative institutions are not weakened when they are still establishing their authority. Both officials and civil society actors therefore agreed on the importance of establishing agreements between public institutions and civil society or citizen groups that clearly set out participatory and monitoring mechanisms and outline the limits to each side's intervention. This is seen as one helpful way to prevent the overlap of mandates and conflict.

4.8.4 Tools vs. Contexts

SA initiatives have come under criticism for prioritising standard tools and their technical aspects to the detriment of paying close attention to the specificities of the context in which they are implemented. As the El Comita case study shows, SA tools cannot simply be transplanted and implemented through a predetermined methodology or 'toolkit'. This echoes critiques in the literature calling for a 'best-fit' rather than a 'best-practices' approach (Hickey & King, 2016) and for distinguishing between 'watchdogs' and 'widgets' (Joshi & Houtzager, 2012). In addition, civil society actors can become enamoured of technical tools to the extent that they seek to monopolise them. For instance, an interesting discussion occurred during the FGD on whether CSOs should seek to copyright an SA tool that they created and to what extent organisations should insist on the implementation of a mechanism in the same way in different regions and localities. In response to the statement by one participant that his organisation was 'trademarking' the SA tools it developed, another civil society representative responded,

> The idea of transfer is important. As civil society, we are working on capitalising on previous experiences … we see what experiences have been done, learn from them, try to implement and improve them … But this attempt to monopolise a concept is not in line with civil society. (project coordinator Al Bawsala, FGD)

Some participants also referred to the tendency to copy tools and mimic models from other countries. One stated, 'Our problem in civil society is we're only focusing on a few mechanisms, like participatory budgeting, citizen score cards. Everyone copies. We're only implementing models instead of developing our own tools' (representative of ANSA, FGD).

This illustrates the tensions between different ways of viewing SA: between a technical approach that focuses on the development and application of tools and a more contextualised approach that focuses on developing specific tools and strategies that respond to local needs and contexts.

4.8.5 *Confrontation vs. Cooperation*

In the period between 2011 and 2021, civil society relations with the state evolved as organisations sought to strike their own balance between cooperative and confrontational approaches and to navigate the line between cooperation, conflict and co-optation. While adversarial tactics were important, most civil society actors covered by this study reflected on their own experience that confrontation needed to be coupled with direct engagement, 'diplomacy' in communicating with officials and building cooperative relations with them. Such approaches might involve civil society working with local authorities to solve local problems by facilitating public meetings, presenting ideas and mobilising local knowledge. Most agreed on the need for both cooperative and adversarial approaches: the latter to build negotiation power and the former to agree on commitments. Research participants viewed as the biggest advances instances where civil society was able to find willing partners among politicians or bureaucrats who could push in the same direction.

4.8.6 *National vs. Local*

As outlined above, SA initiatives in 2011–2021 tended to be concentrated at the local and regional levels, given the greater ease of access to subnational officials and institutions. Nevertheless, local–national linkages were important to enabling civil society to utilise the expertise and networks they gained through local initiatives in order to shape national policies. The experiences of various organisations, such as Action Associative, Al Bawsala and El Comita, show how these organisations—based in Tunis but with local branches in different regions—tested and developed

SA strategies at the local level and then transferred knowledge between their local branches and to the national level through advocacy activities to ministries and Parliament. By having a presence at both the local and national levels, and by building both their policy advocacy and mobilisational capacities, these organisations were able to create linkages between local SA initiatives and national policy. This demonstrates the importance of building national–local civil society linkages and coalitions and linking local mobilisation to national advocacy efforts. Participants viewed this ability to bridge the local and national levels as giving these associations and their activists greater credibility at the local level—due to their presence at the national level and relations with national-level institutions—and greater credibility at the national level, due to their nationwide networks and knowledge of different geographical contexts.

4.9 Conclusion

The large number and range of SA initiatives in Tunisia between 2011 and 2021 demonstrate citizens' desire to establish a more inclusive social contract that delivers social justice, rule of law and basic rights and freedoms for all citizens. Within this struggle, SA initiatives seek to—in the words of their proponents—rebalance state–society relations away from a despotic and clientelist mode towards one based on accountability and equality between citizens.

The experiences of the organisations interviewed for this study demonstrate the importance of four main factors in the success of SA initiatives: first, the need for civil society to build credibility with both citizens and officials over time; second, the importance of tackling both ends of the accountability equation by working with citizens and officials to strengthen the commitment and engagement of both to achieving accountability; third, the need to build coalitions of CSOs and local–national civil society linkages; and fourth, utilising cooperative as well as confrontational strategies towards officials that involve multiple methods, such as media campaigns, community mobilisation and training for officials. When these factors were present, SA initiatives were seen to advance downward accountability and reshape state–society relations. Obtaining 'small wins' was also seen as critical to building credibility, gaining the commitment of citizens to mobilisation and maintaining momentum.

However, SA initiatives face a number of challenges. Resistance by influential actors within or close to the state—politicians, bureaucrats and private parties—continues to stymie efforts to bring about greater accountability. Political accountability is undermined by an electoral system that disperses power between a large number of parties in the government, and legal accountability is often difficult to enforce. Civil society mobilisation is seen to bring about only slow and limited advances in this area, as in the case of economic reforms, regional development and access to information. Civil society faces internal weaknesses that undermine its capacity to effectively push for accountability. Finally, civil society is itself embedded within a governance system based on patronage, which shapes the nature of its relations and cooperation with political officials and citizens' interactions with the state.

The Covid-19 crisis added further challenges, such as obstacles to mobilisation due to bans on public gatherings, compounded by the emergency measures introduced on 25 July 2021 and the subsequent suspension then replacement of the 2014 Constitution. These changes have further undermined accountability, weakened judicial independence and placed executive decisions above judicial review. Twelve years after the 2011 uprising, Tunisia's civil society is once again on the defensive, facing the challenge of preserving the progress made in the past decade while adapting its strategies in the context of a changing constitutional and political regime.

Notes

1. La circulaire n °12 datée 2011 relative à l'encouragement de la participation des citoyens dans le processus de l'évaluation des services publics; la circulaire n°13 de 2011 relative à l'activation de l'approche participative dans la prestation des services publics; la circulaire n °14 datée 2011 relative à la démarche participative dans la légifération et l'évaluation de la qualité des textes juridiques.
2. Indeed, the SA initiatives in the health and education sectors identified during the mapping largely focused on local or regional health and education services, rather than national ones. See International Alert's program in Tataouine (International Alert, 2019).
3. The Access to Information Authority (Instance d'Accès à l'Information, INAI) is an independent public body created by Organic Law no. 22 of March 24, 2016, to oversee implementation of the right of access to information.

4. Some municipalities have a large number of residents, which would mean that a large number of signatories are required for a petition or meeting request to be accepted.

References

Al Bawsala. (n.d.a). *Taqdīm al-munaḍama* [Presentation of the organisation]. https://www.albawsala.com/ar/presentation

Al Bawsala. (n.d.b). *Tartīb al-baladiyyāt hasba miqyās al-shafāfiyya* [Ranking of municipalities according to the transparency index]. https://baladia.marsad.tn/transparence/

Al-Siyāsa. Ḍaʿaf al-mawārid wa ghiyāb al-musāʾala athara ʿalā najāʿat al-ʿamal al-baladī [Lack of resources and absence of accountability impact on effectiveness of municipal work]. (2001, January 9). *Mosaique FM*. https://www.mosaiquefm.net/ar/السياسة-ضعف-الموارد-وغياب-المساءلة-أثرت-على-نجاعة-العمل-البلدي/تونس-أخبار-وطنية/1003712

ʿAmārī, I. (2021, May 22). Tūnis. Jalsa ʿāmma li-musāʾalat khamsa wuzarāʾ [Accountability session in Parliament with five ministers]. *Tunisie Numerique*. https://ar.tunisienumerique.com/تونس-جلسة-عامة-لمساءلة-5-وزراءسياسة/

Amnesty International. (2018, December 13). *Tunisian authorities must sustain progress on transitional justice* [Press release]. https://www.amnesty.org/en/latest/press-release/2018/12/tunisian-authorities-must-sustain-progress-on-transitional-justice/

Amnesty International. (2023, July 24). *Tunisia: Human rights at risk two years after President Saied's power grab*. https://www.amnesty.org/en/latest/news/2023/07/tunisia-human-rights-at-risk-two-years-after-president-saieds-power-grab/

Arab Network for Social Accountability. (2021). Al-wāqiʿ al-qānunī wal-ijrā'ī al-dāʿim llmusā'ala al-ijtimāʿiyya fī tūnis [The legal and procedural context relating to social accountability in Tunisia].

ARTICLE 19. (2014, April 16). *ARTICLE 19 part of a civil society project to improve transparency and good governance*. https://www.article19.org/resources/tunisia-article-19-part-civil-society-project-improve-transparency-good-governance/

Association Associative. (n.d.). *Instruments et mécanismes*. https://www.actionassociative.org/instruments-et-mecanismes/

Association Tunisienne des Contrôleurs Publics. (n.d.). *Publications et rapports*. https://atcp.org.tn/rapports/

Association Tunisienne des Contrôleurs Publics. (2016). *IGOVEP: Indice de gouvernance des entreprises publiques en Tunisie. Analyse et résultats 2016.* http://atcp.org.tn/wp-content/uploads/2019/02/IGOVEP.pdf

Ben Ismail, Z. (2023, July 18). *Free voices silenced by decree 54 in Tunisia.* Inkyfada. Retrieved August 18, 2023, from https://inkyfada.com/en/2023/07/18/free-voices-silenced-decree-54-tunisia/#:~:text=According%20to%20ICJ%2C%20the%20Decree,international%20human%20rights%20law%20and

Booth, D. (2012). *Development as a collective action problem: Addressing the real challenges of African governance.* Overseas Development Institute. https://cdn.odi.org/media/documents/appp-synthesis-report-development-as-a-collective-action-problem-david-booth-o_7un7DOu.pdf

Brett, E. A. (2003). Participation and accountability in development management. *Journal of Development Studies, 40*(2), 1–29.

Cherif, Y. (2017, August 8). The Kamour Movement and civic protest in Tunisia. *Carnegie Endowment for International Peace.* Retrieved August 18, 2023, from https://carnegieendowment.org/2017/08/08/kamour-movement-and-civic-protests-in-tunisia-pub-72774

Classement des municipalités au niveau de la transparence: Khelidia en tête. (2020, January 19). *Réalités Online.* https://realites.com.tn/fr/classement-des-municipalites-au-niveau-de-la-transparence-khelidia-en-tete/

Cleaver, F. (2005). Rethinking agency, rights and natural resource management. In S. Hickey & D. Mitlin (Eds.), *Rights-based approaches to development: Exploring the potential and pitfalls* (pp. 127–144). Kumarian Press.

Constitute Project. (n.d.). *Tunisia 2014 constitution.* https://constituteproject.org/constitution/Tunisia_2014?lang=en

Corbridge, S., Williams, G., Srivastava, M., & Veron, R. (2005). *Seeing the state: Governance and governmentality in India.* Cambridge University Press.

Di John, J., & Putzel, J. (2009, June). *Political settlements.* Issues Paper. http://www.gsdrc.org/docs/open/eirs7.pdf

Espace Manager. (2013, April 16). *Table Ronde sur la redevabilité sociale.* https://www.espacemanager.com/table-ronde-sur-la-redevabilite-sociale.html

Forum Tunisien de Droits Economiques et Sociaux. (n.d.). *Monthly reports on social movements, suicides, violence and migration.* Retrieved 10 December 2021, from https://ftdes.net/en/observatoire/

Fox, J. (2007). *Accountability politics: Power and voice in rural Mexico.* Oxford University Press.

Fox, J. (2015). Social accountability: What does the evidence really say? *World Development, 72*, 346–361.

Hickey, S. (2013). *Thinking about the politics of inclusive development: Towards a relational approach.* ESID Working Paper 1. Effective States and Inclusive Development Research Centre. https://www.effective-states.org/wp-content/uploads/working_papers/final-pdfs/esid_wp_01_hickey.pdf

Hickey, S., & King, S. (2016). Understanding social accountability: Politics, power and building new social contracts. *The Journal of Development Studies, 52*(8), 1225–1240.

Hickey, S., & Mohan, G. (2008). The politics of establishing pro-poor accountability: What can poverty reduction strategies achieve? *Review of International Political Economy, 15*(2), 234–258.

Human Rights Watch. (2021, September 27). *Joint statement: Tunisia: Unprecedented Confiscation of Power by the Presidency.* Retrieved July 20, 2023 from https://www.hrw.org/news/2021/09/27/joint-statement-tunisia-unprecedented-confiscation-power-presidency

Information, de Formation d'Études et de Documentation sur les Associations, Centre de. (2021). *Tableau général des associations au 9 Aout 2021.* Retrieved 10 December 2021, from http://www.ifeda.org.tn/stats/francais.pdf

Instance d'Accès à l'Information. (n.d.). *Faḍāʾ al-nafādh ilā al-maʿluma* [Access to information portal]. http://www.inai.tn/espace-acces-information/

Instance d'Accès à l'Information. (2019). *Ittifāqiyyat sharāka wa taʿāwun bayn hayʾat al-nafādh ilā al-maʿlūma wa jamʿiyyat Tūnis arḍ al-insān* [Partnership and cooperation agreement between the National Access to Information Authority and Tunisia Ardh al-Insaan Association]. http://www.inai.tn/wp-content/uploads/2019/12/convention_inai_Ass_Terre_Hommes.pdf

Instance Nationale de Lutte Contre la Corruption. (2020a). *Stratégie nationale de bonne gouvernance et lutte contre la corruption 2016–2020.* Retrieved 10 December 2021, from https://inlucc.tn/wp-content/uploads/2020/11/isar.pdf

Instance Nationale de Lutte Contre la Corruption. (2020b). *Al-istrātijiyya al-wataniyya lil hawkama al-rashīda wa mukāfahat al-fasād 2016–2020* [National anti-corruption strategy 2016–2020]. https://inlucc.tn/wp-content/uploads/2020/12/Strategie-Nationale-de-Bonne-Gouvernance-et-de-Lutte-Contre-la-Corruption-Decembre-2016.pdf

International Alert. (2019). *Taqyīm mujtamaʿī lil-khadamāt assihiyya alʾumūmiyya b wilayat Tataouine* [Societal evaluation of public health services in the Governorate of Tataouine]. https://www.international-alert.org/sites/default/files/Tunisia_HealthinTatatouine_AR_2018_1.pdf

International Alert. (2021, March). *Community score card: A tool to strengthen mutual accountability and community-police partnership.* https://www.international-alert.org/publications/community-score-card-tool-strengthen-mutual-accountability-community-police-partnership/

Jamaity. (2020, February 4). *Résumé: Al Bawsala.* https://jamaity.org/association/al-bawsala/

Jasmine Foundation. (n.d.). *Nabnī. TN, bunāt al-thiqa* [We Build Tunisia: Building Trust]. http://www.jasminefoundation.org/ar/?p=4020

Jasmine Foundation. (2017, May 30). *YouthAct: Project overview*. http://www.jasminefoundation.org/en/?p=1690

Joshi, A., & Houtzager, P. P. (2012). Widgets or watchdogs? *Public Management Review, 14*(2), 145–162.

Kemp, S. (2021, February 12). *Digital 2021: Tunisia*. Datareportal. https://datareportal.com/reports/digital-2021-tunisia

Kherigi. (2020, January). *'Civil society in a time of transition', EuroMed Survey of civil society and social movements in the euro-mediterranean region* (10th ed.). IEMED.

La Presse. (2017, March 16). *Les dispensaires sous la loupe de la société civile*. Retrieved August 18, 2023, from https://www.pressreader.com/tunisia/la-presse-tunisia/20170316/281526520865302

Landemore, H. (2020). *Open democracy*. Princeton University Press.

Lassoued, H. (2020, November 23). *Hiwār ma'a Munīr Sa'īdanī haula namūdhaj i'tissām al-kāmūr* [Interview with Munir Saidani on the model of the Kamour sit-in]. Nawaat. https://nawaat.org/2020/11/23/%D8%AD%D9%88%D8%A7%D8%B1-%D9%85%D8%B9-%D8%A3%D8%B3%D8%AA%D8%A7%D8%B0-%D8%B9%D9%84%D9%85-%D8%A7%D9%84%D8%A5%D8%AC%D8%AA%D9%85%D8%A7%D8%B9-%D9%85%D9%86%D9%8A%D8%B1-%D8%A7%D9%84%D8%B3%D8%B9%D9%8A%D8%AF/

Ministère de l'Interieur. (2016). *Caisse des prêts et de soutien des collectivités locales : Documents atelier PAI*. https://cpscl2016.wixsite.com/cpscl2016/documents-atelier-autour-du-pai

Open Government Partnership Tunisia. (n.d.-a). *Tunisia: Action Plan 4*. Retrieved June 16, 2023. https://www.opengovpartnership.org/members/tunisia/#commitments

Open Government Partnership Tunisia. (n.d.-b). *National Action Plans*. http://www.ogptunisie.gov.tn/en/?cat=44

Organisation for Economic Co-operation and Development. (2019, September). *Good governance and anti-corruption in Tunisia*. https://www.oecd.org/mena/governance/good-governance-and-anti-corruption-in-tunisia-highlights-en.pdf

Peruzzotti, E., & Smulovitz, C. (Eds.). (2006). *Enforcing the rule of law: Social accountability in the new Latin American democracies*. University of Pittsburgh Press.

Reuters. (2023, March 9). *Tunisian president to dissolve municipal councils months before local elections*. https://www.reuters.com/world/africa/tunisian-president-dissolve-municipal-councils-months-before-local-elections-2023-03-09/

Riahi, L. (2018, February 9). *Manich Msamah: Retour critique sur un moment politique*. Nawaat. https://nawaat.org/2018/02/09/manich-msamah-retour-critique-sur-un-moment-politique/

RTTEM. (n.d.). *Al-shabaka al-tūnusiyya lil-shafāfiyya fī al-tāqa wal-manājem* [Tunisian network for transparency in energy and mining]. Retrieved August 18, 2023, from https://www.facebook.com/profile.php?id=100064806453155

Tunisian Republic. (n.d.). *Bawwābat al-mushāraka al-ʿumūmiyya* [Public Participation Portal]. Retrieved August 18, 2023, from http://www.e-participation.tn.

United Nations Development Programme. (n.d.). *TAMKEEN, pour la promotion de la citoyenneté, le renforcement de la cohésion sociale et de la société civile.* https://www.tn.undp.org/content/tunisia/fr/home/projects/tamkeen--pour-la-promotion-de-la-citoyennete--le-renforcement-de.html

United Nations Development Programme. (2018, July 5). *L'Assemblée des représentants du Peuple lance sa plateforme de gestion des relations entre l'Assemblée et la société civile.* https://www.undp.org/fr/tunisia/news/l'assemblée-des-représentants-du-peuple-lance-sa-plateforme-de-gestion-des-relations-entre-lassemblée-et-la-société-civile

US Embassy in Tunisia. (2021, February 2). *Assistance Unit's project launches the first online platform to link municipalities, deputies, and civil society.* https://tn.usembassy.gov/assistance-units-project-launches-the-first-online-platform-to-link-municipalities-deputies-and-civil-society/

Venice Commission. (2022, May 27). *Urgent Opinion on the Constitutional and Legislative Framework on the Referendum, and Elections Announcements by the President of the Republic, and in particular on the Decree-Law no. 22 of 21 April 2022 amending and completing the Organic Law on the Independent High Authority for Elections (ISIE)*, Opinion no. 1085/2022, Council of Europe. Retrieved 18 August, 2023 from https://www.venice.coe.int/webforms/documents/default.aspx?pdffile=CDL-PI(2022)026-e

Vloeberghs, W., & Bergh, S. I. (2021, March 10). *Weapons of discontent? Sketching a research agenda on social accountability in the Arab Middle East and North Africa.* ISS Working Paper No. 671. https://repub.eur.nl/pub/135292

Webdo.tn. (2019, January 7). *I Watch porte plainte contre Chahed pour corruption.* https://www.webdo.tn/fr/actualite/national/i-watch-porte-plainte-contre-chahed-pour-corruption/151914

Webdo.tn. (2020, July 28). *I Watch dépose une plainte pour annuler le contrat entre l'ANGED et VALIS.* https://www.webdo.tn/fr/actualite/national/i-watch-depose-une-plainte-pour-annuler-le-contrat-entre-langed-et-valis/142936#.YbHy6vHMI-Q

CHAPTER 5

Social Accountability in Lebanon: Collaboration Rather Than Confrontation in Times of Crisis

Hicham Jadaoun

Abstract This chapter brings a case study of social accountability (SA) initiative in Lebanon, focusing on the relationship between community-based committees and municipalities. It explores different meanings of SA, which in this context focuses more on the possibility of people to question the municipality's actions, and latter's openness to this kind of questioning. SA therefore takes a more reactive form, and is more accepted in the case of failure to respond to people's priorities, while steering away from financial accountability. Local actors emphasise direct communication as a primary tool for SA. Collaboration is more valued than confrontation as it seen as more likely to yield positive results and change. During the multifaceted crisis in Lebanon, citizens' expectations of municipalities and their respective roles are shifting towards responding to basic needs. This is coinciding with municipalities' diminished resources to fulfil their duties. Municipalities therefore look to local

H. Jadaoun (✉)
Independent Researcher, Beirut, Lebanon
e-mail: jadaoun.hicham@gmail.com

W. Vloeberghs and S. I. Bergh (eds.), *Social Accountability Initiatives in Morocco, Tunisia, and Lebanon*, EADI Global Development Series,
https://doi.org/10.1007/978-3-031-51322-0_5

citizen committees for support. This opens the door for collaborative planning, if certain boundaries are respected.

Keywords Collaboration · Co-optation · Municipalities · Lebanon · Social accountability

5.1 Introduction

This Lebanon case study is part of a larger research project on social accountability (SA) in the Middle East and North Africa (MENA), including Lebanon, Morocco and Tunisia (see Chapter 1: Introduction in this volume). The three case studies revolve around the overall question of what SA looks like on the ground. In the case of Lebanon, the study presents key findings related to the concept of SA in the country. It links SA practices and activities to several key events in the MENA region and in Lebanon more specifically.

The case study examines local committees in two villages, Baaqline and Baysour, located in the Chouf district (*qaḍāʾ*) of the Mount Lebanon governorate (*muḥāfaza*). Both villages took part in one of the cohorts implemented by 'Peacebuilding in Lebanon', a project run by the United Nations Development Programme (UNDP) since 2007. The collaboration focused on creating mechanisms for social stability for each village. The two villages were selected because they were considered at high risk for tensions due to a population increase (Syrian refugees) and difficult living conditions. The project was implemented in tandem with the municipalities and the Ministry of Social Affairs (MoSA).

I describe the link to SA through the relationship between the local committees[1] and their respective municipalities. I document the role and understanding of local committees acting as local mechanisms to hold the municipalities accountable through the former's identification of priorities, decision-making and implementation of community-based activities. I also examine the different meanings local stakeholders ascribe to SA, document mobilisation methods used by local committees and municipalities, analyse the responses of the latter and shed light on the outcomes. The research revolves around the following main research question: *What does accountability look like for the people on the ground?*

The main question was divided into four subquestions:

1. Multiple meanings: what do locals understand by the word 'accountability'? How do citizens engaged in SA mechanisms refer to it and ascribe meaning to it?
2. Mobilisation methods: how did local activists get the attention of fellow citizens (mobilising them) and of the officials in power responsible for providing certain types of information or services (i.e. how did they get them to listen)?
3. Responses from authorities: how did local activists maintain momentum in terms of mobilisation and how did they get power holders and officials to commit to providing the information and services? What motivated the official(s) to commit?
4. Outcomes: how did activists get power holders to deliver on their commitments? Did they succeed in exacting accountability at all, and if so, to what extent? And are there some signs of their commitments being institutionalised? What are the reasons for successes and/or failures?

5.2 Methodology

The case study was developed with data collected predominantly through qualitative methods. These included a review of relevant documents on SA, its background in Lebanon, the local context and community actors, contributing to a better design and tailoring of the methods and guiding questions. Five semi-structured interviews were conducted with two mayors (of Baaqline and Barbara; the latter is a small village in the Jbeil district in Mount Lebanon), two local committee representatives (Baaqline and Baysour) and one municipality spokesperson (Baysour). The interview with Barbara's mayor was added to better understand findings on the shift in roles and people's expectations from the municipalities during the public health (Covid-19) and economic crises.

An additional interview was conducted with the social policy and management consultant contracted by UNDP, who facilitated the formation and capacity-building processes of both local committees. The consultant worked with the committees for over a year. Support included coaching on participatory needs assessments, planning, capacity-building and implementation. I identified the case study and located both committees with the support of this consultant, who is a former colleague.

I did not previously work or interact with the local committees and their respective municipalities in any way.

One focus group discussion (FGD) was conducted with seven members of Baaqline's local committee, comprising four women and three men: the committee representative and six local activists or delegates of community-based organisations (CBOs). Participation was voluntary, and the invitation was shared in the committee's WhatsApp group. I could not conduct a similar FGD with Baysour's committee due to members' lack of interest and availability.

Before conducting the interviews and FGD, I explained the background and objectives of the case study and collected interviewees' informed consent to their participation and the recording of the interview. Recordings were transcribed and translated from Arabic into English with the help of a research assistant. Findings were analysed manually according to themes based on the research questions. Interviews lasted on average 40 minutes and were conducted online via Zoom or Microsoft Teams, due to the challenges of commuting amidst the fuel crisis in Lebanon, or in person at the municipality.

One additional workshop was organised online to validate the findings, including a presentation of preliminary findings answering the different research questions. The workshop was attended by 10 participants: the local committee representatives, one mayor who had taken part in the research, the UNDP project coordinator for Mount Lebanon, the vice president of a municipality in Mount Lebanon (Jeddayel), the former social policy and management consultant of the project, two local development consultants and one local researcher.

5.3 Accountability in Lebanon in Context

Lebanon was founded as a parliamentary democracy in which power is shared among religious communities according to the concept of confessionalism. Political parties were established reflecting citizens' ideologies and religious beliefs. Politics in Lebanon is highly tied to sectarian elites, who use their positions of power to influence citizens and who have access to the state's resources. The Lebanese system has long been described as 'dysfunctional and problematic' (Haase, 2018, 793) because of the highly clientelist power-sharing relationships between sectarian leaders and citizens. Hence, there is limited space for citizen participation in political life and decision-making. Also, Lebanon has been deeply affected by the influence and domination of foreign powers (Haase, 2018, 793).

Sectarianism is a complex phenomenon, and the sectarian system is deeply rooted in Lebanese politics. This system, first introduced in 1843 in Mount Lebanon, is considered one of the major contributors to the Lebanese civil war, which occurred from 1975 until 1990. Sectarianism was not applied to the rest of the Lebanese territories before the creation of Greater Lebanon in 1920 under the French Mandate and was not fully formed and developed until the country's independence in 1943. The elites in power, representing Maronite and Sunni interests, joined in an unwritten agreement also known as the 'National Pact of 1943'. This agreement distributed power positions on a sectarian basis: the presidency for the Maronites, the premiership for the Sunnis and the parliament speakership for the Shiites (Ofeish, 1999).

As a result of the Pact, sectarian conflicts increased. This, together with the constant influence of foreign powers in the country, triggered the start of the Lebanese civil war in 1975. Foreign interference was highlighted in the Taif Agreement of 1989, when different foreign powers negotiated in Saudi Arabia to find a formal way to end the war. The negotiations resulted in the Taif Agreement, which contained reforms to the sectarian system that did not materialise, however (Ofeish, 1999). The influence of sectarian elites grew even more after the civil war, which tremendously impacted Lebanese politics as people's loyalties remained tied to their sectarian *Za'īm* (male leader) in exchange for services. Thus, there was less regard for national ties (Karam, 2017). Social accountability in Lebanon is affected by all these characteristics.

5.3.1 Legal Context

The Lebanese Constitution states in its preamble[2] that the people are the source of all power, given that the country is a parliamentary democracy. People have the 'authority and right' as citizens to hold public officials accountable. The Constitution also guarantees the practice of accountability through parliamentary elections, in which Lebanese people have the right to choose their representatives ("Lebanese Constitution" n.d.). Moreover, the Constitution acknowledges the importance of internal accountability practices through the principle of separation of powers.[3] In its articles 8[4] and 13,[5] it highlights the importance of 'liberty and freedom', which are major pillars of SA practices (Moukheiber, 2021).

In 2017, the Lebanese Parliament ratified the Access to Information Law. It serves as a valuable legal instrument in the practice of accountability, as it enables citizens to evaluate and monitor the performance of public administrations (Organisation for Economic Co-operation and Development [OECD] et al., 2018). The ratification of the law was considered a breakthrough, giving citizens, journalists, and researchers the right to access all public institutions' files except for 'personal data, state security documents and confidential diplomatic information' (Chehayeb, 2020). In 2020, Parliament adopted Law no.175/2020, which provides legal grounds for fighting corruption in the public sector and requests the establishment of a national anti-corruption commission, 11 years after Lebanon acceded to the UN Convention Against Corruption (UNCAC). The law lays the foundation for accountability practices, highlights the importance of investigations, identifies corruption cases in the public sector and monitors the enforcement of anti-corruption-related laws. It also defines corruption and sets penalties for corrupt practices, 'including up to three years of imprisonment and a fine amounting to at least double the value of the bribe' (Chehayeb, 2020).

5.3.2 *Civil Society Organisations Pre-Arab Spring*

Civil society organisations (CSOs) act as a 'watchdog' and have the power to hold public officials accountable through lobbying, spreading awareness or applying direct pressure (El Mufti, 2015). This section offers a brief description of some CSOs and initiatives that have been active in Lebanon since before the Arab Spring in 2011 on issues related to SA. Two organisations have been mainly concentrating on issues pertaining to the aftermath of the civil war (1975–1990). The Committee of the Families of Kidnapped and Disappeared in Lebanon was formed in 1982 to lobby for clarity on the fate of individuals who disappeared during the civil war. The committee's main aim is to push politicians to officially take into account the issue of missing people (Civil Society Knowledge Centre, 2015). Support of Lebanese in Detention and Exile (SOLIDE) was established in 1990 to work on the issue of the disappearance of victims and arbitrary detention during the civil war.

Other organisations tackle political, legal and human rights issues. The Lebanese Association for Democratic Elections (LADE) was launched in response to Parliament's decision to postpone the elections in 1996 (AbiYaghi, 2012). It has since been active in monitoring and evaluating all proceedings relevant to elections. At a broader level, the Lebanese Transparency Association (LTA) was founded in 1999 in response to the increasing rate of corruption in the country. Its work focuses on encouraging and supporting civil society to hold officials accountable and ensure transparency in public institutions (Transparency-lebanon.org, accessed 10 February 2023). The Legal Agenda in turn was created in 2009 with the hope of bringing a 'critical and multidisciplinary approach to law and justice in Arab countries' (Legal Agenda n.d.). The organisation focuses on political, civil, social and economic rights.

5.3.3 *The Arab Spring and its Spillover Effects in Lebanon*

More than a decade ago, accountability seemed unattainable across Arab states. On 7 December 2010, Mohamed Bouazizi, a Tunisian street vendor, set himself on fire in front of the local government building in Sidi Bouzid, Tunisia (Gelvin, 2015). This incident led to the eruption of a series of civil protests propelled by wide discontent due to the unequal distribution of 'civic, political and social rights of citizenship between different groups and societal classes' (Vloeberghs & Bergh, 2021, 5) that set off what became known as the Arab Spring. A wave of revolutions rippled through the MENA region in 2011 and the following years, in Tunisia and other Arab countries such as Libya, Egypt, Yemen, Bahrain and Syria (Ma'oz, 2014). The Arab Spring is considered an important event in the history of the region, as it united citizens from different countries to demand justice, freedom and 'accountable governance' (Vloeberghs & Bergh, 2021, 5). However, its outcomes varied across countries. In Tunisia, the uprising resulted in the departure of President Ben Ali and political reforms. In Egypt, President Mubarak was overthrown while in Syria, a long-lasting civil war erupted, resulting in a severe refugee and humanitarian crisis that affected many countries (Elagati, 2011).

In 2011, Lebanon shortly became part of the Arab uprisings, as hundreds of Lebanese protested in Beirut calling for an end to the sectarian system. This march was planned on Facebook, with the organisers demanding a 'secular, civil, democratic, socially just and equal state' ("Lebanese protest", 2011). However, the marches and mobilisation did not last long, as the movement did not manage to attract attention outside of the capital (Halabi, 2019) and scepticism among youth about the outcomes of the Arab Spring developed (Rosiny, 2018).

In 2015, civil movements grew stronger as a reaction to the garbage crisis. This crisis started when one of the biggest landfills in the country had to be closed as it had reached maximum capacity and the government failed to find a replacement. A large number of protestors took the streets, demanding an end to the crisis and using the slogan 'You stink' in reference to the country's political leaders, who had left the country 'paralysed' for years (Yahya, 2015). These protests highlighted the importance of civil society movements, shedding light on the concept of accountability with the aim of generating long-lasting change. This paved the way to another mass uprising in the country in 2019.

On 6 May 2018, parliamentary elections took place after a nine-year hiatus, as Parliament had extended its own mandate on more than one occasion (LADE, 2018). A new electoral law enabled the Lebanese diaspora to vote from abroad for the first time in the country's history. However, the election process lacked transparency. According to Transparency International, the Supervisory Commission for Elections operated with 'such inefficiency and poor transparency' that it created an 'unfair advantage for candidates' (Transparency International, 2018, 3).

On 17 October 2019, an evening protest in Beirut grew into a mass uprising. Activists and independent groups formed political parties and came together to mobilise protests. People took to the streets in reaction to the economic decay in the country, with several demands under the slogan 'all of them means all of them'[6] (Saab et al., 2021). Demands encompassed different aspects of Lebanese citizens' lives and highlighted common hardships. The uprising targeted various issues in the Lebanese political administration and system: corruption, inefficiency, unemployment, sectarianism and clientelism (Saab et al., 2021).

This uprising broke through social and sectarian barriers. It was the first time in the history of Lebanon that citizens from all confessions, sectarian and political affiliations, generations, social and economic backgrounds and professions were united. Protestors succeeded in electing Melhem Khalaf to Parliament, and with him a new generation of young leaders and activists as a result of independents winning seats in student elections across different Lebanese universities. However, the scale of mobilisations has clearly decreased. Many observers link this decrease to the economic crisis, the Covid-19 outbreak and state oppression (Comaty et al., 2021).

5.3.4 *The Current Multidimensional Crisis*

Since 2020, Lebanon has experienced a multidimensional crisis, caused by political uncertainty and economic collapse and exacerbated by the Covid-19 pandemic and the fallout from the August 2020 Beirut Port explosion. Aggravated political and economic instability has affected the livelihoods, living conditions and safety of different populations in the country while increasing inequality (Abed et al., 2020). Thousands of people have been thrown into poverty as a result of these interrelated crises (Médecins sans Frontières, 2021). More than 55 per cent of the population is struggling to meet its basic needs and lives below the poverty line. The country is suffering from hyperinflation, with inflation averaging 84 per cent in 2020 (World Bank, 2021b). Salaries in Lebanese pounds have continuously lost value against the rapid cost increase of goods and services (United Nations Children's Fund [UNICEF], 2021). Moreover, around 1.5 million Syrian refugees are currently hosted in Lebanon, equivalent to a quarter of its population. With the highest per capita concentration of refugees in the world, social stability in many municipalities is fragile, as the large numbers of people increase pressure on already stretched services and infrastructure (International Labour Organization [ILO] n.d.). The World Bank categorised the current situation in Lebanon as among the top three 'most severe crisis episodes globally' since the nineteenth century (World Bank, 2021a).

The current situation has fuelled both inter- and intracommunity tensions, which already ran high. Access to jobs, services, resources and humanitarian and international aid has become more challenging (World Vision International, 2015). Relationships among communities are put to the test, with social, economic, geographical and confessional divides widening (El Mufti, 2015). Communal relations are deteriorating, driving tensions along with an increase in incidents and escalations triggered by the worsening economic situation, job losses, rising poverty and deterioration of services (UNDP et al., 2023).

The dysfunctional sectarian system in Lebanon has been the main contributor to the unprecedented economic crisis (Hubbard, 2020). The crisis built up for years due to the flawed political system, which hindered rational policy-making and enabled the growth of widespread of corruption and waste (Hubbard, 2020). Corruption has been a prominent issue in Lebanon for years. According to Transparency International (2022),

Lebanon is ranked 150th out of 180 countries in the Corruption Perception Index, with a score of 24/100 (a country's **score** is the perceived level of public sector corruption on a scale of 0–100, where 0 means highly corrupt and 100 means very clean). Lebanese citizens have lost confidence in government officials, as the former act in pursuit of their personal interests, leaving the public interest on the side. Despite the severe impact of corruption on Lebanese society, the government has made little effort to fight it (Haase, 2018).

In response to the Covid-19 pandemic, the Inter-Ministerial and Municipal Platform for Assessment, Coordination and Tracking (IMPACT)—an e-governance platform owned by the Central Inspection of the Presidency of the Council of Ministers—introduced new modules to fulfil crisis response needs. The government established the platform to facilitate people's access to permits for moving around during national lockdowns. It was later used as the key and only reference for vaccination appointments and delivery. IMPACT is a one-of-a-kind public initiative that offers access to data collected by different public sector agencies (of ministries and municipalities). The overall aim is to enhance transparency and accountability of these institutions through the wider adoption of citizens' right to access to information (https://impact.cib.gov.lb/home, accessed 5 February 2023). Nevertheless, ownership of data generated by IMPACT remains a source of dispute between the Central Inspection and the prime minister (IMPACT team, 2021).

5.3.5 *Local Systems of Governance*

Lebanon is divided into eight governorates, 26 districts and 1108 municipalities. Each governorate is headed by a *muḥāfaz* (governor) appointed by decree by the Council of Ministers (CAS, 2023). Municipalities aim to achieve local development within their area. They are subject to the Municipal Law promulgated by Decree-law no. 118/77 from 1977 and its amendments. They consist of a decision-making authority, embodied in the municipal council elected on the basis of general and direct vote, and an executive authority (Mourad & Al-Siddiq, 2018). The president (mayor) and vice president (deputy mayor) are elected by the municipal council. The municipal council has to have a clear agenda and is tasked with monitoring and planning different development projects in the area (Mourad & Al-Siddiq, 2018).

Article 47 of the Municipal Law states that 'each work of public character or interest, within the municipal area, falls within the scope of the municipal council's competence' (Mourad & Al-Siddiq, 2018, 12). The municipal council has the authority to note its recommendations concerning subjects and projects related to public needs and public policies in its municipal area. It 'is the competent authority in making decisions on subjects that do not fall within the scope of competence of any other authority, be it central or local' (12). Therefore, municipal tasks consist mostly of providing basic infrastructure, such as paving roads, providing lighting and planning public parks. Since municipalities also issue work and building permits, collect fees and taxes and provide/oversee educational and health services, their role is important, as they directly influence the daily lives of their citizens. Hence, transparency and accountability are very important pillars of the municipal council's practices, at least in theory (Gherbal Initiative[7] & UNDP Lebanon, 2020).

5.3.6 *The Peacebuilding Project and Local Committees*

Under the peacebuilding project mentioned earlier, UNDP partnered with the MoSA, aiming to reduce existing tensions between host and displaced communities. The project worked on reaching stability through providing a common space for the local community to express its concerns and participate in resolving conflicts (UNDP, 2018). The project (which is ongoing in other municipalities) aims at enhancing mutual understanding and social cohesion by addressing root causes of conflict. It also works on addressing the impact of the Syrian crisis on social stability in Lebanon. The project supports different groups—from local leaders to educators, youth, media professionals, journalists and civil society activists—in developing both medium- and long-term strategies for peacebuilding, crisis management and conflict prevention (UNDP n.d.).

The project included Baaqline and Baysour among its cohorts between 2017 and 2018. Both areas, unlike others that were part of the project, managed to form committees composed of 15 members each, all of whom were from the Druze sect, and brought together loyal supporters (of the municipality) and representatives from the political opposition (who run against each other during municipal elections or are part of opposing political parties and families). These committees cooperated on a strategic plan for the village. They are two rare cases where different sides came together to work to the benefit of the village in a structured manner. The committees included municipal council members, local activists and representatives of CBOs. They also had a higher representation of women and youth than other committees, which were dominated by men (social policy and management consultant, personal communication, 18 August 2021, online).

Baaqline is located in the Chouf district in the Mount Lebanon governorate and presents a rich and unique combination of cultural, historical and natural heritage. It is characterised by the presence of mostly Druze families and a minority of Christian families, with active yet relatively limited social relationships. It has around 17,000 inhabitants living in 2,870 homes (Ghosseini, 2017). Baaqline is an important Druze town, as it is the seat of the sect's religious leaders. The Druze are a small religious sect (minority) characterised by 'an eclectic system of doctrines and by a cohesion and loyalty among its members (at times politically significant) that have enabled them to maintain for centuries their close-knit identity and distinctive faith' (Editors of Encyclopaedia Britannica, 2022). An estimated 2,800 Syrian refugees reside in Baaqline (social policy and management consultant, personal communication, 18 August 2021, online).

Baysour is a village located in the district of Aley, also an administrative division of the Mount Lebanon governorate. It is more homogeneous in terms of religious groups, as it mainly consists of Druze communities. However, it is surrounded by villages with diverse religious and political backgrounds, with whom relations were tense in the past ("Baysour" n.d.). The total population in the area is estimated to be around 12,000 (Union of Municipalities of the Gharb Aala and Chahhar [Uomgac] n.d.). The village also hosts around 3,500 Syrian refugees since the beginning of the crisis.

5.4 Multiple Meanings

Having provided a background to the political system in Lebanon and the context of the case studies, I now turn to presenting my findings for each of the four sub-research questions. As for the first subquestion, I found that accountability and SA take on several meanings in the local context of Lebanon. In the absence of a clearly designated and synonymous word in Arabic, accountability lends itself to two translations and interpretations. The first is linked to ***muḥāsaba***: the act of holding someone or an entity accountable for their actions (or inaction). This definition has a negative connotation and has closer ties to financial accountability. The second interpretation starts from ***musāʾala*** and is closer to 'questioning'. In the following, the meanings associated with these two interpretations are presented from most to least frequent, as described by the stakeholders interviewed.

5.4.1 Accountability as Holding Authorities to Account

Different understandings and explanations among research participants revolved around the capacity of holding local authorities (municipalities) accountable by asking about their performance and plans. The most common interpretation of SA was constituents asking the municipality or the municipality being asked by constituents about actions or the lack thereof. This openness to being questioned is a major step that municipalities feel they are taking towards SA at the local level. This acceptance is not taken for granted. These actors perceived being open to people's questioning as an effort to be acknowledged by the people they try to serve. This points to the importance of communication as a primary tool for SA in the perception of different stakeholders, as will be established below. As the mayor of Baaqline stated:

> Any citizen has the right to question the municipality. To ask is a duty and to respond is a duty as well. This is accountability. The citizen has to ask and you, as a person holding a position of power, have to respond. (Baaqline mayor, personal communication, 13 August 2021, in person)

Municipalities agreed on the need to be questioned by different actors, but this remains conditional on when, why (which topics) and how (communication rather than confrontation) it is done. Municipalities and CSOs alike felt that they can, or should be, questioned if they fail to fulfil their duties.

The willingness and capacity to hold local authorities to account has evolved after the 2019 uprising. Interviews and the discussion during the validation workshop pointed to the growing sense of accountability, especially among the younger generation. According to a Baaqline local committee representative, young people are less affected by social pressures at the local level, unlike their parents, and have more courage to demand clarity and accountability (personal communication, 9 August 2021, online). There is growing ownership of and demands for holding public servants accountable and responsible for what they have accomplished in their areas, especially for those who have been in office for a long time. This was backed by the social policy and management consultant, who expressed that people feel that their voices can now be heard and that they can make a difference, unlike before (personal communication, 18 August 2021, online). This also contributed to a shift in the mayors' mindset, whereby they began to fear being publicly shamed.

5.4.2 *Accountability as Responding to Local Needs*

For social activists, SA also meant holding a person in a position of power accountable for fulfilling the tasks dictated by their role. According to local committee members, the municipality should provide citizens with their basic rights, and they can hold it accountable in case it fails to do so. Members felt that the mayor is 'someone in a position of power, this person has tasks; we shall hold him/her accountable if he/she did not accomplish the required tasks' (Baaqline local committee FGD, 13 August 2021). They also stated that accountability is achieved when responsible people are questioned adequately and malpractices are not ignored. When people are held accountable, it forces them to do their jobs right. Therefore, SA is closely tied to the municipalities' capacity to identify and respond to local needs. The more a municipality manages to deliver the services needed or expected by their constituents, the less it is subject to being held accountable. Thus, identifying supportand understanding local needs is an essential step in the local understanding of SA. Local committees the municipalities in this process by connecting them with people and active CBOs.

At the same time, stakeholders pointed to the increase in expectations during the multifaceted crisis in Lebanon, with people increasingly turning to municipalities with their requests and demands, given that these are the closest local authorities (Baaqline local committee representative, personal communication, 9 August 2021, online; Baysour municipality spokesperson, personal communication, 11 August 2021, online; social policy and management consultant, personal communication, 18 August 2021, online; Barbara mayor, personal communication,

9 September 2021, in person). In the midst of a national economic crisis and drained public funds, with the aggravation of the situation and especially shortages in essential imported products, municipalities are expected to play an active role in coordinating, facilitating access to or delivering basic needs such as water, electricity, fuel and healthcare required by Covid-19 (such as essential medication and access to hospitalisation). This represents a shift in municipalities' earlier roles and tasks as described above, which were mainly related to administrative services and public infrastructure. This is why a municipality representative stated that people have the right to hold the municipality accountable, but that the latter should not be held responsible for the country's current stagnation (Baysour municipality spokesperson, personal communication, 11 August 2021, online). Similarly, Barbara's mayor shared that people in his village were aware of the current situation and challenges and were no longer holding the municipality accountable for council members' election promises.

5.4.3 *Accountability as Acting in the Case of Failure*

Different stakeholders emphasised the predominant use of SA in cases of failure: situations in which municipalities failed to perform or deliver what citizens were entitled to, did not keep their promises or did not intervene where people felt it was needed. This is a more reactive stance towards SA, with a limited preventative approach or scope concerning what SA could be or contribute to. 'At some point accountability includes receiving critiques. SA is present if the municipality is failing to respond to a crisis' (Baysour municipality spokesperson, personal communication, 11 August 2021, online).

5.4.4 *Accountability as a Legal Measure*

The issue of who has the legal authority and jurisdiction to hold the municipality accountable was one of the key findings emerging from the conversations with mayors. Municipalities took different stands on who can hold them accountable legally. This also varied with governance levels. For example, some mayors concentrate all responsibilities in the hands of the district commissioner (*qāʾim maqām*), believing that they are the main reference for legal (financial) obligations. To quote one of the mayors interviewed:

> If people elected me, they do not always have to hold me accountable and question where I am spending the money; there are experts for monetary issues who get to hold me accountable and not the people. If you put your money in the bank, you do not go and count it every day. (Baaqline mayor, personal communication, 13 August 2021, in person)

Different actors connected accountability to financial decisions or to how municipal or public funds are distributed. Accountability usually includes decisions, decrees or even informal policies enforced by the municipality with a financial implication. According to a committee representative: 'With the current circumstances, there are no projects and thus there is no practice of accountability, because municipalities do not even have a budget' (Baaqline local committee representative, personal communication, 9 August 2021, online). Local committee members also pointed to other facets of financial accountability concerning where the money was spent and what was achieved, as well as whether the funds were earmarked according to a specific priority (Baaqline local committee FGD, 13 August 2021).

5.4.5 *Accountability as Access to Information*

Access to information, which can be achieved by publishing budgets and official decisions, is another meaning associated with holding the municipality accountable. The level of information-sharing varies from one location to another. In Baaqline, local committee members felt that less than 10 per cent of the municipal information was being published, limited to yearly budgets. They were adamant about constituents' rights to have access to this sort of information. On the other hand, municipalities like Barbara expressed that they are one of the few municipalities to publish their decisions, plans and budgets for the public on the municipality's website. For them, this is an essential part of accountability (Barbara mayor, personal communication, 9 September 2021, in person). However, people's awareness of their right to access and demand such information remained minimal.

5.4.6 *Accountability as a Personal Contribution*

Accountability in the perception of activists and municipalities also included the idea of holding oneself accountable. This is translated by questioning their contribution to the community. Taking ownership of one's actions is a key manifestation and exercise of accountability. It starts with the person's level of responsibility. As a local committee representative described it: 'SA is linked to one's contribution to one's society. As a person who lives in a certain area, what is your contribution? How do you hold people in power accountable? How can you add value to your society?' (Baaqline local committee FGD, 13 August 2021).

5.5 Mobilisation Methods and Means for Accountability

Moving on to the second subquestion, there are different methods, techniques and channels for accountability used vis-à-vis local authorities. These are presented according to the order in which they are used, as described by respondents.

5.5.1 Direct Communication

The first and most common channel for accountability is direct communication. Here, the extent to which the municipality, in particular the mayor him- or herself, is reachable through direct communication becomes important. An 'open door' policy was perceived to be the optimal solution for increasing residents' possibilities to engage in conversations with the municipality, mostly to share requests, demands or complaints. This direct contact could also take the form of in-person visits or encounters with the mayor, at the municipality or elsewhere. The latter included social ceremonies like weddings and funerals, religious celebrations or festivals and social visits. Hence, the open door policy was translated as any chance to reach the mayor (or a member of the municipality) in person or over the phone to convey a message. Respondents saw an important link between SA and communication. The possibility of directly denouncing a possibly 'wrong action or decision' or sharing demands or grievances increased accountability in the perception of different parties. According to one of the mayors: 'You have to listen to people. This is the key. You have to listen and respect everyone' (Barbara mayor, personal communication, 9 September 2021, in person).

However, many citizens are (a) not aware of their rights to question the municipality and (b) lack access to the tools, fora and spaces to do so.

This is why members of Baaqline's local committee felt that it is important for citizens to know their rights. This was corroborated by the social policy and management consultant, who supported the call to empower citizens via access to the required tools to hold any type of institution accountable. Yet, there is also a question of access to the municipality and mayor. Opposing parties, residents and refugees (mostly Syrian in these cases) are likely to have less opportunities in this regard. According to the Baaqline mayor, the municipality's door is open for communication, and they are always in contact with citizens. Nevertheless, during the fieldwork I did not observe any active initiatives from his side to inform people or connect with them.

To put the opportunities for SA through direct communication in perspective, it is useful to briefly consider the traditional political accountability mechanism, namely (local) elections. Voting for municipal and parliamentary elections still follows the parental place of birth of the person (in the case of male voters) or the place of birth or registration of the spouse (for married women voters).[8] Residency in another village or city, regardless of the number of years, does not grant the right to vote for the municipal council in that location. Residents not holding a Lebanese passport or official identification document are not entitled to participate in municipal and parliamentary elections. This affects the extent to which the priorities of certain groups, such as Syrian refugees, are represented, communicated or acted upon. When you are not a voter, you have fewer chances to share your priorities or contribute to local accountability.

5.5.2 *Support Rather Than Confrontation*

Local committees adopted internal accountability in their attempts to support rather than confront the municipalities. There is a collaborative sense to this, in line with the preference for direct communication. 'Internal' accountability was described as more effective in some cases and involves communication and the process of questioning taking place behind closed doors, with the aim of finding solutions or improving the situation. Hence, the objective is improvement rather than blaming or shaming. Local committee members acknowledged that some municipal council members might lack experience in development work, and they saw it as the committee's task to reach out to them and offer help. Working to support the municipalities enabled committees to push and influence them to achieve their own priorities or desired changes. Even those who came to the committees from a politically opposing position engaged in close communication with the municipalities. Being involved in the committee offered them a direct channel that provided a better understanding and access to knowledge on the inside. This also allowed for discussions on why certain things took place and why certain decisions were taken, which paved the way for more in-depth talks.

This emphasis on support is exhibited in this Baysour local committee representative's opinion on the matter:

> When you are holding a person accountable, you have two options. You approach this person either directly or indirectly. Directly through heading to the municipality. Indirectly through social media, although I am against it, especially during this time when anyone can create fake accounts and digital campaigns. (Baysour local committee representative, personal communication, 22 August 2021, online)

The municipalities have been welcoming and keeping close coordination with the local committees, as members of the latter have gained a better understanding of the situation in the villages and are better able to reach those who are most vulnerable. This points to the perceived and expected roles of the local committees, which are entrusted with assessing local needs, supporting the planning and execution of projects such as recycling, tourism and awareness of Covid-19, etc. These roles are less about oversight and accountability and more about support of and collaboration with the municipality. Municipal council members insisted that they themselves are the 'decision-makers' and that committees should (merely) take on a coordination role.

5.5.3 *Denouncing on Social Media*

Another, less frequent method of SA is the direct denouncing of the municipality on social media, mainly Facebook. The method is rarely if ever used by local committees and is employed more frequently by community members. Social media could be perceived as an indirect alternative to the direct approach. If the latter is not successful, and the municipality does not respond, social media becomes an option. The municipalities involved in this research have official pages where people can send messages and ask for clarification on issues of interest.[9] They review these messages and try to find adequate solutions. After the

2019 uprising, public shaming and denouncing of political individuals or groups and public servants on social media became more common and somewhat acceptable (social policy and management consultant, personal communication, 18 August 2021, online).

In terms of mobilisation methods, given the challenges of getting around in Lebanon (due to roadblocks and fuel shortages), social media was considered the most common option for activists and municipalities alike to share their questions and priorities and announce their activities or decisions. Activists also considered social media, mainly Facebook, the main tool for mobilisation. WhatsApp groups are used to spread information, news and activities. However, they are less interactive and work mostly as dissemination channels.

5.5.4 *Filing Complaints*

The mayors mentioned filing official complaints or using the complaint box as possible SA means, but there is limited evidence of their use. Instead, those who can or want to access the municipality prefer to seek other, more direct and indirect approaches, as detailed above.

5.6 Responses from Authorities

This section answers the third subquestion on responses from the authorities, outlining responses that are again specific to the collaboration between the local committees and the two municipalities.

5.6.1 *Using SA 'Responsibly'*

When looking at responses from municipalities, it should be kept in mind that people's expectations from municipalities have changed, as explained above. From the municipalities' point of view, SA is welcome as long as it is used 'responsibly'. Municipalities call on those observing their performance to keep in mind the (limited) realm of their responsibilities, any gaps between available budgets and growing needs and the local context and current situation.

> We are heading towards a very difficult situation. We are trying not to spend money to leave a certain budget for emergencies. ...There are no resources available other than the people. What we are noticing is that

people are engaging together and many of them are volunteering. (Barbara mayor, personal communication, 9 September 2021, in person)

'Responsibly' also refers to a preferred method of expression and collaboration. Some committee members in Baaqline and Baysour resigned at an earlier stage of the committees' inception. Allegedly, this was due to repetitive clashes about approaches and points of view with municipal council members, who held traditional beliefs on social work and accountability (social policy and management consultant, personal communication, 18 August 2021, online) or on how people should express themselves (Baysour local committee representative, personal communication, 22 August 2021, online).

5.6.2 *Free Qualified 'Labour' and Access to Funds*

Especially in the current dramatic socio-economic situation, the municipalities see the role of local committees as supporting them with (mostly qualified) 'free labour', in a way as volunteers conducting needs assessments of the most vulnerable and organising awareness-raising campaigns. For example, their work as part of the Covid-19 response included identifying vulnerable families to support, distributing food items and raising awareness to prevent infection. They also supported the municipalities in other areas, for example with recycling and tourism projects. In both study areas, the municipalities benefit from a qualified and specialised group of people (i.e. the members of the local committees) to support them in social and humanitarian initiatives. As a municipal representative elaborated: 'The municipality is a key actor and has many responsibilities, but it also needs support at some point, it needs volunteers during the crisis' (Baysour municipality spokesperson, personal communication, 11 August 2021, online).

Such 'participation' also ensures that as recipients of funds, the municipalities fulfil donors' and local non-public actors' requirements and conditions of community engagement. This means that more funds are channelled to the municipality or the village through the committee. It remains to be seen to what extent this dynamic contributes to a depoliticisation or co-optation of the local committees, pulling them away from their SA roles. 'We are not used to practicing accountability. Sometimes questioning the municipality creates further conflicts. Therefore, people prefer not to ask critical questions to avoid a misunderstanding' (Baaqline local committee FGD, 13 August 2021). By 'misunderstanding', the interviewee probably meant tension with or retribution from the municipality, such as public shaming, pressuring the person's family, halting communication, making it difficult to obtain future services, etc.

5.6.3 *'Soft' Power*

Historically, but even more so in the current situation, a significant portion of residents does not pay taxes to the municipalities. This places them in a latent or 'soft' position of power, even if this is unclaimed or acted upon, with respect to people who wish to complain or hold them accountable. The case study was unable to find more data on this point, given how sensitive it is for the different parties involved. However, it would seem that the old adage of 'no representation without taxation'—which is fundamental to the social contract as understood in the Global North—applies to this case and weakens the position of citizens vis-à-vis the municipalities.

5.6.4 *Contextual Factors*

As outlined above, the national context of widespread corruption determines the responses from authorities to a great extent, including at the local level. Lebanese officials have used certain laws to their advantage and failed to implement others, although the constitution and laws provide legal grounds for strong accountability practices. For example, Lebanese authorities have arguably 'legalised corruption', breaching laws for public appointments[10] and motivating clientelism in public administrations. This strongly impacts accountability, as individuals are appointed on the basis of sectarian affiliations and 'are expected to be loyal to political leaders, and are unlikely to inform/denounce wrongdoings' (Martini, 2015, 4).

Similarly, even though the constitution guarantees freedom of expression and assembly, citizens and activists have faced and are still facing interrogation, detention and censorship at the hands of security forces for sharing different views and pinpointing corruption practices in government institutions (Touma & Zaghbour, 2020). The constitution solemnly declares the principle of equality of all citizens before the law. However, many forms of and mechanisms for immunity specifically favour civil servants and public officials (Moukheiber, 2021). In addition, several recent reports by LADE highlight the lack of transparency, law breaches and violations during recent municipal and parliamentary elections in Lebanon. Despite such documentation, the state continues to use corrupt practices and manipulate election dates and laws in its favour (LADE, 2018).

5.7 Outcomes

Finally, the fourth subquestion asked about outcomes. In light of the findings presented here, it is clear that in the case of Lebanon in general and of the two local committees of the case study in particular, the evidence of clear, concrete and solid results is modest. Nevertheless, the various interviews and discussions suggest that desired outcomes were achieved at three levels. First, the collaborations initiated under the UNDP project increased synergy and coordination between local committees and municipalities, leading to a better capitalisation and use of resources (human resources, access to people and funds). Second, the trust of municipalities in local committees increased both outreach and representation efforts. Third, the close coordination and engagement between the different parties (including the political constituency and opposition) boosted the local acceptance and legitimacy of municipalities and their efforts conducted at the local level. Indeed, this could be an additional factor pushing the municipalities to cooperate with the local committees and offer support.

5.8 Discussion and Conclusion

In the absence of institutionalised means and a lack of interest of the political ruling class to respond to local calls for accountability, the different endeavours and actions of CSOs working to advance SA remain unanswered. This is why CSOs currently focus on mobilising for parliamentary and syndicate elections.

Access to information remains one of the key challenges for SA at local and national levels. Lebanese authorities have failed to implement the Access to Information Law. Many municipalities and state institutions have poor website management and thus fail to a large extent to provide citizens with access to public data (Chehayeb, 2020). The low rates of compliance by and interest from public institutions in response to the Access to Information Law is well documented (Al Moghabat, 2018).

The multifaceted crisis has heightened pressures on local authorities to play a greater role in responding to citizens' needs. This has increased people's demands but has also given municipalities a greater leeway to passively escape accountability obligations. In an extremely resource-scarce environment, the dependency of individuals on bilateral connections with the municipality (in the shape of patron–client relations, co-optation, etc.) increases as they try to satisfy some of their urgent and primary needs.

SA initiatives in Lebanon have taken various forms at the local and national level and yielded different results. At the local level, as is the case with the local committees discussed here, a combination of close coordination, access and communication remains the most effective strategy. Being able to advise and take part in decision-making could be more pragmatic and impactful. Having a seat at the table counts more than protesting from the outside. On the other hand, the impact of formal organisations and CSOs has been weaker at the national level. Advocacy campaigns have mostly been met with negative (or no) responses by the government (Mardini, 2021).

After 17 October 2019, there has been a greater level of awareness of the importance of accountability and transparency, as well as heightened engagement and interest in issues of public interest, especially among youth. The latter's approach has been dominated by direct opposition and confrontation. This pushes local authorities to take a defensive position, increase their inclusiveness or find a middle way, in which they use subtle strategies to co-opt or 'divide and conquer' critical groups of citizens, such as those represented in the local committees discussed here.

Suggestions for future research include the following, mainly shared and discussed during the validation workshop: it would be interesting to explore the extent to which accountability and advocacy have evolved or changed, especially after the 2019 uprising. In particular, if and when the next municipal elections take place (they were scheduled for May 2023 but at the time of writing, their current mandates had been extended by up to a year, see Wood, 2023), it would be useful to assess accountability practices around them, in addition to citizens' and civil society's roles in motivating, supporting and agreeing or disagreeing with the municipality. Will people engage with the new municipal council in the same way as they did with the previous one? In addition, the role of women in the public sphere in general and in the municipal realm in particular needs to be explored, including its challenges (opposition from some religious authorities and conservatives).

Notes

1. A local committee was created in each village with the support of a UNDP consultant. They initially included activists and representatives of grassroots organisations, major families and other civil society organisations. The committees' composition differed according to the nature and dynamics of each village. Their initial role was to develop social stability plans and implement relevant initiatives. In both Baaqline and Baysour, the focus evolved to address larger community needs and priorities in collaboration with the municipalities.
2. Preamble D: 'The people are the source of authority and sovereignty; they shall exercise these powers through the constitutional institutions' ("Lebanese Constitution" n.d.).
3. Preamble E: 'The political system is established on the principle of separation of powers, their balance and cooperation' ("Lebanese Constitution" n.d.).
4. Article 8: 'Individual liberty is guaranteed and protected by law. No one may be arrested, imprisoned, or kept in custody except according to the provisions of the law' ("Lebanese Constitution" n.d.).
5. Article 13: 'The freedom to express one's opinion orally or in writing, the freedom of the press, the freedom of assembly, and the freedom of association shall be guaranteed within the limits established by law' ("Lebanese Constitution" n.d.).
6. Repeating the term 'all of them' served to emphasise and affirm that all politicians are corrupt, not one single party.
7. The Gherbal Initiative advocates for a better adoption by administrations of measures that guarantee access to information and transparency. The Initiative hopes to transform the current political rhetoric to a candid and patriotic dialogue that relies on facts and numbers. See https://elgherbal.org/.
8. From 2018, married women were allowed to run for municipal elections in their registered hometown (following their father's registration) or in the town where their husband is registered.

9. See the Facebook page of Baaqline municipality: Facebook.com/ Baaklinechouf. See also the Facebook page of Baysour municipality: Facebook.com/ بلدية-بيصور-الصفحة-الرسمية.
10. Article 12 of the Lebanese Constitution states: 'Every Lebanese shall have the right to hold public office, no preference shall be made except on the basis of merit and competence, according to the conditions established by law' ("Lebanese Constitution" n.d.).

References

Abed, D., Baroud, M., & Moussawi, F. (2020, December). *Inequality in Lebanon: Questioning labor, social spending, and taxation*. Policy Brief #4/ 2020. Issam Fares Institute, American University of Beirut. https://www.aub.edu.lb/ifi/Documents/publications/policy_briefs/2020-20/20210112_inequality_in_lebanon_english.pdf

AbiYaghi, M.-N. (2012, June). Civil mobilisation and peace in Lebanon. *Accord: An International Review of Peace Initiatives*, *24*, 20–24.

Almoghabat, M. (2018, September). *The right to access information. A study on the Lebanese government's commitment to the Right to Access Information Law (No. 2017/28)*. Gherbal Initiative, with the support of the European Endowment for Democracy. https://elgherbal.org/reports/Edc2fkXSYcGABHzwxeST

Baysour. (n.d.). Retrieved January 31, 2023, from https://www.cityofaley.com/villages/baysour/.

Central Administration of Statistics - about Lebanon (n.d). Retrieved August 08, 2023, from http://www.cas.gov.lb/index.php/about-lebanon-en

Chehayeb, K. (2020, January 7). *New laws, same old practices? Lebanon passes anti-corruption laws, but questions persist over their efficacy*. The Tahrir institute for Middle East Policy. https://timep.org/2020/07/01/new-laws-same-old-practices-lebanon-passes-anti-corruption-laws-but-questions-persist-over-their-efficacy/

Civil Society Knowledge Centre. (2015). *Committee of the Families of Kidnapped and Disappeared in Lebanon*. https://civilsociety-centre.org/party/committee-families-kidnapped-and-disappeared-lebanon

Comaty, L., Fawaz, M., Younan, O., Masri, R., Hassan, N., Tannoury-Karam, S., Geha, C., & Saab, R. (2021, September 21). *Why did the October 17 Revolution witness a regression in numbers?* The Lebanese Center for Policy Studies. https://www.lcps-lebanon.org/articles/details/2462/why-did-the-october-17-revolution-witness-a-regression-in-numbers

Editors of Encyclopaedia Britannica. (2022, December 9). Druze. In *Encyclopaedia britannica*. https://www.britannica.com/topic/Druze

El Mufti, K. (2015, February). *Civil society's role in security sector reform in Lebanon: An asymmetric partnership despite a growing working relationship with security services*. International Alert Background Paper. https://www.international-alert.org/wp-content/uploads/2021/08/Lebanon-SSR-Civil-Society-EN-2015.pdf

Elagati, M. (2011, July 27). The Arab Spring: Common roots, common challenges. *Jadaliyya*. https://www.jadaliyya.com/Details/24246

Gelvin, J. L. (2015). *The modern middle east: A history* (4th ed.). Oxford University Press.

Gherbal Initiative and United Nations Development Programme Lebanon. (2020, May 4). *Transparency in the municipalities and federations: Requests to access to information*. https://www.undp.org/lebanon/publications/transparency-municipalities-and-federations

Ghosseini, N. (2017). Baakline: Towards a Smart City—Leading change into Chouf Souayjani region. In A. Stratigea, E. Kyriakides, & C. Nicolaides (Eds.), *Smart cities in the Mediterranean: Coping with sustainability objectives in small and medium-sized cities and island communities* (pp. 59–84). Springer.

Haase, T. W. (2018). A challenging state of affairs: Public administration in the Republic of Lebanon. *International Journal of Public Administration, 41*(10), 792–806.

Halabi, F. (2019, December 18). *From 'overthrowing the regime' to 'all means all': An analysis of the Lebanonisation of Arab spring rhetoric*. Arab Reform Initiative. https://www.arab-reform.net/publication/from-overthrowing-the-regime-to-all-means-all-an-analysis-of-the-lebanonisation-of-arab-spring-rhetoric/

Hubbard, B. (2020, May 10). Lebanon's economic crisis explodes, threatening decades of prosperity. *New York Times*. https://www.nytimes.com/2020/05/10/world/middleeast/lebanon-economic-crisis.html

IMPACT team. (2021, October 9). Open letter to Prime Minister Najib Mikati: Do not block reform and innovation. *L'Orient Today*. https://today.lorientlejour.com/article/1277417/open-letter-to-prime-minister-najib-mikati-do-not-block-reform-and-innovation.html

International Labour Organization. (n.d.). *Partnership for improving prospects for forcibly displaced persons and host communities (PROSPECTS)*. Retrieved February 3, 2023, from https://www.ilo.org/global/programmes-and-projects/prospects/lang--en/index.htm

Karam, J. G. (2017). Beyond sectarianism: Understanding Lebanese politics through a cross-sectarian lens. *Middle East Brief, 1*(107). https://www.brandeis.edu/crown/publications/middle-east-briefs/pdfs/101-200/meb107.pdf

Lebanese Association for Democratic Elections. (2018, May 9). *Observation mission of 2018 parliamentary elections: Preliminary report summary*. https://lb.boell.org/sites/default/files/uploads/2018/05/180507_prelimreport_overviewen.pdf

Lebanese Constitution. (n.d.). Promulgated on May 23, 1995. English translation retrieved from http://www.presidency.gov.lb/English/LebaneseSystem/Documents/Lebanese%20Constitution.pdf

Lebanese protest against sectarian political system. (2011, February 27). *Reuters*. https://www.reuters.com/article/lebanon-protest-idAFLDE71Q08L20110227

Legal Agenda. (n.d.). *About us*. Retrieved February 12, 2023 from https://english.legal-agenda.com/about-us/

Libandata. (2018, January 08), Baysour (Alay). https://www.libandata.org/ar/almdn/byswr-alyh

Ma'oz, M. (2014). The Arab Spring in Syria: Domestic and regional developments. *Dynamics of Asymmetric Conflict, 7*(1), 49–57. https://doi.org/10.1080/17467586.2014.894249

Mardini, R. U. (2021, July 4). Transparency and accountability in international assistance: The case of Lebanon. *UNDP*. https://www.undp.org/lebanon/blog/transparency-and-accountability-international-assistance-case-lebanon

Martini, M. (2015). *Transparency and accountability in Lebanon's emerging petroleum sector*. Transparency International. https://issuu.com/cmi-norway/docs/150719114858-a5df7191fdb84dcc845d38bb82ec2eb4

Médecins sans Frontières. (2021, January 8). *Overlapping crises in Lebanon increase needs and worsen access to care* [Press release]. https://www.msf.org/lebanon-overlapping-crises-increase-needs-and-worsen-access-care

Moukheiber, G. (2021, July 4). Constitutional challenges and the fight against impunity. *UNDP*. https://www.undp.org/lebanon/blog/constitutional-challenges-and-fight-against-impunity

Mourad, A., & Al-Siddiq, Z. (2018). *Citizen & municipality handbook. Simplified legal rules governing municipal work in Lebanon*. Nahnoo. https://nahnoo.org/wp-content/uploads/2021/09/Citizen-municipalities-handbook-english-1.pdf

Organisation for Economic Co-operation and Development [OECD], MEPI, OMSAR, and Gherbal Initiative (2018). *The right to access information: citizen guide*. https://www.oecd.org/mena/governance/ati-guide-lebanon-en-min.pdf.

Ofeish, S. A. (1999). Lebanon's second republic: Secular talk, sectarian application. *Arab Studies Quarterly, 21*(1), 97–116.

Rosiny, S. (2018, April). *Lebanon: The predecessor of the Arab Spring? The youth is sceptical but not desperate*. FES MENA Youth Study: Country Analysis Lebanon, Friedrich-Ebert-Stiftung. https://library.fes.de/pdf-files/iez/14985.pdf

Saab, R., Comaty, L., Fawaz, M., Younan, O., Masri, R., Hassan, N., Tannoury-Karam, S., & Geha, C. (2021, September 21). *Has the October 17 revolution accomplished anything at all?* Lebanese Center for Policy Studies. https://www.lcps-lebanon.org/articles/details/2463/has-the-october-17-revolution-accomplished-anything-at-all

Touma, A., & Zaghbour, M. (2020). *To speak or not to speak: Tackling recent violations of freedom of expression in Lebanon*. Policy Brief #1/2020. Issam Fares Institute, American University of Beirut. https://www.aub.edu.lb/ifi/Documents/publications/policy_briefs/2019-2020/20200117_freedom_of_expression.pdf

Transparency International. (2018, May 9). *Ineffective election monitoring in Lebanon highlights urgent need for independent body*. https://www.transparency.org/en/press/ineffective-election-monitoring-in-lebanon

Transparency International. (2022). Lebanon Corruption Perceptions Index. https://www.transparency.org/en/cpi/2020/index/lbn

Union of Municipalities of the Gharb Aala and Chahhar. (n.d.). Baysour. http://www.uomgac.org/en/bayssour/

United Nations Children's Fund. (2021, July 1). *Living on the edge in Lebanon: More than half the population is now below the poverty line*. https://www.unicef.org/lebanon/stories/living-edge-lebanon-more-half-population-now-below-poverty-line

United Nations Development Programme. (2018). *The UNDP peace building in Lebanon project's newsletter*. https://www.undp.org/sites/g/files/zskgke326/files/migration/lb/undp_newsletter_20_EN.pdf

United Nations Development Programme. (n.d.). *Peacebuilding in Lebanon project—Phase 3*. https://www.undp.org/lebanon/projects/peacebuilding-lebanon-project—phase-3

United Nations Development Programme, United Nations High Commissioner for Refugees, Government of Lebanon. (2023). *Lebanon crisis response plan*. https://lebanon.un.org/sites/default/files/2023-05/Lebanon%20Crisis%20Response%20Plan%202023_0.pdf

Vloeberghs, W. P., & Bergh, S. I. (2021). *Weapons of discontent? Sketching a research agenda on social accountability in the Arab Middle East and North Africa*. ISS Working Paper No. 671. https://repub.eur.nl/pub/135292

Wood, D. (2023, May 31). *Lebanon needs to hold municipal elections*. International Crisis Group. https://www.crisisgroup.org/middle-east-north-africa/east-mediterranean-mena/lebanon/lebanon-needs-hold-municipal-elections
World Bank. (2021a). Lebanon sinking (to the top 3). *Lebanon Economic Monitor, Spring 2021*. https://documents1.worldbank.org/curated/en/394741622469174252/pdf/Lebanon-Economic-Monitor-Lebanon-Sinking-to-the-Top-3.pdf
World Bank. (2021b, June 1). *Lebanon sinking into one of the most severe global crises episodes, amidst deliberate inaction* [Press release, World Bank]. https://www.worldbank.org/en/news/press-release/2021/05/01/lebanon-sinking-into-one-of-the-most-severe-global-crises-episodes
World Vision International. (2015, November 18). *Social cohesion between Syrian refugees and urban host communities in Lebanon and Jordan*. https://www.wvi.org/sites/default/files/World%20Vision%20International%20DM2020%20Social%20Cohesion%20Report.pdf
Yahya, M. (2015, August 25). *Taking out the trash: Lebanon's garbage politics*. Carnegie Middle East Center. https://carnegie-mec.org/diwan/61102

CHAPTER 6

Conclusion: Social Accountability Initiatives as Sites of Relational Power

Ward Vloeberghs and Sylvia I. Bergh

Abstract In this chapter, we first summarise the findings from the country chapters on the multiple meanings of SA, documenting terms, translations and contrasting understandings between citizens and public officials. Second, we highlight how civil mobilisation tends to be cyclical over time and is often mediated by brokers. Strategies to spur stakeholders

W. Vloeberghs (✉)
Erasmus University College, Erasmus University Rotterdam, Rotterdam, The Netherlands
e-mail: vloeberghs@euc.eur.nl

S. I. Bergh
International Institute of Social Studies, Erasmus University Rotterdam, Rotterdam, The Netherlands

Research Group Multilevel Regulation, Centre of Expertise Global and Inclusive Learning, The Hague University of Applied Sciences, The Hague, The Netherlands

S. I. Bergh
e-mail: bergh@iss.nl

W. Vloeberghs and S. I. Bergh (eds.), *Social Accountability Initiatives in Morocco, Tunisia, and Lebanon*, EADI Global Development Series,
https://doi.org/10.1007/978-3-031-51322-0_6

into action rely on a delicate balance of both collaboration and confrontation. Third, we examine the responses from authorities to SAIs, finding that reactions are uneven and that all civic innovators fear appropriation or co-optation by officials. Fourth, we assess overall outcomes of Arab SAIs and highlight that the transformative potential of SAIs exists especially at municipal level, if four conditions for success are present (trust, proximity, endorsement, evaluation). We also point out that the actual outcomes of SAIs in Arab societies have, so far, been limited due to design deficiencies (emphasising short-term objectives and limited context sensitivity) or because of officials' resistance in active or passive forms. We characterise SAIs as a discursive action format that is best understood with a relational approach to power. In a final section, we formulate recommendations for activists, officials and donors on how to make SAIs more effective.

Keyword Civic space · Social accountability · Middle East and North Africa (MENA) · State–society relations · Citizen participation · Donors

Social accountability (SA), both as a concept and as a tool to repair broken state–society relationships or social contracts, has gained significant traction in the Middle East and North Africa (MENA) region over the past decade. Understood here as formal or informal citizen-led action beyond elections that aims to hold state actors accountable for public decision-making, SA emerged from the fields of international public governance and development studies and is key to healthy citizen–state dynamics.

This volume started from a twofold paradox. First, while the literature on SA has moved beyond area studies focused on Latin America to analyse initiatives across other continents, there has been limited scholarly attention for social accountability initiatives (SAIs) in the MENA region. We find this relative negligence surprising, given the spectacular breakthrough in civic space during the Arab uprisings of 2011 and their resurgence in 2019. This hints at the second paradoxical observation, namely that Middle East Studies has largely ignored insights from international development scholars focusing on SAI as a mechanism of social change.

We argue that SAIs are a mixed and fragmented bag when juxtaposed and assessed in terms of tangible outcomes for advancing the standards of answerability among public decision-makers in Arab societies. While clear victories exist (e.g. the adoption of progressive legislation in Tunisia, awareness-raising in Morocco and improved municipal service delivery in Lebanon), in some SAIs authorities engaged in co-optation tactics and window-dressing—without donors noticing it. We believe, therefore, that SAIs deserve closer attention because they enable us to understand how power relations between various stakeholders play out on the ground. Our case studies moreover document the potential of citizen action when certain conditions are met. Alas, analysing a decade of Arab SAIs also illustrates how citizen voice that lacks teeth can be curtailed by incumbent rulers.

When analysed from a more generic perspective, an SAI is a discursive action format that constitutes a helpful prism for analysing how power relations are produced, maintained and altered in local settings. We conceptualise 'discursive action format' as a package of interventions connected by a more or less coherent narrative of social change and practical arrangements (from regular meetings to physical or digital registration forms) designed to facilitate interaction between ordinary citizens and state officials. In this sense, a SAI can be seen as a 'political artefact, an effect that is made out of processes, which involve both discursive and material components' (Moisio et al., 2020, p. 8). These initiatives reveal interlinkages and surprisingly similar modes of operation and contestation at multiple scales (Global Partnership for Social Accountability [GPSA], n.d.). Since SAIs are increasingly present in the Global South as a tool for civic innovation and participatory democracy, it is important to understand how they greatly vary and yet are comparable across time and space.

6.1 Answering Our Research Questions

In this book, we set out to document what SA looks like for people in three key countries of the Arab world. We divided this overall question into four subquestions, focusing on multiple meanings of SA, mobilisation methods, responses from authorities and outcomes. In the process, we relied mostly on qualitative research methods (interviews with donors, activists and officials; focus groups with project leaders and stakeholders; case studies; participant observation and desk review). Below, we formulate some concluding observations for each of these four subquestions (see Table 6.1) before providing more general lessons and recommendations on SA in the MENA.

Table 6.1 Meanings, mobilisations, responses and outcomes of social accountability initiatives in three Arab societies

	Morocco	*Tunisia*	*Lebanon*	*Overall*
Meanings	• Multiple terms circulate simultaneously (*redevabilité sociale*, *musāʾala ijtimāʿiyya*, *muḥāsaba*) • Polysemy of social accountability (holding decision-makers to account, monitoring public policies, citizen participation)	• SA covers at least six dimensions: transparency, rule of law, citizen participation, answerability of authorities, access to information, monitoring and evaluation) • Whereas activists speak of accountability initiated by citizens or CSOs, authorities rather speak of 'transparency'	• SA is holding local authorities (esp. municipalities) to account • Compliance from public servants remains conditional, cannot be taken for granted • SA requires malpractice to be tackled, not just exposed	• Theory: SA as communal tool for improved public service delivery is 'diverse, malleable, and contested' (Fox, 2022, p. 56) • CASES: multiple terms circulate simultaneously; polysemy of SA concept; state officials hold different understandings than citizens, which affects outcomes
Mobilisations	• Intermediaries (often CSOs) facilitate contact between citizens and the (local) state • Demonstrations raise awareness • Occasional confrontation via litigation	• SA most often led by civil society actors targeting unresponsive officials • SAIs focused on elected officials need combination of persuasive and coercive strategies	• Direct access of citizens to decision-makers is preferred route but limited to taxpaying residents with voting rights • SAIs with municipalities mostly rooted in collaboration	• Theory: gradual rather than constant mobilisation, key role for intermediaries, differences in types of CSOs • CASES: SAIs are trade-offs between collaboration and confrontation, both are needed

	Morocco	*Tunisia*	*Lebanon*	*Overall*
Responses	• Contrasting attitudes: sensitivity to SA calls but also obstruction • Positive response more likely if mobilisation is mediatised	• CSOs are often wary of exploitation, manipulation of SAIs by authorities • Reluctance among officials to share executive powers	• SA is welcome when it is non-threatening; SAIs may create win–win configurations where citizens contribute to public service delivery • Persistent nepotism among officials influences responses	• Theory: authoritarianism constrains accountability but SAIs exist nonetheless • CASES: tokenism (at best) or sabotaging accountability (at worst) not uncommon; scale matters (SA in small localities easier than in big cities) and credible threat (media coverage) of escalation is key to officials' response
Outcomes	• Overall success of SAIs limited due to inefficiencies of institutional protocols, complex ties between authorities and CSOs, discretionary bureaucracy • Occasional concessions	• Ability of SAIs to deliver is a variable, depends on willingness and responsiveness of bottom-up pressure and allies among authorities • Importance of local–national civil society linkages • Need for confrontation ***and*** collaboration	• Evidence of clear, concrete and solid results is modest	• Theory: sandwich strategy, contextual drivers • CASES: citizens or CSOs rarely succeed on their own, need for coalitions of (unlikely) partners; response remains limited, giving citizens impression SA may be window-dressing; defusing threat more important than genuine change or cooperation; civic space evolves in cycles (opening vs closing space)

6.1.1 Meanings

The scholarly literature has a broad definition of SAIs, including citizen monitoring and oversight of public or private sector performance, user-centred public information access systems, public complaint and grievance redress mechanisms and even citizen participation in actual resource allocation, such as participatory budgeting. Consequently, the 'ideas and institutions of SA are diverse, malleable, and contested' (Fox, 2022, p. 56).

When we asked local citizens and civil society activists in Lebanon, Tunisia and Morocco what they understood by SA, we found a broad range of different interpretations connected to the relationship between state and citizens, including transparency, access to information, participation, answerability of public institutions, rule of law, performance monitoring and evaluation of public service delivery.

The term 'accountability' does not have a clear, single equivalent in Arabic. Across all initiatives and in civil society discussions in all three countries, two terms emerged time and again when discussing SA: *musāʾala* and *muḥāsaba*. Activists often used the term *musāʾala*, linked to the notion of questioning (*saʾala*), to indicate the answerability of public officials and their obligation to disclose information and explain their actions (or inaction) and decisions. Meanwhile, the term *muḥāsaba*, derived from the verb 'to settle accounts' (*ḥasaba*), has a more threatening connotation of enforcing accountability, i.e. sanctioning officials, and is mostly used in initiatives focusing on the rule of law and access to justice.

The popularisation of the term 'social accountability' (*musāʾala ijtimāʿiyya*) in recent years has been driven by both local demands for accountability and international donor programmes. In Tunisia, for example, the spread of the term in civil society was boosted by the United Nations Development Programme's (UNDP) Tamkeen programme on 'reinforcing the capacity of civil society' (UNDP, n.d.). However, accountability has been picked up and reappropriated by local actors in their own array of initiatives, which go beyond interventions promoted by international donors. Thus, there is no straightforward process through which ideas or models are transferred. While donors play a key role in circulating concepts, these concepts are often adapted to fit a wide diversity of endogenous demands for accountability.

In all three countries, state officials seem to have understandings of accountability that differ significantly from those of citizens. This polysemy affects the outcomes of SAIs. For example, despite the creation of explicit constitutional principles and institutions ostensibly dedicated to oversight and the eradication of corruption, in practice it remains very difficult for Moroccan citizens participating in SAIs to achieve accountability. One conclusion of this challenging reality hints at a lack of (state) capacity due to bureaucratic inefficiency, coordination problems or resource shortages. Some argue, however, that such a view is naive and that reality is both more complicated and more cynical: accountability is elusive not because of poor capacity but because state officials actively undermine accountability mechanisms. There are good reasons to substantiate such a view when looking, for instance, at how political elites in Lebanon have 'managed to obstruct and even quash the domestic judicial process for holding those responsible for the [2020 Beirut Port] blast accountable' (Nassar & El Machnouk, 2023).

6.1.2 Mobilisations

The impunity of corrupt public decision-makers fuelled Arab societies to revolt against dictators in 2011 and has continued to nourish civic mobilisations across the region ever since. In all three countries analysed in this volume, such spectacular eruptions were the result of the 'gradual build-up of contentious mobilisations witnessed over the past years', in most cases stretching back decades (Daher, 2021; see also Bogaert, 2015; Gobe & Salaymeh, 2016). This suggests that citizen mobilisation is a cyclical phenomenon in which periods of more dynamic mobilisation activity alternate with spells of quiet networking activities in the face of an unreceptive political climate, theorised as abeyance (Geha, 2019). In other words, timing is key in identifying the moment at which the socio-political climate presents opportunities for change.

This book has documented a variety of mobilisation strategies throughout the Arab world over the past 15 years. These strategies were almost always a mix between collaboration and confrontation among officials and citizens. When collaboration alone was chosen, there was a risk of co-optation or appropriation; when only confrontation was privileged as a strategy, the dangers of sidelining or repression loomed around the corner. Effective mobilisation thus seems to require direct, personal ties between citizens and officials as well as indirect (social) media attention; it needs a good balance of both persuasive and coercive tactics.

In nearly all cases, intermediaries from civil society organisations (CSOs) connected providers and recipients of public services, be it via awareness-raising activities among specific target groups (youth, women, illiterate people,...) or through attempts at outright confrontation (from demonstrations to naming-and-shaming campaigns and litigation against corrupt officials). Our cases seem to confirm the findings of recent scholarship suggesting that the role of intermediaries is key (Anderson et al., 2022; Berdou & Shutt, 2017; Kirk, 2023), because such brokers can act as 'translators of accountability' with agency (Marini et al., 2018, p. 1905). Intermediaries' or brokers' political identities should receive more attention from donors as well as scholars, as they determine to a great extent whether SA programmes can challenge clientelism effectively (Kirk, 2023, p. 10).

It is essential, therefore, to properly distinguish between the various actors who intervene in SAIs, as one cannot assume that CSOs are monolithic actors (Kherigi, 2020). Nor can CSOs be seen as one homogeneous group; the sector has become highly professionalised over the past decades and its diversity has only increased. For example, an ad hoc association of villagers demanding access to electricity in rural Morocco differs considerably from an institutionalised multinational donor organisation such as Oxfam or Save the Children.

The Tunisia chapter in this book illustrates how fragmentation among CSOs can cause programme (and outcome) incompatibilities for people on the ground. This finding echoes similar insights about different types of CSOs and the political contexts in which such organisations operate (Mako & Moghadam, 2021). The distinction between different kinds of CSOs and their attitudes to the political regime (adversarial, boycotting or collaborative) profoundly affects how authorities will likely respond to SAIs and can thus be seen as a key variable of SA.

6.1.3 Responses

We know from the theory that accountability initiatives always face the risk of being merely cosmetic, i.e. challenging existing structures of power only superficially rather than profoundly transforming these regimes. Mariz Tadros has labelled this 'the risk of authoritarian accountability':

'Authoritarian systems of governance are kept intact or even strengthened by being associated with Western-style accountability programmes' (Tadros, 2018). Furthermore, more recent scholarship (Hassan, 2022; Khodary, 2022; Sika, 2023) has shown that mobilisation depends on the extent and type of authoritarianism. Fortunately, these studies show how stakeholders can navigate the restrictions imposed by authoritarian regimes: the degree of repression impedes mobilisation but also determines the chances of protesters to obtain concessions from their authoritarian rulers (Sika, 2023). Put simply, the extent of repression influences the degree of policy concessions citizens can extract.

In our case studies, we found that all participants were concerned about authorities' responses to SAIs. Citizens and brokers were wary of the risk of appropriation by authorities. From their side, officials were eager not to expose themselves to sanctions by their superiors—which can occur when they give in too rapidly to calls for accountability or when they underestimate the risk of demands snowballing out of control. We conclude that two factors matter for SAIs hoping to nudge authorities into action: the scale of intervention and the risk of contagion. Indeed, authorities in small localities seemed easier to convince than those in charge of big cities or larger polities. Besides, authorities were more likely to respond favourably to demands when there was a credible threat that such claims would spill over. It is here that (social) media coverage provided valuable leverage. The more autonomous and/or larger the media channel and hence its coverage was, the higher the chances of responsiveness, even though some media attention was already more effective than none.

State capacity proved to be another crucial variable in the way authorities responded to SAIs. In settings where states were strongly institutionalised (like Morocco and Tunisia), SAIs tended to meet more resistance from authorities than in contexts with more fragile state capacity, like Lebanon. This means, surprisingly perhaps, that SAIs may have higher chances of success in fragile than in strong states, because officials in 'stronger' states can perceive SAIs as attempts to curtail their implementation prerogatives or challenge their decision-making powers. By contrast, under conditions of weaker state capacity, SAIs can be perceived as providing municipal actors with complementary, non-threatening assistance to ensure public service delivery. In such cases, participatory initiatives can be a welcome supplement to state action, as long as they do not overtly contest the established hierarchy.

Participants in our project invariably expressed serious concerns about the potential threat of authorities responding with tokenism (at best) and manipulation (at worst). Indeed, the risk of authorities reacting to SAIs with lip service only or with counter-efforts to appropriate campaigns to their own advantage is never absent. Whether aiming to undermine accountability protocols or to present themselves as initiators of participation, authorities' window-dressing responses are well known, corroborated by recent scholarly attempts to theorise them. Fox (2022, p. 74), for example, speaks of 'openwashing' by actors who 'appear to promote transparency but actually hide the persistent abuse of power and impunity', whereas Kirk (2023, p. 9) refers to 'isomorphic activism', which occurs when 'public authorities appropriate others' opportunities to participate in politics and, in the process, undermine democratic norms', based on his fieldwork in a context marked by clientelism.

6.1.4 Outcomes

In an ideal world, SAIs constitute new forms of citizen–state interfaces in which Grandvoinnet's contextual drivers, i.e. state action, information, citizen action and civic mobilisation (Grandvoinnet et al., 2015, p. 12; see also Sect. 2.3 in this book) positively align or realign to generate what Fox calls a 'perfect sandwich strategy'. In such a strategy, citizen voice can equip itself with teeth that ensure shifts in accountability outcomes (Fox, 2022, p 82). On the one hand, our case studies confirm this promise of a new social contract. At a limited scale, tangible results do exist (e.g. new legislation) and municipalities clearly stand out as the most promising level at which to launch SAIs. If all stakeholders accept that real change is often small and slow, civil actors can be successful catalysts of change and become credible partners for both the demand and supply sides of the accountability chain.

On the other hand, the sobering reality we encountered across the region is that outcomes of SAIs are highly variable and that success stories are rare, since pressures from below rarely find responsive allies inside state administrations (see Table 6.2). We found several reasons for these relatively poor outcomes. Before discussing these, however, we highlight four conditions for successful outcomes in SAIs based on our case studies.

First, our findings confirm that civil society actors (whether multinational donors or modest, purpose-built committees) can facilitate connections and commitment between citizens and officials. Repeated

Table 6.2 Promise and limits of social accountability in three Arab societies

	Morocco	*Tunisia*	*Lebanon*	*Overall*
Promise of social accountability	• SAIs can fill legitimacy vacuum: CSOs increasingly replace parties and unions, who lost credibility • Citizens have created tools and platforms to connect with decision-makers • Civil society can raise awareness; has resilience and drive for long-term change	• Important achievements (in legislation) in 2011–2021 • Focus on local politics, especially municipalities • SAIs can rebalance state–society relations away from nepotism towards social justice • Joint trainings helps officials respond to SA demands and activists identify implementation obstacles	• Citizen and (municipal) state collaborations yield better access to public services as well as better use of human resources and funds • Such synergies improve delivery and acceptance (legitimacy) of public goods as well as the credibility of all actors	• Civic innovators *can* be successful drivers of social change as credible partners enjoying legitimacy • Many initiatives have been launched *but* real change is small and slow • Tangible results do exist, often at municipal/local levels • Key condition for successful SAIs is trust between officials, donors, citizens

(continued)

Table 6.2 (continued)

	Morocco	*Tunisia*	*Lebanon*	*Overall*
Limits of social accountability	• Drip system accountability rather than systemic approach to accountable state–society relations • Decision-makers guard their discretionary powers • Duration of funding affects sustainability of SAI outcomes • Response dependent on proximity between authorities and brokers • Officials can obstruct advances and there is reluctance to scale up micro-level successes to nationwide reforms, despite the existence of institutional accountability protocols	• Project-based approach of international donors can undermine accountability outcome • SA cannot simply be transplanted via toolkits; it should rather work on local needs by crafting tools sensitive to specificities • Systematic evaluation of SAIs can inspire more efficient strategies • CSOs and intermediaries face internal fragmentation and a lack of local–national coordination	• Lack of interest and/or sabotaging from officials in SAIs • Only residents enjoying full citizenship rights (nationality, voting registration, taxation) can access participatory initiatives (vulnerable people within a community are not represented)	• Institutionalising SA mechanisms triggers risk of reappropriation or downsizing mechanisms by authorities • Lack of enforcement powers prevents SAIs from gaining 'teeth' • Strategic opacity in chains of decision-making undermines efficiency of SAIs • Who participates and how are key questions in evaluating SAIs • SAIs can be a form of discourse • Copying tools and formats for intervention is unhelpful

interactions can then lead to reciprocal trust, which is needed for initiatives to succeed. Personal ties of proximity bind stakeholders together and motivate them to overcome obstacles. Second, once alliances and shared understandings of SA have been forged at the local level, it is crucial that these are relayed to and endorsed higher up in the respective institutional hierarchies: micro-level success does not guarantee national-level success without backing at the higher echelons. Similarly, advances at the local scale are easily undone, even when formal protocols or bodies exist. Third, for SAIs to be successful, it is essential to learn from failure. Modes and means of participation should be systematically evaluated while taking the context into consideration and providing opportunities for adjustment. If projects do not acknowledge flawed designs and implementation shortcomings, the same blind spots (who participates?) and pitfalls (how is participation measured?) risk being reproduced. Fourth, all successful SAIs combine forms of cooperation and confrontation: letting citizens or activists train officials can be a successful collaboration strategy to strengthen accountability, as CSOs can lend credibility and know-how to state officials. Conversely, allowing officials to cooperate with civic innovators in SAIs enables authorities to point out implementation obstacles when rolling out projects in specific communities. Finally, confrontation strategies (e.g. the shaming of local officials by social media) sometimes appear as the most appropriate pathway towards change.

Alas, all too often, evidence of clear and concrete outcomes where all these conditions are met is scant, as the overall response from authorities remains limited. One reason for this, among others, is that there is less and less space for people to demand SA. Whereas in 2011, citizens broke through the barriers of fear (Weyland, 2012, p. 926), over time rulers have launched counter-strategies to reassert their power that successfully repressed citizens seeking change.

In all three countries, calls for SA have been sidestepped: in Morocco and in Tunisia we clearly saw how the space for civic innovation has considerably evolved over the past 15 years. While in the beginning, spaces opened (Tunisia), even including a moment of invited space (in Morocco during the run-up to the 2011 referendum, leading to the unprecedented capture of executive power by the moderate Islamist party Parti de la Justice et du Développement [Justice and Development Party, PJD]), these spaces gradually closed, culminating in a presidential coup in Tunisia and the restoration of the monarchy's allies in Morocco. In Lebanon, the impunity of public officials responsible for the Beirut Port blast of August 2020 and the downward socio-economic spiral triggered by the massive devaluation of the national currency have been spectacularly evident.

On the whole, incumbents gradually co-opted dissidents or reframed reforms to their benefit. Consequently, authorities and political elites were reluctant to grant initiatives real enforcement powers, prioritising their own survival. Thus, defusing tensions by occasionally giving way was preferred over systemic change. Such drip-system accountability underlines the key role of appointed or elected officials in determining outcomes of SAIs. Another, related reason for the rather meagre outcomes of SAIs in the Arab world is that authorities often perceived projects that included an element of citizen participation as potential threats rather than as opportunities to renew their legitimacy. If initiatives are approached as a nuisance factor to be contained, then a lack of interest—or worse, active resistance—is to be expected. A third reason for the modest harvest of Arab SAIs so far touches on structural vulnerabilities: donor-funded projects were typically short-term interventions involving multiple stakeholders who often had specific standards and modes of operation used to streamline their operations across continents (e.g. particular types of citizen-score-card mechanisms). Such templates can impede successful intervention, as sustainable advances in accountability take time to emerge and often require objectives and tools that are context-dependent (Anderson et al., 2022; Bergh, 2019; Harb, 2018; Loewe et al., 2021; Tadros, 2020).

6.2 SAIs as Relational Sites of Power

While this book is organised into several chapters that discuss SAIs in settings using national boundaries as a unit of analysis, we explicitly encourage readers to also look at our case studies transnationally and seek out recurrent patterns and themes. We believe that SAIs can best be understood via a relational approach that views them as a 'discursive action format' that, despite its many manifestations, has a number of common features and understandings. Studying SAIs from a grounded perspective illustrates how they are relational sites of power: they not only shape their environment but are also shaped by the particularities of their respective environments. Thus, paraphrasing Eyben's study on international aid (2008, p. 20), we can say that a relational understanding of

[SAIs] would not see [them] as a thing. Rather, SAIs would be understood as a particular pattern of social relations shaped by context-specific and historically derived configurations within the broader fields of power and meaning in global and local politics.

Such a relational approach to SAIs furthermore makes it possible to take into account that power dynamics are relational: they are 'a complex and polymorphous reality that is best analysed from several entry points' (Silvester & Fisker, 2023, p. 3, citing Jessop, 2016, p. 51). SAIs are affected by notions of reach and connection as well. Power is

> exercised through the interactions of different sets of actors and institutions whose relationships—both proximate and distant—are conditioned to attain certain political ends. Presence and proximity are no longer simply about physical distance; rather, thinking about reach and connection bring into view how institutions and movements also change *what* can be demanded politically and *how* it may be brokered, contested and countered. (Clark et al., 2022, p. 270, emphasis in original)

Therefore, we view SAIs as various manifestations of a globally circulating discursive action format that enable us to excavate often implicit power relations that can contribute to the 'operation of state power in the micro-geographies of the state' (Moisio et al., 2020, p. 8). As such, we maintain that the SAIs analysed in this volume reveal politics at multiple scales (local, regional, national, international, global) and 'enrich our understanding of how local politics operate and are produced, navigated, negotiated, contested and challenged, and thus how local power is (re)shaped' (Clark et al., 2022, p. 258).

Looking critically at SAIs as manifestations of relational power—integrating various levels of governance and aligning modes of governance across entities—puts the spotlight on a fundamental risk of SAIs when they are promoted as an instrument of intervention, namely that the modus operandi becomes more important than the quality of public service delivery itself. In this sense, emulating tools and methods across countries can be counterproductive. While transposing SAIs from one setting to another may enable experts and international donors to streamline and compare projects more extensively, their specific set-up can become a straitjacket for local participants, citizens, CSOs and officials alike. Stakeholders on the ground need time to develop mutual trust and measures adapted to their respective communities or environments, rather than having forms of collaboration imposed on them. They need continuity and long-term stability in resources and commitment, rather than short-lived campaigns or temporary project managers eager to make 'their' project a successful step in a globetrotting career.

What we observe, then, is a lesser-known aspect of SAIs as a discursive action format that becomes a blueprint for intervention in settings with imperfect accountability. Here, SAIs can be seen as sites of relational power, in which SA mechanisms or tools appear as a form of discourse espoused by global organisations (such as the World Bank, UNDP, Cooperative for Assistance and Relief Everywhere [CARE] or Transparency International) and shared with—or imposed on—local 'partners', authorities, CSOs and citizens. The professionals (be they regular staff or consultants) are often interlinked and expose a form of assembled power that projects its instruments (know-how, deliverables) onto local communities with very diverse needs and backgrounds. SAIs in this view are relational sites of power because they present a discursive format of action that performs globalising tendencies of governance (i.e. a set of steps to be rolled out aimed at 'more responsive governance', the 'fight against corruption' and 'enhanced delivery of public goods'). SAIs easily circulate far beyond the MENA region thanks to this shared discourse and because of their ontological character as a template that can be used by projects fostering citizen participation elsewhere in the world and that other initiatives and practitioners can *relate to* precisely because they understand this discourse and partake in this shared format of action.

6.3 Grounded Lessons and Recommendations

In this final section, we formulate insights and recommendations based on our findings. We set out to examine what SA looks like on the ground. First, we found that the very notion of SA is so malleable that all stakeholders bent it to their interests. The malleability of SA and its contested nature are both a threat (giving rise to obstruction and openwashing) and an opportunity (to reformulate claims and demands) for civic innovators.

Not surprisingly then, we found that what SA looks like greatly depends on local conditions and specific circumstances. SA has potential and appeal in the MENA region (and other contexts marked by democratic deficiencies) because it holds the promise of providing ordinary citizens with agency to monitor authorities, thereby empowering them as a key actor in a relation of mutual trust between state and society. In other words, there is a glimmer of hope in SA for despondent citizens who wish to combat impunity and tackle corruption. In practice, however, we have reason and evidence to believe that it is exactly this potential of SA that pushes authorities, officials, politicians and bureaucrats to sabotage, hollow out or undermine SAIs by any available means as soon as they fear losing their ill-gained privileges or one-sided clientelist relationships. Indeed, we found that officials used SA as a public relations strategy at best and sabotaged its mechanisms at worst. A preferred tool here was the strategic, i.e. intentional, opacity in hierarchies of decision-making, which undermined the efficiency of SAIs. The detailed reviews in the country chapters show that situations where the conditions for effective SA were met were rare. Most importantly, there was no one-size-fits-all format: the trajectories we encountered were never the same, often winding and reversing, indirect and 'partial, incomplete, and temporary' (Fox, 2022, p. 97).

Despite the overwhelming variety in what SAIs look like on the ground, we would like to offer a concise set of recommendations to policy-makers and practitioners. First, keep in mind that actual change is often more modest and slower than initial ambitions. Consequently, to avoid losing the momentum of mobilisation and achieve advances in SA, all actors should acknowledge erstwhile opponents as potential coalition partners, however uncomfortable or unlikely this scenario may seem ex ante. This is because neither citizens nor intermediaries or authorities can achieve success on their own. While civic innovators may be most resilient and drive to push the boundaries of state–society relations and improved public services, they need persuasive mediators and subtle coercion to convince officials to use their executive power or nudge their superiors towards institutional reform. Measures that build trust between citizens and authorities appear as the most promising glue to achieve tangible accountability results. It is here that (international) donors as well as (local) ad hoc associations can make meaningful contributions, as they have the resources and legitimacy to bridge gaps in know-how and/or funding, provided they commit to a long-term (four to eight years) rather than short-term investment, as is often the case. Such a longer-term presence would also enable them to draw more heavily on the relational character of SAIs by strengthening the local–national linkages of committees, associations and civil society actors and ensuring alignment between headquarters and teams on the ground or between programme managers and staff working with local communities on the ground.

To conclude, SAIs in the three countries under study have proven to yield mixed results so far. On the ground, we saw that projects either remained limited to mere discursive devices for politicians and managers to muster goodwill through interventions that were partial or superficial or yielded concrete socio-economic advances for local communities but failed to be implemented at larger scales and/or with sustainable impacts.

Nevertheless, despite the overall disappointing evidence of the effectiveness of SAIs in the MENA region, we hope that this book will encourage scholars, practitioners, officials, donors and activists to critically question and, where possible, strengthen SAIs and push initiatives fostering accountability in the Arab world. Civic innovation holds major opportunities for imagining future societies based on equality, accountability and social justice. This will require extending the debate from a programmatic one (how to promote accountability at local and national levels) to one that includes legal reforms and a political praxis focused on enforcing laws against individuals, institutions and private companies. This requires changing organisational behaviour to create a more accountable culture of public decision-making, in which malpractice is not merely exposed but also tackled and sanctioned.

References

Anderson, C., Gaventa, J., Edwards, J., Joshi, A., Nampoothiri, N. J., & Wilson, E. (2022). *Against the odds: Action for empowerment and accountability in challenging contexts* (A4EA Policy and Practice Paper). Institute of Development Studies. https://opendocs.ids.ac.uk/opendocs/handle/20.500.12413/17189

Berdou, E., & Shutt, C. (2017). *Shifting the spotlight: Understanding crowdsourcing intermediaries in transparency and accountability initiatives* (Making All Voices Count Research Report). Institute of Development Studies. https://opendocs.ids.ac.uk/opendocs/bitstream/handle/20.500.12413/12836/RReport_ShiftingSpotlight_Online.pdf

Bergh, S. I. (2019, June). *Enhancing social accountability through Community Score Cards? Evidence from the education and health sectors in Morocco and India* [Conference presentation]. Third Annual GLD Conference, Varberg, Sweden.

Bogaert, K. (2015). The revolt of small towns: The meaning of Morocco's history and the geography of social protests. *Review of African Political Economy, 42*(143), 124–140. https://doi.org/10.1080/03056244.2014.918536

Clark, J., El-Kazaz, S., Harb, M., & Salman, L. (2022). Towards a relational approach to local politics. In M. Lynch, J. Schwedler, & S. Yom (Eds.), *The political science of the Middle East: Theory and research since the Arab uprisings* (pp. 256–280). Oxford University Press.

Daher, S. (2021). *Unpacking the dynamics of contentious mobilisations in Lebanon: Between continuity and evolution.* Civil Society Knowledge Center, Lebanon Support. https://doi.org/10.28943/CSKC.002.90001

Eyben, R. (2008). *Power, mutual accountability and responsibility in the practice of international aid: A relational approach* (IDS Working Paper 305). https://gsdrc.org/document-library/power-mutual-accountability-and-responsibility-in-the-practice-of-international-aid-a-relational-approach/

Fox, J. (2022). *Accountability keywords* (Working Paper 11). Accountability Research Center. https://accountabilityresearch.org/wp-content/uploads/2022/01/Working-Paper-11_Keywords_May-24.pdf

Geha, C. (2019). Politics of a garbage crisis: Social networks, narratives, and frames of Lebanon's 2015 protests and their aftermath. *Social Movement Studies, 18*(1), 78–92. https://doi.org/10.1080/14742837.2018.1539665

Global Partnership for Social Accountability. (n.d.). *Strengthening inclusive education in host communities through collaborative social accountability processes in Jordan.* https://thegpsa.org/projects/strengthening-inclusive-education-in-host-communities-through-collaborative-social-accountability-processes-in-jordan/

Gobe, E., & Salaymeh, L. (2016). Tunisia's 'revolutionary' lawyers: From professional autonomy to political mobilization. *Law & Social Inquiry, 41*(2), 311–345. https://doi.org/10.1111/lsi.12154

Grandvoinnet, H., Aslam, G., & Raha, S. (2015). *Opening the black box: The contextual drivers of social accountability*. World Bank Publications.

Harb, M. (2018). New forms of youth activism in contested cities: The case of Beirut. *The International Spectator, 53*(2), 74–93. https://doi.org/10.1080/03932729.2018.1457268

Hassan, Y. (2022). The evolution of the Sudanese authoritarian state: The December uprising and the unravelling of a 'persistent' autocracy. In O. Topak, M. Mekouar, & F. Cavatorta (Eds.), *New authoritarian practices in the Middle East and North Africa* (pp. 252–275). Edinburgh University Press.

Jessop, B. (2016). *The state: Past, present, future*. Polity Press.

Kherigi, I. (2020). Civil society in a time of transition. In *Civil society and social movements in the Euro-Mediterranean region* (pp. 58–65). European Institute of the Mediterranean (IEMed).

Khodary, Y. (2022). Social accountability in challenging environments: Case studies from Egypt. *Middle East Law and Governance, 15*(2), 129–152.

Kirk, T. (2023). Intermediaries, isomorphic activism and programming for social accountability in Pakistan. *Global Policy*. https://doi.org/10.1111/1758-5899.13218

Loewe, M., Zintl, T., & Houdret, A. (2021). The social contract as a tool of analysis: Introduction to the special issue on 'Framing the evolution of new social contracts in Middle Eastern and North African countries.' *World Development, 145*, 104982. https://doi.org/10.1016/j.worlddev.2020.104982

Mako, S., & Moghadam, V. M. (2021). *After the Arab uprisings: Progress and stagnation in the Middle East and North Africa*. Cambridge University Press.

Marini, L., Andrew, J., & van der Laan, S. (2018). Accountability practices in microfinance: Cultural translation and the role of intermediaries. *Accounting, Auditing & Accountability Journal, 31*(7), 1904–1931.

Moisio, S., Jonas, A. E. G., Koch, N., Lizotte, C., & Luukkonen, J. (2020). Changing geographies of the state: Themes, challenges and futures. In S. Moisio, N. Koch, A. E. G. Jonas, C. Lizotte, & J. Luukkonen (Eds.), *Handbook on the changing geographies of the state: New spaces of geopolitics* (pp. 1–28). Edward Elgar.

Nassar, F. N., & El Machnouk, S. (2023, August 4). *The Beirut blast three years on: The case for international accountability*. Middle East Institute. https://mei.edu/publications/beirut-blast-three-years-case-international-accountability

Sika, N. (2023). Mobilization, repression and policy concessions in authoritarian regimes: The cases of Egypt and Jordan. *Political Studies*. Advance online publication. https://doi.org/10.1177/00323217221141426

Silvester, B. R., & Fisker, J. K. (2023). A relational approach to the role of the state in societal transitions and transformations towards sustainability. *Environmental Innovation and Societal Transitions, 47*, 100717. https://doi.org/10.2139/ssrn.4224462

Tadros, M. (2018, March 27). *Authoritarian accountability and accountable authoritarianism*. Institute of Development Studies. https://www.ids.ac.uk/opinion/authoritarian-accountability-and-accountable-authoritarianism

Tadros, M. (2020). *Eleven recommendations for working on empowerment and accountability in fragile, conflict or violence-affected settings* (Policy Briefing). Institute of Development Studies. https://www.ids.ac.uk/programme-and-centre/action-for-empowerment-and-accountability-a4ea/

United Nations Development Programme. (n.d.). *TAMKEEN, pour la promotion de la citoyenneté, le renforcement de la cohésion sociale et de la société civile*. https://www.tn.undp.org/content/tunisia/fr/home/projects/tamkeen--pour-la-promotion-de-la-citoyennete--le-renforcement-de.html

Weyland, K. (2012). The Arab Spring: Why the surprising similarities with the revolutionary wave of 1848? *Perspectives on Politics, 10*(4), 917–934. https://doi.org/10.1017/S1537592712002873

Index

W. Vloeberghs and S. I. Bergh (eds.), *Social Accountability Initiatives in Morocco, Tunisia, and Lebanon*, EADI Global Development Series,
https://doi.org/10.1007/978-3-031-51322-0

T

U

FSC
www.fsc.org
MIX
Papier | Fördert gute Waldnutzung
FSC® C083411

Kolibri 360 GmbH
Ferdinand-Jühlke-Straße 7
99095 Erfurt, Deutschland
produktsicherheit@kolibri360.de